FACING JUDICIAL DISCRETION

Law and Philosophy Library

VOLUME 49

The titles published in this series are listed at the end of this volume.

FACING JUDICIAL DISCRETION

Legal Knowledge and Right Answers Revisited

by

MARISA IGLESIAS VILA

Professor of Legal Theory,
Department of Legal, Moral and Political Philosophy,
Pompeu Fabra University,
Barcelona, Spain

KLUWER ACADEMIC PUBLISHERS

DORDRECHT / BOSTON / LONDON

A C.I.P. Catalogue record for this book is available from the Library of Congress.

ISBN 0-7923-6778-2

Published by Kluwer Academic Publishers,
P.O. Box 17, 3300 AA Dordrecht, The Netherlands.

Sold and distributed in North, Central and South America
by Kluwer Academic Publishers,
101 Philip Drive, Norwell, MA 02061, U.S.A.

In all other countries, sold and distributed
by Kluwer Academic Publishers,
P.O. Box 322, 3300 AH Dordrecht, The Netherlands.

English translation of El problema de la discreción judicial.
Una aproximación al conocimiento jurídico, Centro de
Estudios Políticos y Constitucionales, Madrid, 1999,
translated by S.C. Mendlewicz.

Printed on acid-free paper

Printed in the Netherlands.

For Nuri Vila,
the noblest dreamer

TABLE OF CONTENTS

CHAPTER 5: COHERENCE IN LEGAL INTERPRETATION

CHAPTER 6: HARD CASES AND LEGAL DETERMINACY

ACKNOWLEDGEMENTS

This book began life as a doctoral thesis, submitted at the Universitat Pompeu Fabra, Barcelona, in 1997, which I completed thanks to the financial support of the Generalitat de Catalunya. It is the result of several years of study, reflection, and persistency with ideas that only hesitantly assent to leave darkness.

Special thanks are due to all those who made its publication possible both in its Spanish as well as in its English version, in particular, to the managing editors of Centro de Estudios Políticos y Constitucionales and Kluwer Academic Publishers. I am grateful to the translator, S. C. Mendlewicz, for her work and for the long hours of detailed discussion. Her observations have helped me clarify a number of points.

Intellectual activity is not the product of mere individual effort. Philosophy benefits markedly from hard questions, criticism and discussion. I have greatly benefited from the intellectual atmosphere I was privileged to enjoy at the Department of Legal Philosphy of the Universitat Pompeu Fabra. I wish to express my gratitude to its director and my supervisor, Albert Calsamiglia, who provided not only the support, which means so much, but constant guidance and invaluable criticism from the beginning to the end. His striking ability to create a fruitful environment for philosophical exchange afforded me a unique opportunity to meet and learn from thinkers such as Ernesto Garzón Valdés, Carlos Santiago Nino, and Eugenio Bulygin.

I am deeply indebted to José Juan Moreso, Ricardo Caracciolo, Cristina Redondo and Maribel Narváez for the many stimulating and fruitful discussions on the issues addressed in this book, and for reading and commenting upon large portions of earlier drafts. Their incisive criticism and fine observations have led to many improvements.

Many thanks must go to Jordi Ferrer, Josep Maria Vilajosana, Teresa Pascual, José Luis Pérez Triviño, Jorge Malem, Pablo Navarro, Daniel Mendonca, Roberto Gargarella, and Víctor Ferreres for their patience and encouragement. I have been the grateful recipient of their suggestions in developing the ideas in this book. Most importantly, I have had the pleasure of sharing with them my passion for philosophical inquiry.

I wish to thank Neus Torbisco, and all my friends for their unfailing support. They have been wise to remind me the other strands in my life during the difficult moments in the writing of this book. And, of course, I shall not forget to mention Africa.

Finally, and most of all, my everlasting gratitude goes to my parents and sisters, Cristina and Elisabeth, without whose affection, warmth and generosity this book would never have seen the light of day.

INTRODUCTION

In response to ETA's 1997 kidnappings and murders thousands of Spaniards attended mass demonstrations to express their contempt for violence as a means of political pressure. The demand that public authorities prosecute and condemn those who directly or indirectly support ETA and its terrorist attacks was one of the most prevalent slogans in the marches. Indeed, the social response was aimed not only against the terrorist group, but also against Herri Batasuna (HB), the political party that openly endorse ETA's armed actions in the Basque Country.

From the legal point of view, it is interesting to examine what it is citizens are requesting from the government in the above-mentioned case. How do these collective claims translate into legal language? One may think it fit to answer that Spanish citizens want violence to be met with the institutional punishment prescribed by the legal order. Nonetheless, it could also be argued that citizens in fact demand that certain kinds of behaviour be regulated by the law in their country. While from the latter viewpoint citizens wish for the creation of new legal norms, from the former they are just calling for the application of the law. What reasons may render us inclined to sympathise with one of these two views rather than the other? Which one of these two options is most appropriate?

At first sight, this may appear to be a simple question. Answering it requires no more than consulting the normative texts and determining what is prescribed by the Spanish law with regard to this point. If it is the case that support to terrorism falls into a delictive category, citizens just claim an effective application of the law. Otherwise, they are demanding that a new criminal figure be created.

However, there is more to it than that. Let us inquire about what would make support to terrorism a legally regulated action. The literal meaning of normative texts is usually malleable. How would otherwise members of HB have eluded convictions of an offence of conniving at terrorist acts by expressing approval of them, or co-operating with armed terrorist organisations? Precisely the legal qualification of the conduct of HB's members has been widely debated in connection to the limits of free speech, and the room for political action as a sign of democratic pluralism. Thus, the answer to which alternative better describes citizens claims against the support of violence is not obvious at all - it very much depends on the conception of law we choose to embrace;

but law is a dynamical social practice that involves argument and discussion, and in which interaction is driven by some specific purpose. We know what law is when we are able to account for this complex social practice.

This book is an attempt to address this issue from an epistemic point of view. I will explore some of the assumptions that account for particular conclusions of certain legal theories about which behaviours are legally regulated. My discussion will develop in the context of legal adjudication. Over the last few decades, legal philosophy has paid much attention to the analysis of judicial reasoning. This has proven an interesting starting point to explore questions of a wider scope such as what is law, how do we come to know it, and what are its limits. For this reason, investigating judicial discretion and legal interpretation will ultimately enable us to identify some of the elements that a view of law should incorporate to warrant its viability. The main question I will attempt to answer to is how to ensure the existence of objectively right legal answers. With a view to doing so, I will investigate some of the difficulties encountered by a theory of the truth conditions of legal propositions that assumes, at least, partial legal determinacy. I will suggest an answer along the lines of Dworkin's theory, the thesis of internal objectivity, as to how to justify the existence of right legal answers, and yet avoid falling into semantic realism. Moreover, I will hint at reasons that prevent the determinacy of law in all cases.

The first chapter outlines the different meanings ascribed to the expression 'judicial discretion' in the context of legal theory. The features of each one of these uses are described and particular attention is paid to weak and strong discretion. Each of these two uses of discretion yields a separate model about what is law and how it is identified.

In the second chapter, the 'strong discretion model', mainly endorsed by Hartian positivism, is introduced. The distinguishing features of this model can be summarised in the four postulates: I) the thesis of the social sources of law; II) law as communication; III) meaning as settled use; and IV) the partial indeterminacy of law. The purpose of an analysis of these theses is to show the difficulties met by Hartian positivism and its conventionalist semantics to overcome the sceptical challenge of rule-following without falling into semantic realism. Additionally, I point to certain deficiencies in the justification of the positivist claim that semantic disagreement necessarily leads to legal indeterminacy.

The third chapter is devoted to an analysis of what I shall call 'the weak discretion model', whose chief exponent is Ronald Dworkin. I develop three aspects of this theory of law: I) the relationship between legal theory and normative adjudication; II) the interpretive view of law; and III) law as integrity or narrative coherence. The purpose of this chapter is to illuminate the epistemic assumptions of Dworkin's theory and to point to the main objection that can be pressed against his model, namely how to justify optimism about the possibility of eliminating the need for strong discretion in adjudication.

The starting point of the fourth chapter is the idea that every theory supportive of the existence of right legal answers ought to account for the distinction between interpretation and invention. The ultimate goal of this chapter is to provide an answer as to how to draw this distinction objectively and simultaneously avoid externalism or semantic realism. To this end, I set forth the epistemic grounds of the interpretive theory of law and evince the advantages of such an approach over Quine's holism and Davidson's epistemic coherentism. This leads to the conclusion that the best way to distinguish between invention and interpretation is by adopting a theory of truth as assertability for legal statements in line with Putnam's internal realism.

The purpose of the fifth chapter is to advocate a theory of truth as assertability that adopts coherence as the criterion to determine what it is we are entitled to assert. I consider coherence as a property and as a relationship. Moreover, as far as coherence as a relationship is concerned, I distinguish between vertical and horizontal coherence. My claim here is that for a coherentist theory to avoid both foundationalism and a too strict form of holism it should take into account vertical and horizontal coherence, as suggested by the idea of reflective equilibrium. I argue that coherence within a complex interpretive scheme can warrant legal determinacy, albeit only partially. Thus, although judges always require a weak form of discretion when they adjudicate norms, there is evidence to support the need for strong discretion in the resolution of certain cases.

Finally, Chapter 6 relates the postulates of Hartian positivism to those of Dworkin's theory, and shows their differences and similarities. I favour Dworkin's view on the grounds of its epistemic accessibility and its higher explanatory output. I specifically stress that Dworkin's position permits a viable strategy to overcome the problem of rule-following, and distinguish interpretation from invention. This leads to the conclusion that legal indeterminacy does not necessarily follow from semantic disagreement.

CHAPTER 1

THE CONCEPT OF JUDICIAL DISCRETION

1.1 INTRODUCTION

The debate on judicial discretion and its limits gained considerable attention from legal theorists in the 1930's. One of the reasons accounting for this increase in interest was the loss of influence of certain maxims of theoretical positivism as a way of describing the structural characteristics of legal orders[1]. Some currents of thought such as American legal realism challenged completeness and the formalist perception of the role of judges as simply implementing the will of the legislation[2]. Extreme realism, which presents legal theory as a mere psychological theory of adjudication, did not have a lasting influence. However, it did trigger an interest to analyse judicial decision-making and its connection to normative production. Particularly in the 1970's, intense debate arose about the problem of adjudication of norms. Controversy focused on two main issues: the technical necessity for judicial discretion on the one hand, and the justification of discretionary decisions on the other.

The technical necessity for judicial discretion has been studied by means of different approaches to the limits of law in connection with the judicial obligation to render a decision. In this context, the necessity for judicial discretion emerges as a result of a restrictive understanding of the limits of law. Legal positivism, for example, advocates the rule of recognition and the social sources of law as criteria to identify law as well as to establish its limits. It has thus forged a framework for discretionary activity[3]. However, some authors have downplayed the importance of judicial discretion, and some even claim that there is no such thing as judicial discretion. Their conclusions follow either from accepting a much less restrictive thesis on the limits of

[1] See Bobbio (1995, 37-66) for a characterisation of theoretical positivism.

[2] See Frank (1930; 1949) and Llewelyn (1951).

[3] See Hart (1994, Ch. VI) and Raz (1982, Ch. III).

law, or from envisaging the possibility of judges incorporating moral criteria when they identify norms[4].

The second point of interest is whether discretionary acts on the part of officials can be justified. There are typically two objections to the idea that judges may, by means of discretion, create new norms that confer rights and impose duties. The first objection invokes the democratic deficit of the judicial body. Citizens do not directly elect judges and therefore the latter are not subject to direct account giving to the former. Judges are therefore only legitimated to make decisions that ensure the implementation of the will of those institutions that have been democratically elected. Otherwise, separation of powers would be undermined. Consequently, judicial discretion understood as the existence of room for choice between alternative courses of action and as an act that can result in the creation of new norms is not justifiable from the standpoint of institutional design[5]. The second objection concerns legal certainty and the retroactive character of discretionary decisions. New norms created by the judiciary would determine rights and duties *ex post facto*, and this would entail putting legal certainty at risk[6]. Both of these criticisms have received much attention and generated a large amount of literature with a twofold goal: on the one hand these works seek to devise a structure of restrictions that will allow to forge a framework for a justifiable exercise of judicial discretion[7]; on the other, they attempt to provide general arguments to justify the existence of discretion. Sometimes these arguments aim at proving that judicial discretion is a suitable mechanism to recognise certain implicit individual rights. On other occasions, however, they seek to show the usefulness of judicial discretion to obtain just results in particular cases as well as to get around the rigidity of law and its inability to adapt promptly to changing social practices in the community[8].

Despite justification of discretionary decisions constituting an essential element in any theory on institutional design, this book will devote most of its attention to elucidating the extent to which discretion is necessary for the adjudication of norms by the judges. Up to the 1980's, the debate about this question focused on issues such as the content of the rule of recognition, the role of legal principles and of moral criteria in the

---

4 See Dworkin (1977, 31-39, 68-71) and Sartorius (1971, 151-160).

5 See Greenawalt (1975, 392-393; 1977, 1004-1007), Dworkin (1977, 84-86), Barak 1989, 192-203) and Sartorius (1971, 158-159).

6 See Aarnio (1987, 3-8), Dworkin (1977, 84-86), Barak (1989, 167-171, 203-206) and Burrows (1976, 15-18).

7 See Isaacs (1933, 344-352), Galligan (1986, 4-14), Traynor (1978, 1025-1040) and Barak (1989, 235-260).

8 See Wellman (1988, 153-165), Davis (1969, 216-217), Aarnio (1991, 31-35) and Kadish and Kadish (1973, 40-45).

identification of law, and the obligations inherent in the judicial function. However, over the last decade this debate broadened to include the semantic and epistemic dimension of the problem of judicial discretion, and of legal interpretation. In this respect, legal theorists have made considerable effort to endow legal analysis with a well-developed philosophical background, and a conceptual structure that will take into account current developments in epistemology and semantics. The study of the problem of judicial discretion is thus placed in a wider context. It has been related to other fundamental questions, such as the knowledge of social phenomena and the status of social ontology, the relationship between language and law, and the problem of rule-following. In this new context, Ronald Dworkin's interpretive theory has been one of the most controversial and relevant approaches to law ever since Hart's work[9]. Dworkin's particular conception of law and legal knowledge has generated remarkable interest from both those who agree and those who disagree with his views. His interpretive theory challenges some of the basic philosophical postulates of legal positivism. Positivists such as Raz, Bix, Greenawalt, Schauer and Marmor have replied to the interpretive theory of law by developing and further refining Hart's conception of law.

Before we go on to this discussion in the context of adjudication, it is essential to specify the meaning of 'judicial discretion', the different uses given to this expression, and what arguments have been put forward to justify the necessity or non-necessity for judicial discretion in any of its senses. For this reason, in the remaining of this chapter, we will outline the different uses of the term 'discretion' and consider the different conceptual proposals for their characterisation.

1.2 USES OF 'DISCRETION'

In ordinary, non-technical language, the term 'discretion' has two meanings: on the one hand it connotes certain personal qualities such as sensibility, reasonableness, caution and good judgement. On the other, it refers to the freedom to decide what is the thing to do in a particular situation. Legal theory has incorporated this term into its vocabulary by appropriately specifying it further for its use in the legal context. 'Judicial discretion' reflects a type of legal difficulties faced in adjudication, i.e. the process of settling conflicts by means of the law[10]. However, the different senses of this expression strongly depend on the legal conception maintained. For this reason, the conceptual

[9] For a detailed account of Dworkin's interpretive theory, see Dworkin (1985, 1986).

[10] See Hawkins (1992, 32-35) and MacCormick (1978, 242).

characterisation of judicial discretion raises some analytic difficulties that sometimes appear intractable[11].

Nevertheless, we should not be led to underestimate the relevance of a detailed study of discretion: on the grounds of its close connection to the limits of law's institutional control, judicial discretion emerges as a basic element in legal theory. In order to grasp the nature of the problems that underlie the debate about the existence of judicial discretion, a conceptual analysis of the different senses of this term in legal theory becomes crucial.

The problem of discretion has been extensively investigated in connection with administrative acts and delegated legislation. This work, however, is a study of discretion in the context of judicial adjudication[12]. We will characterise this concept from an analysis of legal interpretation and the application of law by the courts. Nonetheless, the resulting characterisation will be wide in scope.

1.2.1 Senses of judicial discretion

The first meaning given to 'judicial discretion' is based on the first usage of the term 'discretion' in ordinary language. It suggests certain personal qualities in the performance of the judicial function. A judge who is to take action in accord with the prescriptions of law should display sensibility and good judgement[13]. It appears reasonable to expect judges and courts to have these qualities regardless of the clarity with which normative guidelines are expressed. Admittedly a judge who carries out her institutional role with discretion, i.e. sensibly and with good judgement, is a responsible judge, and thus a good judge[14].

However, this meaning of discretion is secondary and we will give it no further consideration. Most authors agree that the need for good judgement and reasonableness arises from the difficulties to understand law and legal language in those cases where abstract or imprecise standards apply. Dworkin for example has proposed a characterisation of judicial discretion along these lines that has remarkably influenced the theory of adjudication. The description of what in his view is a first meaning of discretion follows:

> Sometimes we use 'discretion' in a weak sense, simply to say that for some reason the standards an

---

[11] See Barak (1989, 3-5).

[12] With regard to administrative discretion, see Davis (1969) and Galligan (1986).

[13] Isaacs (1933, 339, 341-342).

[14] Here 'responsible' is meant in a laudatory sense. Lucas states that an individual is responsible in this sense when he or she acts reliably. For further details see Lucas (1993, 11-13).

official must apply cannot be applied mechanically but demand the use of judgment. We use this weak sense when the context does not already make that clear, when the background our audience assumes does not contain that piece of information. Thus, we might say 'the sergeant's orders left him a great deal of discretion', to those who do not know what the sergeant's orders were or who do not know something that made those orders vague or hard to carry out. It would make perfect sense to add, by way of clarification, that the lieutenant had ordered the sergeant to take his five most experienced men on patrol but that it was hard to determine which were the most experienced[15].

We will call this sense of discretion 'weak discretion'. In our account, this will be the second meaning of discretion. 'Weak discretion' refers to those situations in which, although law offers an answer to the case under consideration, this answer is not obvious. A complex intellectual process is necessary to identify the course of action prescribed by the law. The law is expressed by means of language and the interpreter may meet with epistemic difficulties in understanding the language. Weak discretion reflects the need for good judgement and sensibility to reach the right legal answer when the written law does not obviously indicate what it is.

Those theories of interpretation that do not allow for the possibility of law being indeterminate due to semantic reasons tend to relate weak discretion to the fact that legal language is ambiguous and imprecise. However, in Dworkin's theory of adjudication weak discretion has implications of a wider scope[16]. This is partly due to Dworkin's particular conception of law as an interpretive phenomenon.

Some legal theorists use this sense of discretion to refer to the scope of freedom judges have to determine the material facts of a case. This does not by any means mean that judges have the power to construct or invent the material facts. Rather, discretion comes into play when assessing what constitutes sufficient evidence to ascertain that a particular event took place[17]. However, when establishing the judicial syllogism factual premise, it is assumed that there is a single right answer: the event either took place or did not. For this reason, this meaning of discretion reflects epistemic difficulties to

---

[15] Dworkin (1977, 31-32). Pattenden's 'concealed discretion' refers to this idea. See Pattenden (1990, 2). See also Greenawalt (1975, 365-366), Galligan (1986, 14), Skubik (1990, 26-27) and Sartorius (1971, 152).

[16] This is one of the reasons that account for the confusion in the controversy over the relationship between weak and strong discretion, particularly between Dworkin and authors such as Greenawalt and Galligan. There seems to be some implicit conceptual disagreement about the meaning of weak discretion. As we shall later see, most authors agree on the above characterisation of weak discretion, but they emphasise different aspects of this concept: some highlight the linguistic indeterminacy of language, whereas others stress the existence of a right answer that is not obvious to the interpreter.

[17] See Barak (1989, 13-14), Isaacs (1933, 339) and Pattenden (1990,3-4). This meaning of discretion also appears in the works of some classics of the analysis of the judicial process. See Cardozo (1921, 100) and Frank (1949, 57-58).

determine the account of the facts that is closest to reality when information is incomplete.

The third use of 'judicial discretion' puts emphasis on the nature of judicial decisions that are not subject to further review. Typically these correspond to decisions made by the highest judicial authority in a given matter. The resolution is thus final and no other authority is entitled to revise it[18]. This meaning of discretion does not necessarily presuppose difficulties in understanding the law or the existence of judicial autonomy to decide on the content of a resolution. Discretion as finality refers to the power of the institution that is ultimately responsible for declaring what the law is. As pointed out by Pattenden, this can only be *de facto* discretion since there exists no mechanism to alter or to overturn the final decision, even if the final decision is legally wrong[19].

Lastly, the fourth and foremost sense of 'judicial discretion' is what Dworkin calls 'strong discretion'[20]. This sense lies at the heart of most debates on this subject. Strong discretion can be defined as the possibility to choose among different equally valid or legally admissible courses of action[21]. This meaning of discretion presupposes that there exist certain contexts in which law leaves room for the interpreter to determine the standards that will guide his or her decision[22]. Most authors agree that discretionary

---

18 Dworkin uses discretion in a further weak sense to speak of the irreversibility and finality of certain judicial decisions. See Dworkin (1977, 32). See also Isaacs (1933, 339, 341-342), Pattenden (1990, 2), Greenawalt (1975, 365 and ff.), Galligan (1986, 14), Shiner (1992b, 32), Guest (1992, 214-215, 220-221) and Rosenberg (1971, 637).

19 See Pattenden (1990, 2). Rosenberg (1971, 637) refers to this meaning of discretion as 'secondary discretion'.

Legal realism takes this meaning of judicial discretion as its starting point to reach the conclusion that it is the judiciary who determines the content of law. Both American and Scandinavian realism have been interested in a factual approach to the legal phenomenon, that is to say, in law as it is applied in reality. Hence, they tend to argue that legal norms exist only in so far as judges to settle conflicts use them. Judicial decisions that are not subject to review become the very contents of law. About this point see Hart's remarks (1994, 141-142) on the difference between the 'finality' and the 'infallibility' of a judicial decision and his criticism to scepticism.

20 See Dworkin (1977, 32-33). For a detailed analysis of Dworkin's meaning of strong discretion, see Waluchow (1983).

21 The distinction between valid and admissible courses of action will be established in the next section, which is devoted to strong discretion. This definition of strong discretion is generally accepted although sometimes with slight differences in meaning, or even a different terminology. See Hart and Sacks (1958, 126), Barak (1989, 7), Greenawalt (1975, 363-366), Galligan (1986, 6-8, 21-22), Davis (1969, 4), Burrows (1976, 1), Raz (1972, 843), Rosenberg (1971, 637), Bell (1992, 92) and Shiner (1992b, 33).

22 This is why Dworkin defines strong discretion as that action which is not subject to standards set by the legal authority. See Dworkin (1977, 32-33) and Galligan (1986, 6, 8, 22).

proceeding continues to be subject to standards of rationality and justice although strong discretion by definition implies the absence of a single right answer. Of course, all discretionary decisions exhibit some extra-legal element, either because they create a new norm, or because they establish a subjective criterion to choose between different legal alternatives. Nevertheless, they are still subject to justification[23].

This meaning of discretion is different from what Luzzati calls 'explicit discretion' in his study of Kelsen's work. For Luzzati, 'explicit discretion' embraces those instances in which the competent authority specifically awards the judges the freedom to decide. Thus, explicit discretion can be seen as a case of legislative delegation in a particular subject matter. Strong discretion applies to those situations in which there is no explicit provision of freedom for the judge to decide autonomously. Therefore, strong discretion is closer in meaning to Luzzati's 'implicit discretion', i.e., those contexts in which the judicial body itself has to make a decision between different courses of action although it has never been explicitly granted such freedom[24].

So far, I have outlined the main uses of the term 'discretion' in legal literature and some of their relevant features. In what follows, we will focus on two of the meanings previously considered: strong discretion, and weak discretion. These two uses and their implications are at the heart of the controversy between the different theories of judicial adjudication about legal knowledge and its limits. I shall pay no further attention to the first use of the term 'judicial discretion' because it appears in conjunction with the epistemic problems faced by the judge in instances of weak discretion. Discretion in the determination of material facts can be seen as an instance of weak discretion too - it is indeed one such instance in the configuration of the factual premise of the judicial syllogism. This does not detract from its importance: indeed, establishing the material facts of a case is an essential part in the application of law - a necessary condition to proceed to the legal qualification of conduct. However, the present work is concerned with the knowledge of law and of legal language.

Lastly, discretion as finality is not linked to the problem of legal indeterminacy nor

---

23 This idea is very clearly outlined by Raz (1972, 847). See also Hart (1980, 9), Galligan (1986, 7-8) and Barak (1989, 24-27).
The demand for general justification of a discretionary decision allows for distinction between strong discretion on the one hand, and a further sense of discretion that links this concept to arbitrariness, on the other. This point will be discussed in detail later on, when we define and analyse arbitrariness and its relationship to discretion. It is worth noting that some authors consider strong discretion to be synonymous to arbitrariness. See, for instance, Hayek (1960, 228, 453) and Dicey (1945, 188).

24 For a detailed distinction between explicit and implicit discretion, see Luzzati (1990a, 130-137). For Kelsen's distinction between intentional and non-intentional indeterminacy in the application of law, see Kelsen (1970, 349-351).

to the difficulties in understanding law, but to the exercise and control of the power to ultimately declare what is the content of law. Recall the distinction between 'finality' and 'infallibility' that Hart put forward in response to legal realism. According to Hart, these two concepts are independent of one another and refer to distinct problems. As he clearly points out, a judicial decision does not constitute the content of law just because it is a final decision. Finality does not mean freedom to choose the course of action to be undertaken. Final judicial decisions are not necessarily infallible. Otherwise, we would be accepting that law is what courts say it is. Hart argues that we can only claim infallibility when law is indeterminate and the judge must choose one among different open alternatives[25].

1.3 STRONG DISCRETION

In a first approach, we defined 'strong discretion' as the possibility to choose among different equally lawful and admissible courses of action. This definition, however, is still incomplete. Although it does include some of the most relevant features of this concept, further investigation is necessary to grasp the problems underlying the debate about the technical necessity for strong discretion in the exercise of the judicial function.

1.3.1 The context of strong discretion

Strong discretion is often invoked in the context of some decision-making institutional role. In the case at hand, it is the application of law[26]. Moreover, strong discretion is confined to the normative framework the decision-making body is subject to. Thus, although at first sight strong discretion may appear directly antithetical to the application of legal norms, this term is not used when the decision-maker is subject to

---

25 See Hart (1994, 141-147), Aarnio (1987, 217). Every judicial decision establishes rights and duties, but only in the sense that it creates an individual norm for the instant case. See also Dworkin (1977, 31-33), Isaacs (1933, 339, 341-342), Greenawalt (1975, 365-367), Galligan (1986, 14) and Sartorius (1971, 152).

26 'Application of law' is the use of legal norms to justify judicial decisions. For the time being, I will not use this term to refer to the meaning of 'application' proposed by Ross in connection with validity. As Bulygin points out, Ross considers that a norm is being applied when there is a certain normative ideology, a certain intent that induces the judge to follow a rule. External conduct is not sufficient to determine whether the judge is using a normative standard. The judge should feel internally obliged to follow that pattern of conduct. Bulygin claims that Ross uses both meanings of 'application' without realising the differences between them. Usually, conceptual proposals for strong discretion understand 'application of law' in the first meaning set out above, that is to say, they only take into account the external conduct of judges when they use norms to back up their resolutions. On this point, see Bulygin (1991a, 346-348). For Ross' different meanings of 'application', see Ross (1958, 37-38).

no restrictions. As pointed out by Greenawalt, it would be rather strange to view a child's freedom to choose the flavour of its ice cream as a case of discretion[27]. For Dworkin, strong discretion is a relational concept that appears always linked to the existence of a system of rules. He reports about discretion: 'Discretion, like the hole in a doughnut, does not exist except as an area left open by a surrounding belt of restriction'[28]. This aspect of strong discretion enables us to discriminate those decision-making contexts that are irrelevant to the domain of law, from those which are relevant to law but for which there is no legal answer. The choice among different flavours for an ice-cream, or whether one wishes to take tea or coffee at breakfast are examples of the latter situation. Following Dworkin's metaphor of the doughnut, they would not embody a case of strong discretion because they would fall not inside the doughnut's hole, but outside the doughnut itself. Strong discretion is always a relational concept because it refers to what the decision-maker is entitled or obliged to do according to a system of rules and her institutional position within this system. Thus, it is only meaningful to talk about strong discretion insofar that the judicial role arises from the judge's duty to apply the law, to settle every case taken to court, and to justify her verdicts[29].

1.3.2 Discretion as choice

The core feature of the different conceptual proposals about strong discretion is the possibility for choice[30]. We will define 'choice' as a voluntary act that entails opting for one, and only one, course of action when it is the case that there exist several mutually exclusive possibilities for action[31]. The possibility for choice arises when a decision-maker has freedom to determine unilaterally the outcome of her decision[32]. Even though this freedom for choice implies that a judicial decision is not totally subject to

---

[27] See Greenawalt (1975, 365). See also Galligan (1986, 2-3).

[28] Dworkin (1977, 31). For a similar example, see Bell (1992, 93-94).

[29] A clear account of the three duties of the judicial role is given in Alchourrón and Bulygin (1971, 151-153) and Mendonca (1997, 49-61). They distinguish among the duty to dispose of every dispute, the duty to provide justification to every resolution, and the duty to apply the law.

[30] See, for instance, Hart (1994, 127), Barak (1989, 8-9) and Rosenberg (1971, 636-637).

[31] The concept of choice has been widely developed in Economic Theory, more specifically within the analysis of rational action. The defining features of choice are: voluntariness, preferences, different real possible courses of action, and mutually exclusive options. See, for instance, Afriat (1987, 14-15), and Hollis and Sudgen (1993, 2-7).

[32] About this point, see Galligan (1986, 8, 21) and Bell (1992, 92-94).

the control of law[33], it should be born in mind that this kind of autonomy and freedom is parasitic on a certain institutional duty. Freedom only exists in so far as it is necessary for judges to comply with their duty to render a decision, i.e. their obligation to settle every conflict taken to court.

In most contemporary systems, passing judgement on every case taken to court is an obligation inherent in the judicial function[34]. Nevertheless, it is worth noting the difference between the duty to render a decision, and that to decide in accord with the law. As will be discussed in chapters to come, strong discretion is fundamentally dependent on the absence of what is generally known as 'right legal answer'[35]. Thus, it is obvious that strong discretion is incompatible with the obligation to decide in accord with the law. Clearly, one speaks of strong discretion when it is the case that it is logically impossible to satisfy the institutional duty to pass judgement in accord with the law[36]. This conclusion can be easily reached by means of one of Kant's maxims: 'ought' implies 'can'[37]. From this point of view, only those actions whose realisation is factually or logically possible are normatively qualifiable. It is pointless to prescribe, for example, that stateless individuals should produce a national identification card to enter Spain because this prescription rests on the false logical presupposition that stateless persons bear a national identification card[38]. Therefore, a stateless individual cannot satisfy this prescription. This example embodies the above-mentioned Kantian maxim. Similarly, if a situation requires strong discretion, the judge cannot be subject to the obligation to solve conflicts by means of law because there exists no legal answer.

It could be argued that, when faced with a choice among different legally valid options, as is the case when there exists normative contradiction, whatever the final decision, the judge satisfies the requirement to decide in accord with the law. For the time being, we shall assume that the obligation to solve conflicts by means of law requires not only that law provides a right answer, but also that it provides criteria to choose among different legally valid solutions. Otherwise, it is the judge's responsibility

---

[33] Dworkin claims that in cases of strong discretion the decision-making agent is not subject to standards set by the legal authority. See Dworkin (1977, 33).

[34] For a discussion on the importance that such a judicial duty should exist, see Shapiro (1985, 577-578).

[35] An overview of the concept of right answer can be found in Aarnio (1987, 158-161). The absence of right answer is usually encountered when a) there exist several legal solutions for a case and the judge must decide in favour of one of them by means of extra-legal criteria, or b) there exists no legal solution for the case and the judge makes her choice among different extra-legal solutions.

[36] See Alchourrón and Bulygin (1971, 154-157).

[37] On this maxim, see Hoffsmaster (1982, 27-28). A detailed analysis can be found in von Wright (1970, 123-132).

[38] On the concept of false presupposition, see Ross (1958, 133-134).

to lay down the reasons that justify her choice. This, in turn, prevents full compliance with the obligation to decide in accordance with the law.

It should be emphasised that discretionary proceeding becomes meaningful in connection with the judge's general duty to render a decision. The persistence of this duty in all cases is undoubtedly what allows relating the absence of a right answer to strong judicial discretion. Nonetheless, the duty to decide does not merely require the judge to give an answer to every legal question. It is among the judge's fundamental obligations to provide a justification to her sentences and resolutions[39]. As we shall see later on, the relationship between these two standards is important to understand some of the restrictions imposed by legal theory upon discretionary action so as to distinguish discretionary acts from arbitrary ones.

So far we can claim that the possibility for choice featured by strong discretion entails a restricted autonomy which arises from the duty to render a justified decision. Hence, the room for choice cannot easily be conceived as a power, permission or, authorisation granted to the judge by the law[40] - it should be viewed as a legal duty to decide when law does not provide a univocal solution.

In most definitions of strong discretion, choice among different courses of action is considered to be a permission or power[41]. Confusion arises on this point if one intends to say that a judge who has strong discretion on a particular subject matter is entitled to choose among different alternatives. That an agent is empowered to perform x (where x means choosing among different courses of action) implies that the agent is also empowered not to do x. This creates a contradiction with the obligation to render a decision to which this sense of discretion relates according to those authors that consider the choice an authorisation or a power. Thus, it seems more appropriate to say that a judge has strong discretion when she is obliged to choose among different options. This has been called 'alternative obligation', that is to say, an obligation whose content is a disjunction of actions[42]. The judge must choose between open alternatives

---

39 This judicial duty is acknowledged in most legal orders. See, for instance, article 120.3 of the Spanish Constitution.

40 Along the lines of the conceptual proposals that address this question in the context of strong discretion, 'permission' and 'power' are assumed to be synonymous. But their equivalence is much debated. Thus, an individual is empowered to do x when the relevant authority explicitly neither forbids her to perform x nor forbids her not to do x. See von Wright (1970, 100-107).

41 See, for instance, Hart and Sacks (1958, 126), Barak (1989, 7), Bell (1992, 92), Lemper (1992, 185) and Greenawalt (1975, 366).

42 Alchourrón and Bulygin note that in these instances the judge has no specific obligation to condemn the defendant or to dismiss the claims. The general obligation to render a decision is what actually prevails, and the judge complies with this obligation both in the event of a conviction as in that of an acquittal. In

but she is entitled to set the standards that determine her decision. This is precisely where the freedom and autonomy typical of discretionary decisions come into play. Thus, although the judge is subject to the obligation to choose, there is no legal obligation as to which options she should favour[43].

1.3.3 Open alternatives

Up to this point, choice has been presented as a central feature to strong discretion. However, as pointed out by Hawkins, every choice entails the existence of different alternatives wherefore the antithesis to strong discretion is that situation in which law provides a precise and univocal solution to a case[44]. It is claimed in the latter situation that the determination of the normative premise of the judicial syllogism is free of controversy. It does not require a process of evaluation, nor a genuine choice between different courses of action. Hence, these are easy cases[45]. There is a single due course of action, a single right legal answer, and therefore there is no space for judicial autonomy. Legal philosophers generally link the existence of alternative options to difficulties in the interpretation of law. These difficulties result from the properties of the language in which law is expressed as well as from the indeterminacy of the legislator's purposes[46]. However, this claim is much debated. Dworkin, for instance, has been strongly criticised for excluding semantic problems from his characterisation of strong discretion[47]. He spares this sense of discretion for instances of legal gap, the situation when a legal proposition is neither true nor false. In his opinion, only if there is a legal gap is it legitimate to claim that the decision-maker is not subject to standards set by the legal authority. In instances of ambiguity and vagueness of the legal language, Dworkin argues that law seeks to provide guidelines to the judicial decision by means

---

this sense, this obligation is an 'alternative obligation', Alchourrón and Bulygin (1971, 157). Von Wright refers to this kind of obligation as 'disjunctive order'. See Von Wright (1970, 168).

43 See Rosenberg (1971, 637).

44 Hawkins (1992, 21).

45 These situations are referred to as 'easy cases' or 'clear cases' by legal theorists because, as pointed out by MacCormick (1978, 197), in such cases 'justification of decisions can be achieved by simple deduction from clear established rules'. See also Aarnio (1987, 1-3). We shall discuss in detail the distinction between 'easy cases' and 'hard cases' in Chapter 2.

46 See Galligan (1986, 1).

47 For this criticism, see Greenawalt (1975, 365, 366), Galligan (1986, 19-20) and Waluchow (1983, 330, 331; 1994, 190-207).

of standards the judge is obliged to apply, and it is not appropriate to say that there exists a possibility for choice among different courses of action[48].

Dworkin's claims prompt us to examine carefully those factors usually associated to the need for choice typical of strong discretion. Before we embark on a full analysis of these factors, it is worth noting that it may be the case that law determines explicitly a framework in which the judge has a specific margin of autonomy in the final decision. As an example, take those cases in which the legal prescription merely states a general goal or the ends to be pursued. In these cases it is the judge's responsibility to determine which is the best way to attain this goal. On other occasions, the judge has the power to decide according to the circumstances of the case and her own judgement. The regulation in what regards the admission and pertinence of evidence for a trial in the Spanish legal order constitutes a clear example of this[49]. However, these sorts of explicit power are of little relevance to strong discretion. Besides, they are limited in scope and subject to control[50]. The discussion about this sense of discretion turns on those mechanisms needed to comply with the judicial obligation to render a decision when law is imprecise, remains silent, or, prescribes contradicting courses of action. Hence, the existence of open alternatives is closely related to the absence of a right answer[51].

The relationship between existence of open alternatives, and absence of a right answer sheds light on the most common sources of strong discretion. In what follows, those sources that have received most attention from legal theorists and, in particular, from positivists, will be discussed.

---

48 Dworkin's rejection of semantic problems as instances of no right answer, and hence, as instances of strong discretion, is to be found throughout his work. See, in particular, his references to the problem of the 'semantic sting'. Dworkin (1986, 45, 46; 1987, 14-17; 1977, 33-38, 68-71).

49 See article 566 of the Spanish Rules of Criminal Procedure.

50 As pointed out above, Luzzati refers to this kind of power that judges may be granted by law as 'explicit discretion'. It was also mentioned that the present book would be focusing on implicit discretion and its connection with legal knowledge. See Luzzati (1990a, 130-137). It may be of interest to note that, in cases of no right answer, some legal orders explicitly empower the judges to act as a legislator. See article 1 of the Swiss Civil Code. This criterion completes the legal system by means of authoritative decisions that solve any particular conflict. Hence, the existence of a right legal answer can be ascertained for every individual case. Its only distinguishing feature would be that the judge is empowered to determine what it is. For this reason, it seems inappropriate to include this explicit power as an instance of strong discretion.

51 Cases for which there is an absence of right answer are often considered to be instances of 'hard cases'. This common term in the theory of adjudication has been defined in several ways. Later on I will discuss in detail the relationship between no right answer, hard cases, and strong discretion with a view to determining whether they can be considered coextensive.

Semantic problems

Hartian positivism has devoted much effort to the analysis of the semantic problems that cause indeterminacy in law[52]. A typical concern of this theory is that a legal system ceases to be an effective guide to conduct when the language in which the normative standards are expressed can be legitimately interpreted in several ways. It is assumed that semantic problems lead to strong discretion insofar as difficulties in the assignation of meaning to legal terms and expressions generate a variety of alternatives for action. The most important sources of indeterminacy are vagueness of concepts and ambiguity of terms[53]. Vagueness arises when the meaning of a term is imprecise, i.e. when it is not clear whether a certain case is included in or excluded from the scope of the term[54]. This is the case for terms such as 'reasonable' and 'prudent' whose definitory features do not permit to elucidate whether they embrace a certain case or not[55]. The meaning of terms such as 'bald' or 'rich', which apply to reality in a whole range of gradual intensities also entails vagueness. The distinguishing feature of such concepts is that the

---

52 'Indeterminacy of law' is the lack of deontic qualification of a certain conduct, that is, the absence of a right legal answer. Navarro observes that it is important to distinguish between legal indeterminacy in generic cases, and in individual ones. A generic case is a combination of properties, whereas an individual case is a particular instance of a generic case. If a legal system has a closure mechanism, it guarantees a right answer to every particular case. However, this does not ensure avoidance of legal indeterminacy with respect to generic cases. On this distinction see Navarro (1993, 249-252, 262-266).

53 In this context, I am referring to linguistic indeterminacy. Adjudication can involve other forms of legal indeterminacy such as indeterminacy of purpose, or what Kelsen called 'intentional indefiniteness'. Intentional indefiniteness is met in those instances where the appropriate authority has empowered the judiciary to determine the standards that guide its decisions in a particular subject matter. Luzzati claims that this is the only sense of indeterminacy in Kelsen's theory of law. See Kelsen (1970, 349-351) and Luzzati (1990a, 125-137). On the different sources of legal indeterminacy, see also Coleman and Leiter (1995, 212-219).

54 In this work, the problem of vagueness will be examined in the context of the theory of meaning as use. This is the most common semantic setting of positivist theories based on Wittgenstein's theory of meaning. If we accept that the meaning of a term or expression depends on the usage within the community of speakers, vagueness occurs when there is no well-established convention on whether a case is embraced by a certain concept or not. See, for instance, Luzzati (1990b, 12-13, 34-39).

55 Note that vagueness arises only when a concept is used to refer to some aspect of reality. Thus, concepts as such are not vague. They become vague when the conceptual system is measured against reality. The use of the term 'reasonable' raises no difficulty in a wide variety of cases where it functions in a precise way. The meaning of this term is vague only in those cases in which the conditions for its use do not include in or exclude from the concept the case under consideration. Every concept has a zone of certainty and a zone of penumbra. The zone of certainty covers all those cases to which the term clearly applies, as well as all those cases to which it clearly does not apply. In cases in the penumbral zone it is no longer clear whether the term applies or not. These are borderline cases. See Hart (1994, 122-127; 1958, 607-615).

frontier between the cases in which the property 'being rich' applies, and those in which it does not, is not sharp[56].

The vagueness of a concept is to be distinguished from what Hart, following Waismann, called the 'open texture' of language[57]. The latter expression refers to the fact that it is always possible to find a case whose inclusion in a concept is indeterminate. This problem is inherent in every concept, even in the most precise ones, and is due to the impossibility of comprehensively establishing the necessary and sufficient conditions for the use of a term (its intension[58]) when it is to be applied to reality. The open texture of language could only be avoided by taking into account in the definition of a term every single possible past, present and, future, as well as real and hypothetical applications. By contrast, we face vagueness when the case in question is a penumbral case. It is essential to distinguish between vagueness and the open texture of language, since strong discretion is linked to the occurrence of indeterminacy in law, and not to the mere possibility of its occurrence. The open texture of language is relevant to discretion insofar as it shows that there is always room for vagueness no matter how precisely law is expressed. As a consequence, discretion is inevitable.

The ambiguity of legal terms is a further source of legal indeterminacy. Ambiguity originates in the homonimy of words[59]. Take 'pole' as an example. A 'pole' is a long, slender, rounded piece of wood or metal, typically used with one end placed in the ground. 'Pole' can also be either of the two locations on the surface of the earth which are the northern and southern ends of its axis of rotation. That a word has more than one meaning, however, does not necessarily imply ambiguity. Ambiguity only arises when the linguistic context does not clarify which meaning of a word is intended. Likewise, ambiguity appears when a normative text may be expressing different propositions, and its legal context is of no assistance to determine its meaning.

In the study of strong discretion, vagueness has received preferential attention. Therefore, whenever we refer to the relationship between semantic problems and the absence of right answer, this source of legal indeterminacy will usually be invoked.

---

56 With regard to these cases of vagueness, see, for instance, Carrió (1965, 31-35).

57 See Hart (1994, 123, 127-129). For Waissman's characterisation of the open texture of language, see Waismann (1951, 119-120). On open texture, see also MacCormick (1991, 72-74), Bix (1991, 51-72) and Carrió (1965, 35-36).

58 The well-known distinction between the 'intension' and the 'extension' of a term was first proposed by Carnap. Briefly, when considering a predicate, its extension is the class of objects to which it applies, whereas its intension is the property it expresses. See Carnap (1947, 18-23).

59 A useful account of homonimy and how it differs from polysemy can be found in Lyons (1981). On the ambiguity of the legal context, and the difference between semantic and syntactic ambiguity, see Aarnio (1987, 111-112), Ross (1958, 115-125) and Carrió (1965, 28-31).

Vagueness is interesting as a source of strong discretion to the extent that getting to grips with it requires a choice among different options for interpretation. Raz claims that overcoming the difficulties raised by vagueness does not necessarily demand judicial discretion. If a legal rule is linguistically imprecise, the judge can appeal to principles as a way of selecting among alternative assignations of meaning[60]. Hence, the truth, falsity or lack of truth-value of a legal proposition does not only depend on each rule as an isolated item, but also on wider semantic considerations about the principles and the general contents of law. On some occasions, one or more principles will determine the meaning of a normative formulation that includes some vague concept or ambiguous term. In this case, the official is obliged to assign the meaning that most closely accords with the principles governing that particular normative context[61]. Similarly, when the rules of interpretation provided by the law can be effectively used to favour one among the possible assignations of meaning, the judge is obliged to choose that particular alternative[62].

---

60 Raz (1972, 846) also points out that appealing to principles does not eliminate the need for strong discretion. Principles are expressed by means of language, and their propositional contents may, too, be vague.

61 Even though both rules and principles are often considered to be correlations between generic cases and normative solutions, on some occasions a structural difference between the two is said to exist. It has been argued that rules are applicable in an all-or-nothing fashion whereas principles have a dimension of weight: they are reasons guiding conduct, but they do not establish the conditions for their own applicability. This is the distinction Dworkin (1977, 22-28) and Alexy (1993, 86) appear to support. Some authors, such as Atienza and Ruíz Manero (1991, 108-109) have taken this logical distinction further by saying that rules shape a case in a closed manner, whereas principles do it in an open manner. In this work, no special attention will be paid to the structural aspect of this distinction. It is not clear to me how a rule that is expressed linguistically, can conform a case in a closed manner, i.e. how a complete list of conditions of applicability can be drawn. Perhaps, as suggested by Laporta (1985, 5) and Aarnio (1987, 96-97), rather than setting forth a structural distinction between these two types of norms, it is more appropriate to establish a gradual one that respects the higher degree of generality and abstraction usually displayed by principles. It could also be said that principles are norms of a very fundamental nature and, as such, they reflect the basic guidelines and the core decisions that govern a normative system and justify its existence. See Prieto Sanchís (1992, 58-59). It seems to be the case that no criterion allows drawing a clear distinction between rules and principles. We probably do not even need such a criterion. It suffices to show that certain normative standards are more fundamental and abstract than others; that the more fundamental ones serve as criteria to justify the existence of other norms; and that they are used to interpret them. Whether these remarks reproduce the distinction between principles and norms may be viewed as a mere verbal issue.

62 Hart (1994, 126) claims that rules of interpretation may reduce the need for judicial discretion, but they cannot eliminate it since they, themselves, may be stated vaguely and require interpretation.

A number of alternative courses of action appear when linguistic problems such as vagueness and ambiguity cannot be overcome by means of legal mechanisms[63]. The interpreter faces a range of possibilities for interpretation. We shall investigate the relationship between this range of possibilities and the absence of a right legal answer. The question of how semantic problems affect the conditions of truth of legal propositions is a matter of concern for current legal theory[64]. The most common view within Hartian positivism is that a proposition, whose linguistic indeterminacy cannot be solved by means of law, has no truth-value, i.e. nothing can be ascertained about its truth or falsity[65]. In such a situation, none of the alternatives appears to be a right answer[66]. Dworkin's example on sacrilegious contracts is a useful example at this point. If we admit that the concept of sacrilegious contract is vague in what regards those contracts agreed on a Sunday, it follows that it is impossible to determine a right answer as to whether a particular contract that has been signed on a Sunday is sacrilegious or not[67].

In line with this argument, which is typical of a positivist characterisation of strong discretion, there is no right answer for those cases of ambiguity and vagueness that cannot be solved by means of legal tools[68]. Hence, linguistic indeterminacy may not become an epistemic problem. The only way to overcome these difficulties is by

---

63 If we adopt intentionalist semantics, accepting ambiguity and the existence of alternative actions implies admitting that the speaker has no specific intent when uttering a statement. If, however, we accept that an intent underlies every utterance, then ambiguity is an epistemic difficulty arising from incomplete information about the mental state of the speaker, and can therefore not be considered a source of strong discretion. As it is being described, discretion is dependent on the absence of a single right answer. If, however, intentionalist theory of meaning is replaced by conventionalist semantics, irresolvable ambiguity always generates semantic indeterminacy.

64 A legal proposition is the meaning of a normative statement, i.e. a statement describing the existence of a legal norm. On different approaches to the relationship between semantic problems and legal indeterminacy see Dworkin (1985, 119-145).

65 See Raz (1979, 70-74).

66 This idea can be easily grasped from the following passage by Hart (1994, 127): 'Here something in the nature of a crisis in communication is precipitated: there are reasons both for and against our use of a general term, and no firm convention or general agreement dictates its use, or, on the other hand, its rejection by the person concerned to classify. If in such cases doubts are to be resolved, something in the nature of a choice between open alternatives must made by whoever is to resolve them'.

67 On this particular example and the different versions of the thesis on the absence of a right answer, see Dworkin (1985, 119-137).

68 From this point of view, vagueness fits Raz's definition of legal gap. Legal gaps result from those situations in which some legal questions subject to jurisdiction have no complete answer. See Raz (1979, 70-71).

establishing a new normative pattern resulting from a new meaning ascription to the legal term or expression concerned[69].

The relationship between strong discretion and semantic problems is admittedly one of the most controversial points between Hartian positivism and Dworkin's theory. Dworkin views semantic problems as a source of weak discretion, and claims that cases of ambiguity or vagueness do not require strong discretion[70]. Strong discretion is limited to those cases in which there are no standards serving as guidelines to judicial decisions[71]. Dworkin backs up his claims with the following much-debated two arguments: firstly, a standard, however imprecise, aims at determining the judicial decision[72]; secondly, ambiguity and vagueness do not prevent the existence of a unique right answer. Dworkin claims that there is a single right answer to the problem of sacrilegious Sunday contracts because it is either true or false that a contract agreed on a Sunday is sacrilegious. If the contract is indeed sacrilegious, the judge ought to declare it invalid, and she is obliged to declare it otherwise, if this is not the case. Thus, the judge is effectively not exempt from her obligation to solve the conflict on the basis of the correct normative premise[73]. Indeed, the elucidation of the course of action demanded by the law requires good judgement, as is typical of weak discretion[74]. This,

---

[69] See Coleman and Leiter (1995, 216). Note that if it is assumed that semantic problems cause an absence of right answer, discretion may not be defined as the possibility for choice among different equally valid alternatives. 'Valid' here means 'belonging to the legal system'. We are thus urged to determine whether strong discretion can be characterised in terms of validity, which would limit its scope to cases of normative contradiction, or whether it is more interesting to use looser standards such as acceptability.

[70] Dworkin (1977, 32-33, 70).

[71] Dworkin (1977, 33).

[72] Dworkin (1977, 32) argues that: "if the sergeant is told to take the five most experienced men, he does not has discretion in this strong sense because that order purports to govern his decision. The boxing referee who must decide which fighter has been the more aggressive does not have discretion, in the strong sense, for the same reason'.

[73] On this point, see Dworkin (1977, 68-71).

[74] In order to exemplify the kind of judicial activity required in the context of weak discretion, Dworkin makes up the figure of Hercules. Hercules is an ideal judge with outstanding abilities, no time constraints, and a sound knowledge of law and of the justifying role of legal principles. Hercules has an extremely well-developed conception of law that allows him to provide the right answer even in those cases in which there are important epistemic difficulties to grasp the solution prescribed by the law. Dworkin maintains, in accordance with his own epistemic approach to law, that Hercules' answer is interpretive, i.e. it is theory-dependent. Therefore, the fact that Hercules is able to find the right answer, Dworkin claims, does not mean he has the ability to contrast legal propositions with reality independently of his own conceptual schemes. It is particularly important to keep the latter consideration in mind to avoid some of the most common misunderstandings of Dworkin's theory. On the figure of Hercules, see Dworkin (1977, 105-130; 1986, 239-275).

however, does not discard the possibility of controversy as long as different interpreters may disagree about the outcome of the decision[75].

Several authors have criticised both of these arguments. Waluchow devoted a paper to proving that Dworkin's attempt to characterise strong discretion excluding semantic indeterminacy is not successful. His criticism of Dworkin's first argument is particularly interesting[76]. He argues that there is a fundamental difference between purporting to control a decision, and actually controlling it. Strong discretion as a choice among different courses of action arises when a standard proves unsuccessful in guiding a resolution[77]. This situation implies that there exists a range of possible conclusions, and that law does not offer an answer as to which one should be handed down. An authoritative standard may purport, but fail, to control a decision. Thus, according to Waluchow, purporting to control a decision is not sufficient to prevent having to exercise strong discretion to comply with the judicial obligation to render a decision[78]. This argument shows the weakness of Dworkin's attempt to exclude semantic problems from the scope of strong discretion. An important aspect of this concept is the freedom to decide. This freedom can only be exercised when there exists more than one possible course of action, i.e. whenever the judge lacks an effective guide to the decision. Unless it is proven that semantic problems always have a unique right answer, a standard may, due to linguistic reasons, fail to control the outcome of a resolution. Thus, Dworkin's position should rest on his second argument, i.e. that a legal proposition is always either true or false and therefore, that there always is one correct answer[79].

---

75 This point will be relevant to later chapters. It is worth noting that Dworkin does not claim that disagreement about the meaning of words implies an absence of right answer. Neither does disagreement on the sources of law imply such an absence. In fact, interpretive disagreements lie at the very heart of his view of law as a dynamical and interpretive concept.

76 See Waluchow (1983, 321-331).

77 Waluchow claims that making strong discretion dependent on the existence of standards that pretend to control a decision is equivalent to expecting the interpreter to act as if there exist a single right answer. Moreover, it would entail obliging her to accept that there is, indeed, such an answer, and urging her to find this answer, in spite of her conviction that such an answer does not exist. See Waluchow (1983, 326). It should be borne in mind that this criticism of Dworkin's characterisation is confined to a particular interpretation of Dworkin's theory and of his thesis on the right answer. In chapters to come, the context of Dworkin's discussion of the problem of strong discretion and that of the right answer will be specified.

78 See Waluchow (1983, 325-328). On this point, see also Galligan (1986, 20).

79 On this point, see Galligan (1986, 17). The claim that legal propositions are either true or false has recently been replied. Dworkin argues that linguistic indeterminacy can be avoided by making use of the legislative principle that states that all legal propositions that are not true, should be considered false. His critics claim that if this principle is interpreted as the statement that all legal propositions that are not true are false, then this interpretation implies bivalence only insofar as it is assumed. On the other hand, this

The second of Ronald Dworkin's arguments raised great controversy and met with strong positivist objections. On the one hand, to authors such as Greenawalt or Galligan it seems pointless to claim that there exists one right answer if no qualified interpreter is able to identify it, or if there is genuine disagreement about the meaning of legal expressions. Such a situation requires making a choice, and therefore falls within the scope of strong discretion[80].

On the other hand, some critics of Dworkin argue that strong discretion cannot be avoided by taking as the truth condition of legal propositions their consistency with a coherent set of propositions that offer the best interpretation of the legal phenomenon. Marmor claims that Dworkin's theory neglects the possibility for a number of incommensurable alternative reconstructions to portray the phenomenon in its best light[81].

The debate about whether linguistic problems are a source of strong discretion requires detailed analysis. It is not a mere verbal question, but one that conceals deep disagreements between different approaches to law. The relationship between semantic indeterminacy and strong discretion is very much dependent on both the importance attached to consensus about the meaning of terms when establishing the truth conditions of legal propositions, and on whether it is assumed that there exists a single correct

---

principle as a standard addressed to judges has a contingent character, i.e. it may or may not be contained in the legal order. On these and other criticisms to Dworkin's thesis on bivalence, see Endicott (1997) and Moreso (1998, 63-72).

80 Greenawalt argues that it is legitimate to talk about strong discretion in those cases in which, although it is accepted that a right answer might exist, it is epistemically impossible to identify it. See Greenawalt (1975, 368, 374-375). For a discussion on Dworkin, see Galligan (1986, 17-18). Dworkin has responded to this criticism in two ways: firstly, he claims that a right answer may exist despite the impossibility to empirically prove so. This argument is complex and will be discussed later on. For the time being, let me just point out that Dworkin holds a view on the truth conditions of legal propositions that significantly differs from Galligan's and Greenawalt's. Dworkin claims that a proposition is true when it coheres with the set of propositions that offer the best interpretation of a given phenomenon. Thus, Dworkin does not agree that in order for a proposition to be true it has to accord with certain hard facts, i.e. material facts and other facts concerning human conduct. See Dworkin (1985,137-142). About this point, see also Bix (1993, 107). Secondly, Dworkin argues that semantic disagreement does not necessarily imply an absence of right answer for interpreters may continue to think that such an answer exists. They may put forward arguments in favour of a particular interpretation but they may disagree on what the right answer is. This argument has also been misinterpreted. It does not simply blur the distinction between the existence of a right answer and the belief that such an answer exists. It should be analysed within a coherentist theory of knowledge that takes the distinction between what is subjective and what is objective to be less sharp. See Dworkin (1986, 6-15), Waluchow (1983, 332-333, 335-336) and McDowell (1981, 151-152).

81 See Marmor (1992, 54-55), Finnis (1987, 371) and Putnam (1995a, 6-7).

answer to every case. Generally speaking, the theory of truth, of knowledge, and, of interpretation assumed will have fundamental implications on the relationship between semantic indeterminacy and strong discretion. A close look at the disagreements on these subjects will provide insight into the concept of strong discretion, and shed light on the different models about the role of strong discretion in adjudication. We shall devote further attention to these matters in Chapter 2.

Legal gaps

Legal gaps are regarded as a source of strong discretion because the interpreter must make a choice between alternatives. The problem of legal gaps often relates to that of semantic indeterminacy. According to the view that in case of vagueness legal propositions are neither true nor false, legal gaps result from semantic indeterminacy. Yet, legal gaps may also arise in cases where there is no relevant semantic difficulty. For this reason, we will engage in a separate analysis of legal gaps.

Most legal philosophers use 'Gap' in a wide sense. It is defined as the absence of a normative solution for a particular legal question[82]. In this sense, legal gaps are no more than those cases of absence of a right answer. Dworkin claims that a gap arises when a legal proposition is neither true nor false[83]. But we should define the idea of legal gap more precisely to exclude from its scope instances of no right answer such as whether it is permitted to take tea or coffee at breakfast. Dworkin's metaphor of the normative doughnut may be useful to characterise the idea of legal gap: the absence of correct answer should occur within the normative context that makes sense of the judicial function. Hence, 'legal gap' does not designate those cases of no right answer occurring in legally irrelevant aspects of social life[84]. Similarly, Joseph Raz states that a legal gap in its strict sense arises when 'some legal questions subject to jurisdiction have no complete answer'[85].

One could think that Alchourrón and Bulygin's distinction between normative gaps and axiological gaps might help to grasp the idea of legal gap. There is a normative gap

---

[82] On this wide sense of legal gap see, for instance, Raz (1979, 70-74) and Barak (1989, 83).

[83] Dworkin (1989, 127-128).

[84] Although any situation is liable to be legally regulated, we are compelled to accept that law does not govern every aspect of social life. It thus seems reasonable to claim that certain domains of human life fall outside the domain of law.

[85] Raz (1979, 70). Raz defines 'complete answer' as the answer provided by the law. Raz (1979, 70-72) distinguishes between these gaps and what he calls 'jurisdictional gaps' which arise when courts lack jurisdiction about a particular legal matter.

when a generic case has no normative solution[86]. In such a situation, the legislator awarded some relevance to a particular property or set of properties, but he or she forgot to explicitly assign a legal answer to it in the writing of the law. By contrast, an axiological gap occurs when the legislator has devised a generic case without paying attention to a particular property, which the interpreter considers relevant to law[87]. According to Alchourrón and Bulygin, axiological gaps are not instances of no right answer because there exists a generic case to which there is a solution[88].

Generally speaking, gaps are regarded to be cases of absence of right answer to a legal question from a different point of view. The reason for this is that 'legal question' includes situations excluded from 'generic case'. The latter arises as a result of the interpretation of normative formulations whereas the former refers to the interpretation of normative material as well as to the result of interpretation. Raz's definition of legal gap clearly reflects this point: a legal gap is a legal question that has been taken to court and which has no right legal answer. As such, this notion includes situations of linguistic indeterminacy[89] as well as irresolvable normative conflicts, both of which are excluded from the strict concept of normative gap[90].

Thus, we shall call this wide sense of gap 'legal gap' so as to distinguish it from 'normative gap'. 'Legal gap' is relevant to the present discussion because of the connection often established between the absence of right answer and strong judicial discretion. Here discretion is deemed necessary when law does not provide an answer to the legal question in hand. Authoritative judicial decisions should overcome law's shortcomings. One meets with this situation when: a) semantic indeterminacy cannot be

---

86 A more technical definition can be found in Alchourrón and Bulygin (1971, 62,). A generic case is that combination of properties whose occurrence or non-occurrence has an implication on the normative solution and which is identified on the grounds of the thesis of relevance assumed by the legislative body. See Alchourrón and Bulygin (1971, 62, 146) and Navarro (1993, 250-252).

87 Alchourrón and Bulygin (1971, 106-107).

88 Alchourrón and Bulygin (1971, 106-111).

89 For Alchourrón and Bulygin, linguistic indeterminacy creates recognition gaps and does not imply an absence of legal answer. Recognition gaps generate semantic-epistemic difficulties, but not legal incompleteness. In these borderline cases, legal propositions may continue to be true or false. See Alchourrón and Bulygin (1971, 33).

90 Recall that Raz divides legal gaps into two types: a) those cases in which it is neither true nor false that law conclusively requires an action, or permits its omission; b) instances for which it is true that law neither requires conclusively a certain action, nor conclusively permits its omission. Linguistic indeterminacy and irresolvable normative conflicts are instances of the former type and are, according to Raz, inevitable. Raz denies the latter type of gap because the principle that everything that is not legally prohibited is legally permitted applies to these instances. This is an analytical truth if we accept the social sources thesis, i.e. that the existence and contents of law shall be determined with reference to social facts. For an account of this argument, see Raz (1979, 72-77).

settled by means of legal mechanisms. In this case, a legal proposition is neither true nor false; or, b) a generic case has no normative solution[91].

In the former situation it is not possible to offer a correct interpretation of the normative material to obtain a generic case. In the latter, by contrast, interpretation results in a generic case for which there is no solution.

A choice between alternatives is required to fill the legal gap. The distinguishing feature of this choice is precisely that, by the very definition of gap, it is made among extra-legal alternatives. Gaps thus allow us to establish an important link between strong discretion and invention of norms by judges[92]. Hence, accepting or rejecting the existence of legal gaps has a direct impact on the role attributed to strong discretion in the judicial decision-making process and on the room allowed for judicial legislation[93].

Normative contradiction

Ross writes that there exists a contradiction or an inconsistency between two rules 'where incompatible legal effects are attached to the same factual conditions'[94]. In these cases, law speaks with many voices[95]. Some authors claim that irresolvable normative contradictions result in absence of right answer. However, this statement requires further consideration[96]. A contradiction presupposes the existence of incompatible

---

91 What Raz has called 'irresolvable normative conflicts' will be excluded from our account. Their inclusion as cases of absence of right answer requires further consideration. See Raz (1979, 75). I shall moreover point out that our characterisation of legal gap does not presuppose any particular position with respect to the thesis of the existence of legal gaps. So far, I am only interested in a conceptual analysis of strong discretion and in those elements conceptually related to this kind of discretion, regardless of whether the existence of both strong discretion and of legal gaps is accepted at all.

92 Hart calls the creation of norms by the judiciary in instances of legal gaps 'interstitial legislation'. See Hart (1983, 138).

93 When speaking of the possibility that judges may create norms when they have discretion, we do not mean that judges may create individual norms when applying the law - they always do so. Although sentences have a declarative dimension in cases of discretion, they also have a constitutive dimension for the particular case in hand (except for declarative sentences). The problem of judicial creation of norms by means of discretion turns on the question of whether judges are entitled to determine or create the general normative premise rather than on whether they are entitled to put forward an individual norm that derives from a general norm. On this point, see Kelsen (1970, 236-242). For a discussion of Kelsen's views, see Bulygin (1991b, 362-366).

94 Ross (1958, 128).

95 See Raz (1979, 77).

96 'Irresolvable normative contradiction' refers to that situation in which different norms impute different incompatible legal solutions to the same facts, and in which legal mechanisms of interpretation and principles solving antinomies (*lex superior, lex posterior, lex specialis*) are of no assistance to select one among the different possible courses of action. On the idea of contradiction as a situation of absence of right answer, see Raz (1979, 74-77), Peczenik (1989, 25), and Moreso (1998, 56-57).

legally valid answers. If the propositions referring to those rules were not all true, we would not meet with a contradiction between legal rules. At this point note that there is an important difference between this case, and that of a legal gap, in which, by definition, law remains silent. Why, then, should the cases of contradiction be considered instances of absence of right answer? Inclusion only makes sense if 'right answer' is understood as *single right answer*. Coleman and Leiter point out in this respect that if more than one legal source applies to a case, there will be more than one norm controlling the decision. They stress that ' there may, then, be too may standards available for adjudicating a case to claim that there is only one uniquely warranted outcome. Arguments for indeterminacy, then, can be grounded on considerations of law's internal and unavoidable inconsistency' [97]. Accordingly, the judge's decision will be predetermined only in those instances where there is a single legal answer. If there exist several answers, the decision-maker herself has the autonomy to establish the criteria governing her decisions. In that case, the criteria that allow to solve the normative conflict and to choose among different possible courses of action are not laid down by the law[98]. Nevertheless, the legal character of the conflicting alternatives remains unaffected. Therefore: given the judicial obligation to decide according to the law on the one hand, and that to provide justification to every verdict on the other, we can conclude that, although each one of the conflicting answers is legally valid, the preference for one of them over the others cannot be justified legally. In short, if there is normative contradiction, the judge cannot comply with her obligation to decide in accord with the law. Under such circumstances it is plausible to think of contradiction as an instance of absence of right answer, not because there is a lack of legally valid solutions, but because law specifies no criterion to select among the different legal options. Given that the judge is expected to provide a single answer that accords with law, her decision is not completely determined by the legal order[99].

1.3.4 The zone of reasonableness

Both the idea of a gap in the law, and the thesis that links linguistic indeterminacy to an absence of right answer face serious conceptual difficulties if strong discretion is merely defined as the possibility for choice among different, and, equally valid courses of

---

[97] Coleman and Leiter (1995, 218).

[98] See Bix (1993, 25-26).

[99] A similar argument applies to conflicting principles. Leaving aside for the time being the question of whether there is any structural difference between principles and rules (and the potential consequences of such a difference), the solution of an irreducible conflict between legal principles requires strong discretion for the same reasons that the solution of an irresolvable conflict between rules does.

action[100]. If there is no correct answer, no alternative is a valid course of action. With a view to overcoming this difficulty, some authors have replaced the requirement that the alternatives be 'valid' for that which requires them to be 'admissible' or 'reasonable'[101]. The advantages of this looser requirement are twofold: on the one hand, every instance of no right answer can be included in the concept of strong discretion; on the other, the range of available options for action remains limited. Strong discretion is thus conceptually linked to a range of acceptable answers among which the decision-maker must make her choice. This bounded region is what Barak very appropriately called 'the zone of reasonableness'[102]. The zone of reasonableness embraces all those answers that, although not legally valid, are legally acceptable[103].

Yet, 'reasonableness' is rather obscure as a criterion. In the present context, its meaning is closely related to consistency with the guiding principles of the legal order, and the legal order as a whole[104]. This criterion stresses the need for discretionary judicial decisions to remain as close as possible to the established system of sources and to the linguistic uses in the legal community[105]. Thus, the degree of reasonableness of an option that lies in the zone of reasonableness is rarely conceptually related to its moral acceptability or to its political appropriateness[106]. The aim of the zone of reasonableness is, in line with positivist thought, to characterise strong discretion by

---

100 A course of action is a valid course of action if there exists a legal norm that justifies it or, equivalently, when it is the result of applying a valid legal norm that has been created by the competent authority in accordance with the prescribed procedure. For a discussion on the different meanings of 'validity' see Kelsen (1970, 10-15), and Alchourrón and Bulygin (1979, 41-43).

101 See Hart and Sacks (1958, 126), Greenawalt (1975, 366), MacCormick (1982, 282), and Bix (1993, 26-27). Davis stands as an important exception to this line of thought. He defines discretion as room for freedom to choose among the different courses of action that are within the effective limits of an official's power. Davis seeks to thus show that neither 'validity' nor 'admissibility' are adequate concepts to describe strong discretion and discretionary activity as it occurs in reality. In Davis's opinion, remarkable proportions of discretionary decisions are in fact legally questionable, if not unlawful. See Davis (1969, 4, 12).

102 Barak (1989, 115-118).

103 If there is normative contradiction, the different alternatives in the 'zone of reasonableness' are legal answers. This, however, does not imply that the choice among these options is free of constraints.

104 See, for instance, MacCormick (1978, 250-255).

105 See Isaacs (1933, 347-348), Traynor (1978, 1032-1033), Rosenberg (1971, 643) and Galligan (1986, 321-322). Galligan draws a distinction between reasonableness with respect to the aims of law, and reasonableness as 'moral acceptability'.

106 The concept of reasonableness as moral acceptability has been developed in the theory of legal argumentation and practical discourse. Sometimes reasonableness is linked to the factual consensus on the moral correctness of a specific course of action. On other occasions, it is linked to a hypothetical consensus within an ideal discursive context. On this point, see Aarnio (1990, 33-38) and Alexy (1989, 119-124, 160-164, 287-292).

means of a minimal legal control that allows to distinguish those options which accord with the general goals and aims of law, from those which are not based on the system of legal sources[107]. Certainly, the actual control mechanism may be imprecise and for this very reason, the zone of reasonableness may turn out to be controversial. The determination of its contents may itself be subject to discretion[108]. Even the existence of a zone of reasonableness may be questionable when it is the case that the legal order does not provide correct answers. Accepting the existence of a zone of reasonableness suggests an understanding of strong discretion as an activity that is not subject to specific legal rules predetermining the outcome of a decision, but still linked to general legal standards and guidelines. In this sense, Raz and Soper draw a distinction between substantive legal principles, and principles of discretion. The former predetermine the outcome of the judicial decision, whereas the latter specify the values, criteria and goals to be taken into consideration by a judge when there is no right legal answer. They only establish a set of considerations that the judge ought to respect, but they do not prescribe a solution to the case[109]. Underlying this position is a restrictive conception of discretion: only legally reasonable acts will qualify as discretionary. Such a conception imposes strict limitations on the role of discretion in adjudication. Although this conception deviates from the formalist view that holds that all judicial activity is either strictly mechanical or exempt of legal control, it is in great contrast to wide conceptions of law such as Ronald Dworkin's, who claims that elements such as reasonableness and coherence with a structure of legal standards are features inherent in legal knowledge. His idea of validity of a particular course of action does not coincide with the one presented here. In fact, Dworkin believes the present discussion to fall within the scope of weak discretion.

1.3.5 The demand for justification

The way in which a particular choice among alternative options is to be made places a further restriction on the concept of strong discretion. Unlike arbitrary decisions, strong discretion does not only entail making a choice among different courses of action, but

---

107 MacCormick claims that judicial discretion is restricted by the following three requirements: a) the judicial decision should use legal principles and construct analogies; b) standards such as consistency and coherence should be taken into account; c) consideration should be given to the consequences of the final decision. See MacCormick (1978, 249-251). Similarly, Ruíz Manero (1990, 185-189). It is worth noting that most of these criteria are clearly conservative methods of normative integration for they all aim to draw the reasons justifying the decision as close as possible to settled law.

108 Barak (1989, 117).

109 See also Soper (1984, 3-7).

also providing a justification for the final decision[110]. This statement rests on the following two arguments: firstly, a justification is required for every decision that affects the interests of individuals; secondly, it is part of the fundamental duties of the judge to provide justification to every resolution, in other words, the judge is obliged to put forward reasons for her choice. Raz writes:

> Even when discretion is not limited or guided in any specific direction the courts are still legally bound to act as they think is best according to their beliefs and values. If they do not, if they give arbitrary judgement by tossing a coin, for example, they violate a legal duty. A judge must always invoke some general reasons. He has no discretion when the reasons are dictated by law. He has discretion when the law requires him to act on reasons which he thinks are correct, instead of imposing its own standards'[111].

The demand for justification is one of the features of most conceptual characterisations of strong discretion. Strong discretion is not only about making a choice between the different options in the 'zone of reasonableness' - the choice itself requires a general justification. Consequently, both arbitrary decisions, and those that are made on the basis of particular reasons (i.e. those which do not entail the commitment to act in the same way under identical circumstances) are excluded from the scope of strong discretion. Thus, even if discretionary decisions are not subject to the principle of legality, they should respect that of universality. In other words, and following Alexy's idea of universality, the choice has to be based on a general normative premise applicable to all those cases that share the same relevant characteristics in the discursive context in hand[112]. Furthermore, acting according to

---

110 Galligan asserts that understanding discretion as a mere choice between courses of action is too simplistic a view. Decisions are to be made on the basis of reasons because no course of action can be separated from the reasons that justify it. Thus, it would be irrational to follow the course of action X when there are compelling reasons to believe that the course of action Y is better, Galligan (1986, 7-8). Isaacs points out that proceeding without justification would entail an abuse of discretion. In his opinion, this idea is closely related to another basic idea in the conceptual analysis of discretion, namely that asserting the possibility of discretionary proceeding does not mean submitting the case to the arbitrary will of the judicial body. See Isaacs (1933, 349-350). Similarly, Barak (1989, 118-121) points out that judges are not entitled to decide by flipping a coin. The judge must: a) evaluate factors relating to the structure and development of the legal system; b) take into consideration institutional factors; c) take into account the inter-relations among the different institutions. In a similar line of thought, see Wasserstrom (1961, 23-25), Lord Hodson (1961, 1-19), Bell (1992, 96-97), Dworkin (1977, 33) and Pattenden (1990, 395).

111 Raz (1972, 847-848). See also Hart (1980, 9; 1994, 127)

112 Alexy's definition of the rule of universality rests on the assumption that a speaker can only make those normative judgements that he or she would make in every situation that is identical in all relevant aspects to the one under consideration. See Alexy (1989, 190, 225-228, 275-276), MacCormick (1978, 83-86, 97-99), and Peczenik (1989, 172). Universality can be considered a minimal requirement in

reasons does not merely mean using a standard to justify one decision when several possibilities exist - it requires that the outcome of a decision be based on those reasons that the interpreter ultimately believes to be the best[113].

If the idea of discretion embraces the need for justification, it is easy to distinguish discretion from arbitrariness. Discretionary decisions are never unlawful. Like every other judicial decision, they must be based on reasons. By contrast, arbitrary decisions are irrational and unlawful due to the lack of justifying reasons for action. Hence, it is important to stress that the notions of discretion and arbitrariness are incompatible with one another[114].

The demand for justification substantially reduces the range of activities that qualify as discretionary. The key point now is to what extent this is a legal constraint. Although the need for justification is associated to the institutional function of judges, the grounds for it lie on criteria of rationality[115]. This may generate difficulties when attempting to separate the legal context from practical discourse within the sphere of discretion. Thus, when positivists construct a restrictive conceptual framework of strong discretion, they may appear to be establishing a link between legal discourse and general practical discourse. Nevertheless, positivism only tacitly comes near practical discourse. It is therefore hard to reach a conclusion as to the consequences of the alleged legal constraints to strong discretion, particularly because one of the central theses of positivism is the separation of the legal context from any other normative context. Perhaps, one way to grasp positivist thought to its full extent as far as the theory of adjudication is concerned is by distinguishing between simple positivism and sophisticated positivism, as Shiner indeed suggests. They both have different theoretical

---

formal equality in instances in which formal equality cannot be warranted by means of the principle of legality.

113 On this point, see Raz (1972, 848) and Galligan (1986, 7-8). This demand in fact amounts to the rule of general practical discourse proposed by Alexy, which reads that an agent may only claim what he or she believes. This standard guarantees honesty in practical discourse. See Alexy (1989, 188-189).

114 It was pointed out earlier that Davis's view on the relationship between discretion and illegality is an exception to this opinion. See Davis (1969, 4-30). See also Dicey (1945, 188) and Hayek (1960, 228, 453). It should be noted, however, that Davis, Dicey and Hayek assume different notions of discretion and arbitrariness. It turns out that these concepts are mutually exclusive only when strong discretion is understood in a restrictive sense, and arbitrariness as a lack of rationality. Thus, an arbitrary decision is that which does not result from a reasoning process based on a general normative premise. On this point, and other meanings of 'arbitrariness' as inadequacy of means to ends, or as a lack of predictability of a decision, see Galligan (1986, 143-152) and Aarnio (1987, 3-5).

115 Alexy (1989, 179) writes: ‘Discourses are sets of interconnected actions devoted to testing the truth or correctness of the things we say. Discourses concerned with the correctness of normative statements are practical discourses’.

and practical implications[116]. Use of this distinction will be made in Chapter 2 to evaluate the extent to which the different versions of current legal positivism maintain the thesis of strong discretion.

What has been presented up to now permits a positivist definition of strong discretion: a decision-maker has discretion when, in a case for which there is no single right legal answer, she must make a justified choice among different admissible courses of action. This definition will prove useful to distinguish between the situation in which one has discretion, and that in which one believes to have discretion. This distinction will shed light on the differences between having discretion, and exercising discretion.

1.3.6 Having discretion and exercising discretion

In line with what has been presented so far, discretion comes into play if there is no single right answer to the legal question in hand. Therefore, strong discretion is logically independent of the interpreters' beliefs about the existence of a right answer[117]. A judge may wrongly believe that there is or is not a right legal answer to the case. It then becomes important to distinguish between 'having discretion' and 'believing that one has discretion'. Judicial discretion is dependent on the occurrence of certain facts closely related to the linguistic behaviour of a community and to the normative acts of a particular authority. If the truth-value of legal propositions is conditional on the occurrence of these facts, the interpreters' beliefs may not become the factor determining whether there is a need for judicial discretion in the solution of a case. This idea leads to a further distinction: having discretion and exercising discretion. For a judge to exercise strong discretion, three elements must come together: a) an external element, namely the absence of a right answer, which calls for a choice among alternatives; b) an internal element: the agent's belief that no right answer exists; c) the act of choosing among admissible alternatives. Hence, the exercise of strong discretion,

---

116 Shiner considers that one of the main differences between simple and sophisticated positivism is their respective conceptualisations of strong discretion. Simple positivism accepts that the extent to which a discretionary act is rational can be evaluated in terms of morality and efficiency. However, it does not understand evaluation against these standards to be of a legal nature because they do not derive from the competent authority through the prescribed procedure. Sophisticated positivism, on the other hand, approves of the separation between law and other normative contexts. Nevertheless, it accepts that a discretionary decision is legally constrained by the obligation to provide reasons, and denies arbitrary proceeding. For an account of these different perspectives see Shiner (1992b, 30-35, 80-87).

117 See Waluchow (1983, 335-336). See also Greenawalt (1975, 384-385). Barak observes that strong discretion is not a mental or emotional state, but a legal situation in which the judge is free to decide between alternatives because law does not determine the course of action to be undertaken. See Barak (1989, 8).

in contrast with the existence of strong discretion, is not separable from the interpreters' beliefs since the compliance with a duty, or the exercise of a power, as is the case here, requires the agent to be aware of the existence of such duty or power. According to the present conceptualisation of strong discretion, the judge's exercise of discretion is in fact compliance with her duty to choose among alternative courses of action.

Some authors disagree about this distinction between having and exercising discretion. Waluchow, for instance, agrees that there is a difference between having strong discretion and believing that one has strong discretion, but claims that judges exercise discretion whenever they genuinely believe that there is no right legal answer to the matter in hand. Thus, judges exercise discretion even if they are mistaken in their belief that there is no right answer. If a judge believes she has discretion, she feels compelled to choose among different courses of action in the same way as when she truly has discretion, even though, in fact, she does not. Waluchow's opinion is summarised in the following two paragraphs:

> Even if it were true that judges believe that controls never runs out, this would provide little in the way of support for the claim that they do not have strong discretion. The judges might simply be wrong about whether their decisions are always controlled. The truth of a proposition does not, as a rule, follow from the fact that it is widely accepted'[118].

> The exercise of strong discretionary judgment does not entail that the decision on X is uncontrolled. [...] Suppose a case in which S sincerely believes after much hard thought that his decision is not fully controlled and that he is therefore at liberty, because ha has no other alternative, to choose between two answers neither of which is ruled out by the relevant authoritative standards. Suppose further that S's belief is incorrect, and that one of the two answers is in fact the right one [...]. S will, given his beliefs, be forced to make the sort of choice he is entitled to make when he has strong discretion'[119].

It is worth enquiring why this author assumes that it is possible for a judge to exercise discretion even if she has no discretion. It seems a counterintuitive idea. It would appear rather strange for someone who does not have the right to vote, to exercise this right. (On the other hand, this situation is clearly distinct from the one in which someone, who does not have this right, acts as if he or she did). Noting the following ambiguity in Waluchow's notion of discretion helps to understand his thesis. He uses this term with two different meanings: one relates to the absence of right answer; the other appears in connection with epistemic difficulties to identify the right answer. His notion of exercising discretion makes implicit use of the second meaning. Both meanings seem to be equally central to his analysis of judicial activity. He shows

---

[118] Waluchow (1983, 334). The same idea is presented in Shiner (1992b, 32).

[119] Waluchow (1983, 333).

that judges often face a choice among alternative options, and it cannot be claimed that their choice is unnecessary or improper. According to Waluchow, given that judges are always subject to the obligation to render a decision, it is improper to expect them to go beyond their epistemic abilities to do so[120].

That judges find themselves forced to make decisions whenever they genuinely believe that there is an absence of right answer does not imply that their decisions are discretionary unless it is accepted that strong discretion is dependent on the epistemic abilities of the interpreter. However, this idea seems incompatible with Waluchow's claim that having discretion is quite a different matter from believing that one has discretion. This seems to show a conflict between two different theses on the limits of law: on the one hand, that which claims that the limits of law are independent of the interpreters, and, on the other, that which argues that the limits of law to a considerable extent depend on the interpreter's epistemic abilities.

This conflict is implicit in Greenawalt's, Shiner's and Galligan's proposals on strong discretion. For instance, Galligan defines strong discretion on the basis of two elements: the absence of right answer, and the judge's belief that such an answer does not exist[121]. It is obvious that these elements may conflict with each other. The only way to overcome the inconsistency in these proposals of strong discretion is by considering that strong discretion only occurs in those cases in which the body of adjudication is right in its belief that there exists no right legal answer.

The problems encountered in Waluchow's distinction between having discretion and exercising discretion illustrate one of the challenges faced by legal theory, namely that of devising a conception of law and legal knowledge accessible to both, decision-makers and lawyers. We will discuss this point further in Chapter 2. So far, the notion of right answer in our characterisation of strong discretion is based on a correspondentist theory of truth according to which the truth-value of legal propositions depends on specific facts whose occurrence transcends the epistemic abilities of the agents to identify them[122]. From this point of view, having discretion depends on certain facts and its exercise is conditional on certain mental states whose content corresponds with these facts. The conviction that there is no right answer may compel the interpreter to make a choice among open alternatives, but this is not the kind of choice typical of the concept of strong discretion that has been outlined so far. The view

[120] Waluchow (1983, 333-337). See also Greenawalt (1975, 375) and Galligan (1986, 12-14, 20-22).

[121] See Galligan (1986, 12-14, 20-22).

[122] For the time being, the question whether the truth of a proposition may transcend the epistemic abilities of an individual agent without transcending the epistemic abilities of a community of speakers will not be discussed. We will postpone this discussion until later chapters.

that takes into account the epistemic abilities of the interpreters in its characterisation of strong discretion is meaningful only if an alternative theory on the truth conditions of legal propositions is accepted. These two views are incompatible with one another, and they appear closely intertwined in the conceptual proposals of positivist theorists such as Waluchow, Greenawalt, Shiner and Galligan.

1.4 WEAK DISCRETION

Weak discretion was earlier defined as the need for good judgement in normative adjudication. We further pointed out that weak discretion is often linked to the difficulties in elucidating the legal answer in instances where law only provides abstract or imprecise standards subject to a variety of interpretations[123]. The distinguishing feature of weak discretion is the assumption that there exist legal mechanisms to solve this type of epistemic problems. Thus, there is a single right answer although incomplete information may call for a complex reasoning process to identify it[124].

There are two main approaches to weak discretion that differ in whether or not the existence of a right answer is assumed independent of the epistemic abilities of the interpreters. The next two sections will be devoted to sketching each one of them.

1.4.1 An approach to weak discretion

For those who understand the existence of a right answer to be independent of the epistemic abilities of interpreters, two features characterise weak discretion: the occurrence of discretion depends firstly on 'the structural relationship between pre-existing authoritative standards, and the decision that has to be taken in the instant case'[125], and, secondly, on the difficulties to identify the course of action required by these standards[126]. From this point of view, it is worth noting the difference between discretionary decisions in the weak sense, the so-called 'mechanical decisions', and strong discretionary decisions. Mechanical decisions, in contrast with the former, involve no epistemic difficulties in identifying the solution prescribed by the law. Aarnio refers to this type of decisions as 'routine decisions', and he understands them to depend on the structure of the case. In these situations, ' the decision-maker is aware of the details of both the legal norm that is to be applied and the fact which has occurred.

---

123 On this meaning of judicial discretion, see Dworkin (1977, 31-32, 69-70) and Isaacs (1933, 339, 342-343).

124 In this sense, Sartorius points out that cases of weak discretion are controversial cases in which the judge is liable to make mistakes since there exists a right legal answer which she may fail to identify. See Sartorius (1971, 152-153).

The decision is literally the application of the law'[127]. Strong discretion differs from weak discretion in that no unique right legal answer exists in those cases falling under its scope. In fact, the distinguishing feature of weak discretion is the existence of a right legal answer whose identification requires an interpretive process in which the intellectual ability of the interpreter is challenged.

Barak's proposal to divide cases into three categories, namely easy, intermediate, and hard cases, proves useful to distinguish weak discretion from mechanical decisions and from strong discretion. In Barak's opinion, easy cases are those in which the meaning of normative formulations is clear. Determining the right legal answer to these cases is straightforward. The decision-maker obtains the normative solution simply by means of an unconscious process of interpretation[128]. Intermediate cases are those for which there is a single right answer, but whose identification requires an elaborate process of interpretation because there appears to be more than one appropriate answer. A detailed analysis eventually shows that only one among them is right[129]. Finally, hard cases are those for which there exist several or no legally right course of action. In these situations, even a sophisticated process of legal interpretation fails to provide a right answer, and the judge must decide discretionarily. Hence, hard cases call for strong discretion[130].

Barak's distinction shows the kind of interpretive process that, from his point of view, characterises weak discretion as opposed to strong discretion and to mechanical decisions. The solution of intermediate cases demands analysis, but it does not require an autonomous choice. According to this first approach to weak discretion, having discretion is a matter of degree: the greater the epistemic difficulties, the greater the need for weak discretion. Notwithstanding, the distinction between strong and weak discretion is clearly not a matter of degree: unlike for strong discretion, the existence of a right answer is always assumed in cases of weak discretion, however arduous a task its identification may prove. Hence, even the case entailing maximal difficulties to identify

---

125 See Shiner (1992b, 32).

126 It is assumed at this point that epistemic problems are not due to the interpreter, but rather to the language in which standards are expressed. Thus, epistemic difficulties will emerge when a normative text can be interpreted in several ways, depending on the use of language in the community, rather than on the individual considerations of the interpreter.

127 Aarnio (1987, 1). See also Peczenik (1989, 19).

128 See Barak (1989, 36-39).

129 See Barak (1989, 39-40).

130 See Barak (1989, 40-41).

the right answer is a case of weak discretion as long as such an answer is assumed to exist[131].

Authors such as Greenawalt and Galligan[132] have objected to the idea that the characterisation of weak discretion should rest on the existence of a right answer being independent of the epistemic abilities of the interpreters. Greenawalt, for instance, strongly disagrees with Dworkin's first sense of weak discretion: in Greenawalt's opinion, such a notion implies admitting that a judge is obliged to reach the correct answer 'even if we recognize our own inability and the inability of the most intelligent people we know to identify with any assurance which is the correct decision'[133]. Such a view reveals some of the problems encountered by the approach to weak discretion that associates the existence of a right answer to elements external to the epistemic abilities of the interpreters. Now, is Dworkin's first sense of weak discretion liable to this criticism? It assumes the existence of a right legal answer, and the judge's obligation to follow the prescribed course of action. However, Dworkin's idea of right answer does not seem to depend on the presence of pre-existing standards that the interpreter is expected to discover, but rather on the interpreters' conceptual schemes. We shall discuss the different approach to weak discretion this thesis leads to in the next section.

1.4.2 A further approach to weak discretion

Dworkin's characterisation of weak discretion should be considered in the wider context of his general theory of law. Although he introduces some of the main aspects of his theory of law in *Taking Rights Seriously,* it is in *Law's Empire* where he presents a thorough exposition of his interpretive conception of law. For Dworkin, the idea of a right legal answer is linked to the truth conditions of legal propositions. A legal proposition is true if it figures in or follows from the best constructive interpretation of legal practice as the justification of governmental coercion[134]. According to Ronald Dworkin, however, the interpretation that is best depends on the conceptual structure in which a judgement is made[135]. The question of whether a right answer exists is theory-dependent in the sense that it can only be answered from within a certain way of

---

131 Maximal epistemic difficulties may cause hardship in adjudication because they may prevent the interpreter from making a legal decision. This perspective of weak discretion thus faces a serious problem.

132 See Greenawalt (1975, 365-375) and Galligan (1986, 15-20).

133 Greenawalt (1975, 375). On this point, see also Waluchow (1983, 332-338).

134 For Dworkin's views on the truth conditions of legal propositions, and of interpretive propositions in general, see Dworkin (1986, 13-15, 49-51, 225; 1985, 131-139, 146-149).

135 On this point see Dworkin (1986, 86-90; 1996, 118).

interpreting the legal phenomenon.

These remarks have important implications for the concept of weak discretion, and allow us to construct a different characterisation of it from that presented in the previous section. The distinguishing feature of weak discretion according to this second approach is the theory-dependent character of every judgement about law. Weak discretion is about the production of interpretive statements on the contents of the legal practice. Every time an agent addresses the question of whether a given legal proposition is true or false, he or she produces an answer based on a particular version or interpretation of law[136]. This interpretation requires discretion in a weak sense because it is the product of an intellectual process by which every proposition of the agent's theoretical apparatus interrelates with all the others.

From this point of view, mechanical decisions can be considered simply as a subclass of weakly discretionary decisions. The fact that it may seem obvious to the interpreter which is the right legal answer to a certain case does not mean that she can reach this answer independently of her conceptual scheme. Dworkin writes

> When there is no doubt, the statute is clear, not because Hercules has some distinction, outside his general method, for distinguishing clear from unclear uses of a word, but because the method he always uses is then so easy to apply. It applies itself[137].

And further[138]:

> It adds nothing to say that each knows that his judgment represents a choice rather than a decision forced upon him by reason. His choice is a choice of (what seems to him) the best characterization; it is a choice forced upon him by his judgments just as surely as when the case is controversial, and others disagree, as when it is easy and the do not.

Underlying these quotations is an epistemic approach that endows weak discretion with a wider scope than that which considers the right answer to be a datum external to the interpreters. This new conception will be discussed in detail in Chapters 4 and 5, for it is one of the most important current challenges for legal positivism, in particular, for the thesis of the social sources of law. As we shall see, the interpretive theory of law establishes a distinction between weak and strong discretion in terms of the

---

[136] Dworkin considers that these judgements are strictly speaking neither descriptive nor evaluative. They are interpretive statements because they seek to show the object, which they refer to, in its best light. See Dworkin (1985, 146-151; 1986, 65-68).

[137] Dworkin (1986, 353).

[138] Dworkin (1977, 282).

relationships among propositions within a conceptual scheme rather than the occurrence of certain social facts. Thus, the context of weak discretion is that in which the interpreter can structure her theoretical apparatus coherently to reach an interpretive conclusion about the legal answer to a particular case. Strong discretion, by contrast, comes into play when the best interpretation of law leads to legal indeterminacy. In this case the interpreter must make a choice among open alternatives. We will address this issue again later when analysing the difficulties encountered by the positivist model of strong discretion.

For the time being, I would like to stress that the theory of truth and knowledge adopted has direct implications on both the thesis on the existence of discretion (in either sense) and the concept of discretion defended. The next two chapters will be devoted to a detailed exposition of two models of judicial adjudication: the strong discretion model will be dealt with in Chapter 2. Chapter 3 will be concerned with the weak discretion model. These two models offer different answers to the problem of judicial discretion. The strong discretion model seeks to show that strong discretion is necessary for adjudication, whereas the weak discretion model rejects this claim, and advocates the existence of only a weak sense of discretion. Emphasis will be placed on the conceptual and philosophical assumptions of each one of the models, as well as on the main objections to claim or to deny the existence of judicial discretion in either of its senses. In order to do this, it will be essential to place this debate within the wider context of the different general conceptions of law on which the differing positions on judicial discretion rest.

CHAPTER 2

THE STRONG DISCRETION MODEL

2.1 INTRODUCTION

In the previous chapter we outlined the most common uses of 'judicial discretion'. It became clear that discrepancies in the notions of strong and weak discretion are a consequence of different approaches to the truth conditions of legal propositions. When investigating judicial discretion, legal theorists do not only propose a characterisation of this concept, but also defend a particular thesis on judicial discretion, that is, they hold a specific position about whether or not discretion is necessary in judicial adjudication. Moreover, every thesis on judicial discretion ought to be considered in the wider context of a theory of law and its limits. Every such theory involves a certain position on the existence of right legal answers, and on how these answers can be identified. This is an essential point to bear in mind when analysing theoretical disagreement about the existence of judicial discretion. On some occasions, the differences between those who advocate and those who oppose the need for strong discretion are merely a matter of degree. On other occasions, however, they reflect deeper disagreements on how we come to understand normative standards. Incidentally the role that judicial discretion is assumed to play in adjudication may introduce certain changes in the legal theory embraced. Consequently, a scrutiny of the thesis on judicial discretion maintained by a particular legal theory permits us to examine its internal coherence.

This chapter will focus on the theoretical shaping of the concept of strong judicial discretion. We defined strong discretion as the judicial duty to make a justified choice among different admissible courses of action when there is no right legal answer. The concept of strong discretion is restrictive: arbitrary decisions, as well as decisions made when the judge mistakenly believes to have discretion, are excluded from its scope. As such, this notion of strong discretion does not appear conceptually incompatible with the idea of absolute discretion proposed by sceptics. One of the distinguishing features of sceptics theories is the idea that judges must always make a choice between different courses of action because there never is a right legal answer determining the outcome of their decision. Thus, the idea of strong discretion as limited discretion is to be linked to a theory of law that accepts the need for discretion only in some cases.

What we shall call the 'strong discretion model' is a model of positivist descent. It posits the technical need for strong discretion, if only as a secondary aspect of judicial adjudication. Moreover, it advocates several general theses about law that strongly influence its particular view of discretion[1]. Firstly, this model contends that law is the product of certain social facts[2], that is, it assumes the 'social sources thesis'. Secondly, it asserts the existence of right legal answers in the identification of law[3]. Finally, it posits the so-called thesis of partial indeterminacy, which advocates the need for discretion whenever law does not determine the outcome of the judicial decision[4].

As pointed out in the previous chapter, authors such as Greenawalt, Waluchow and Galligan accept that strong discretion is closely linked to the absence of right answers, but stress the relevance of the epistemic abilities of interpreters in evaluating whether they have discretion or whether they exercise it. Hart and Raz, for instance, insist that law offers means to control discretion even though, by definition, discretion falls outside the domain of law. Ideas such as the zone of reasonableness, standards of rationality, and argumentative honesty serve to restrict the range of decisions that qualify as discretionary[5]. In what follows, these remarks on the scope of strong discretion will be shown to shed light on the latest developments of positivism. The following analysis of the main theses of the positivist model of strong judicial discretion will clarify the positivist view on this issue.

---

[1] We will concern ourselves with the version of positivism that offers an answer to the questions what is law, how do we identify it, and what is its structure. In my view, this version turns on Hartian legal theory because current positivism adopts a Hartian approach to law: it seeks to articulate the main aspects of Hart's perspective in a more sophisticated way.

[2] See Raz (1979, 37-51) for a detailed discussion of this thesis. For Joseph Raz, the social sources thesis implies, in the main, that what is considered to be part of law is a matter of social facts, of human activity and, therefore, of the practices and conventions in the community. Thus, the identification of law can be done on the basis of the social sources regardless of the interpreter's morality. The existence of these sources is the basis for truth of a proposition about what is, legally, the thing to do. In a similar sense, see Hart's conception of the rule of recognition as a social practice in which certain criteria for legal validity permitting the identification of law are accepted. See Hart (1994, 100-117). See also Páramo (1984, 379-415).

[3] See Hart (1994, 124-136).

[4] See Hart (1994, 124-154) and Raz (1979, 70-77).

[5] See Raz (1972, 847-848).

2.2 A FIRST LOOK AT THE STRONG DISCRETION MODEL

It is commonplace within legal positivism to argue that, as a tool to guide human behaviour, law has limits. This accounts for the fact that what is actually being regulated by the law at times differs from what was originally intended to be regulated. For this reason, law does not dispose of every particular dispute taken to court. Notwithstanding, positivists understand the final outcome of the judicial decision to be prescribed by law in a significant number of cases. In their view, the contents of law is determined by pre-existing normative standards and semantic rules fixing the meaning of the linguistic formulations by which these standards are expressed. The necessity for judicial discretion arises from the judicial duty to render a decision when either there are no univocal normative standards, or semantic rules fail to determine the meaning of legal formulations. In both of these cases the judge must choose between a number of open alternatives.

Hartian positivism, in spite of assuming a restrictive notion of strong discretion, conceives discretion as a complex process that always involves extra-legal elements. In situations that require discretion, the judge acts as an interstitial legislator: she stipulates new semantic rules and creates new norms on the basis of her values and beliefs[6]. But it may be worth considering to what extent the proposed criteria of rationality and reasonableness as constraints to strong discretion eventually reduce it to an instance of weak discretion[7]. Accepting this reduction would imply that the possibility for choice arises when the legal order fails to provide a specific answer to the case under consideration and judicial standards such as rationality and reasonableness fail to determine a unique admissible answer. Reducing strong discretion to a form of weak discretion would lead to the conclusion that positivist efforts to distinguish strong discretion from arbitrariness have perverse results, namely that positivism should accept the existence of right answers in hard cases. If that were the case, judges would continue to be legally obliged to identify *the* right answer. Accepting these consequences leads to a view on the role of weak discretion in hard cases and on the limits of law far from that prompted by the social sources thesis.

In my view, Hartian positivism does not lead to these conclusions. It does not purport to maintain the existence of weak discretion in hard cases because such a position would entail methodological assumptions that do not conform to its semantic approach. Certainly, positivism has generally paid little attention to the parameters governing judicial discretion. Its main concern has been to devise a legal framework to

---

[6] See Hart (1983, 138; 1980, 9-10) and Schauer (1991, 222).

[7] See Shiner (1992b, 85-87, 98).

determine when a legal proposition is true or false. In this sense, positivism can be seen as a theory concerned with easy cases. At first sight, it seems to be the case that positivist approaches rest on two common assumptions: on the one hand, that the truth-value of a legal proposition depends on the occurrence of certain facts; on the other, that ascribing meaning is an empirical task. These assumptions, however, are much debated. A detailed study may suggest that perhaps they are not as widespread among positivists as they are usually thought to be. Shiner, for instance, reviews the main difficulties encountered by the positivist analysis of discretion and distinguishes between versions of positivism that rest on distinct ontological and epistemic assumptions. In my opinion, although this distinction is important to understand some of the problems faced by the strong discretion model, Shiner's reconstruction of sophisticated positivism misrepresents current positivist thought.

2.3 SIMPLE AND SOPHISTICATED POSITIVISM

Shiner presents a detailed analysis of the main features that characterise a positivist view of law[8]. He distinguishes between two ideal types of positivism that differ in their understanding of the role to be attributed to judges in hard cases: simple positivism and sophisticated positivism. Thus, there emerge two different perspectives on the implications of asserting that an official has discretion. In his opinion, simple positivism holds the view that discretion as an activity that develops outside the limits of law cannot be subject to any legal restrictions. Sophisticated positivism, in contrast, claims that general legal restrictions apply to discretion and allow us to distinguish discretionary decisions from arbitrary ones. The restrictions being referred to here concern the duties inherent in the judicial role and the range of courses of action that may qualify as legally reasonable. According to Shiner, these differences between simple and sophisticated positivism have important theoretical consequences[9]: while simple positivism accepts the existence of genuine strong discretion in hard cases, sophisticated positivism contends the existence of a weak sense of discretion only. These differences result from the differing semantic conceptions adopted by simple and by sophisticated positivism. Simple positivism relies on realist or correspondentist semantics[10]. This view makes the truth-value of a legal proposition dependent on its

---

[8] Shiner (1992b, 19-99; 1992a, 59-65).

[9] Shiner (1992b, 30-35, 80-87).

[10] Dummet distinguishes between the realist and the antirealist thesis in what concerns the meaning of statements (descriptive sentences). Realism claims that the meaning of a statement relies on certain states of affairs independent of our means to verify their existence. Thus, the correspondence with these facts is

correspondence with a certain state of affairs such as, for instance, that Parliament enacted a particular law. For simple positivism, the truth-value of a legal proposition is thus independent of our epistemic abilities to verify the facts. Adjudication under this light becomes a mechanical task when there is a right answer, and a purely creative one when such an answer does not exist. Thus, understanding law consists merely in describing the propositional contents of normative texts formulated by legal authorities. The propositional contents depends on facts such as the intention of the author and the meaning inherent in the normative text[11].

By contrast, sophisticated positivism concedes that the open texture of language creates a need for strong judicial discretion. However, discretion in hard cases still is controlled by legal standards. In Shiner's view, this position is a consequence of the fact that sophisticated positivists assume antirealist semantics. According to antirealist semantics, the meaning of normative statements depends on the conditions that make them true. Therefore, legal propositions have truth-value[12]. But truth conditions are not seen to depend upon facts but on the epistemic abilities of interpreters for verification[13]. The truth-value of a proposition is conditional on its assertability conditions; in other words, it depends on what elements we count as sufficient evidence for asserting or for denying the proposition. We can thus conclude that some legal propositions are neither true nor false because they do not fulfil the conditions for asserting or for denying them. According to Shiner, sophisticated positivism contends that in easy cases assertability conditions reduce to correspondence with the legal facts[14]. In hard cases, however,

---

what renders our statements true or false. Antirealism, by contrast, understands that the meaning of a statement is tied directly to what we count as evidence for it. See Dummet (1978, 146). Moreso (1998, 49-50, 133-134) presents a clear exposition of the dichotomy between realism and antirealism.

11 Shiner (1992b, 35-38).

12 Note that semantic theories for which the meaning of propositions relies on their truth conditions have traditionally been related to semantic realism, while constructivist or antirealist theories reject a semantic theory based on truth conditions, and favour one based on conditions of assertability. Nevertheless, Baker argues that certain articulations of constructivism accept the semantics of truth conditions but adopt a concept of truth as assertability. See Baker (1977, 50-51) and Dummet (1978, xxi, xxiii). Perhaps this new formulation of antirealism appears in response to scepticism, the theory of radical indeterminacy that rejects the very possibility of talking about truth conditions. Hence, this does not seem to be a merely terminological discussion about whether it is preferable to talk about 'truth' or 'assertability' to refer to what we are entitled to assert. It would be interesting to analyse whether the different formulations of antirealism diverge in some significant way. Unfortunately, such an enquiry is beyond the scope of this work.

13 Shiner (1992b, 87-90).

14 Shiner (1992b, 89-90) points out that, according to sophisticated positivism, one of the rules governing the judicial role takes correspondence to the institutional history to be what actually warrants the assertability of a proposition in easy cases. This idea is rather odd for it seems to imply that only

assertability depends on legal principles, on general acceptability standards, and on the judicial duties[15].

In my opinion, Shiner's reconstruction leads to conflicting conclusions. On the one hand, his remarks seem to suggest that sophisticated positivism believes in the existence of a right answer even in hard cases, and that therefore, legal propositions have truth-value even in these cases. This would advocate a weak sense of discretion and would result in positivism distinguishing between hard cases and instances of no right answer. Thus, a proposition is neither true nor false, that is, it has no truth-value, not when we face a hard case, but only when assertability conditions are not met. On the other hand, however, Shiner points to the open texture of language as one of the elements that sophisticated positivism takes into consideration to construct its theory of hard cases and judicial discretion: discretion emerges insofar as legal propositions are indeterminate[16]. Accordingly, sophisticated positivism sets forth a genuine theory of strong discretion in hard cases that denies unlimited discretion[17]. Instances of no right answer (hard cases) are thus dissociated from the possibility of absolute discretion in their resolution.

In effect, Shiner's account of sophisticated positivism seems to conceal the following ambiguity: on the one hand, sophisticated positivism seems to rest on a theory of truth as assertability that maintains the bivalence principle even in hard cases. The possibility of legal indeterminacy becomes marginal. On the other hand, it could be concluded from Shiner's presentation of sophisticated positivism that, whether in terms of truth as correspondence or of truth as assertability, only for easy cases does sophisticated positivism maintain the principle of bivalence. In hard cases, i.e. in those cases in which legal propositions have no truth-value, this theory only offers guidelines to limit the range of open alternatives based on a theory of conditions of acceptability for a proposition about what the law should be.

Such an ambiguity works against the attempt to differentiate two forms of positivism that coincide in their claim that law can be separated from the moral and other normative contexts. Holding that sophisticated positivism, unlike simple positivism, accepts a theory of truth-assertability for hard cases implies assuming the first reconstruction of sophisticated positivism, and that hard cases relate to weak discretion. Sophisticated positivism, which we will henceforth call 'Hartian positivism', cannot be reconstructed on the grounds of a theory of truth as assertability that affirms

---

propositions which in fact are true can be taken as true. It will be shown how this is in conflict with an antirealist position.

[15] Shiner (1992b, 76-90).

[16] Shiner (1992b, 80-87).

[17] Shiner (1992b, 84, 87).

bivalence in hard cases. In my opinion, a careful reading of the views of some of the most significant Hartian positivists leads to a different account of this theory[18]. I am not claiming that there is no difference between simple and sophisticated positivism. I will argue that the elements accounting for the antirealist nature of Hartian semantics are different from those proposed by Shiner. A general antirealist position on meaning is not a necessary consequence of a theory that supports restricting strong judicial discretion in hard cases.

2.4 JUDICIAL DISCRETION AND HARTIAN POSITIVISM

The origin of Hartian positivism lies in H.L.A. Hart's *The Concept of Law*. It has been further developed by legal philosophers such as Joseph Raz, Andrei Marmor, Frederick Schauer and Brian Bix, to name but a few. Initially it sought to overcome the shortcomings of the simplistic model of the legal structure proposed by Austin and Bentham for whom law consists of direct commands from a sovereign to her subjects and certain obedience habits based upon prudential reasons for action[19]. Current Hartian positivism seeks to account for the complex phenomenology we come across in legal reality. In this context, one of the distinguishing features of Hartian positivism is its interest in language as a means to communicate normative standards. Law is expressed by means of language - language is a means of communication. According to Hart, what is to be transmitted are general normative standards referring to classes of individuals, and not to particular individuals[20]. Thus, understanding law to a great extent involves understanding the language in which law is expressed, and its specific use in the legal context.

2.4.1 The law-communication thesis

Hartian positivism conceives law essentially as a communicational phenomenon, i.e. as a mechanism to guide conduct by means of language. Nevertheless, it does not reduce

---

[18] Interestingly, Shiner thinks both Hart's and Dworkin's legal theories to belong in sophisticated positivism. Two approaches to the legal phenomenon that had traditionally been considered radically opposed to one another are thus regarded as similar. It appears possible to make a new interpretation of the controversy that has for many years developed between Hart and Dworkin: either there was never a genuine disagreement between these authors or else, Hart's theory of law has evolved into Dworkin's. In my opinion, none of these interpretations can be correct. See Shiner (1992b, 90 footnote 56).

[19] See Hart's reflections on Austin's and Bentham's legal theories in Hart (1994, Ch II, Ch IV). See also Hart (1982, Ch VI, Ch X).

[20] See Hart (1994, 124-125) and Schauer (1991, 25-27).

legal communication to a direct linguistic relationship between a speaker and a listener. Communication is usually established on the grounds of general rules formulated in normative texts[21]. In this sense, language limits our understanding of the contents of law. On the one hand, communication requires that the meaning of normative formulations be predetermined to a considerable extent[22]; on the other, 'there is a limit, inherent in the nature of language, to the guidance which general language can provide'[23]. As discussed in the previous chapter, Hart links this limit to the open texture of legal rules, i.e. the possibility of finding cases whose inclusion within the scope of applicability of the rule is not clear.

From this point of view, understanding law is primarily a matter of semantics. In order to identify the rights and duties of the citizenry, one needs to know the socially accepted normative sources and, hence, the conventional meaning of terms such as 'law'. In addition, one needs to identify the meaning of the linguistic formulations by which the citizens are conferred rights and imposed duties[24]. According to Hartian positivism, these semantic considerations are essential to establishing the truth conditions of legal propositions. Moreover, this link between language and law allows for a justification of legal indeterminacy when a normative source is to some extent linguistically indeterminate. In these instances, there is no right legal answer[25]. Hartian positivism can thus be thought of as a semantic theory of law[26]. However, what is the theory of

---

21 This communication technique is a paradigmatic case in continental legal orders and, for this reason, will be taken as the starting point for the present chapter. This, however, does not by any means imply that there exist no other techniques of communication. For example, legal precedent and custom are extremely relevant factors when accounting for the structure of any normative system.

22 See Hart (1994, 126-127, 135-136).

23 Hart (1994, 126). Hart claims that indeterminacy is an inevitable feature of any attempt to guide human conduct by means of linguistically formulated general rules. It will always be possible to find cases for which no previous definition of the general classifying terms appearing in the rule allows us to decide whether the case falls within its scope of applicability or not. See Hart (1980, 9).

24 See Hart (1983, 33, 35). It is not intended that the truth of a legal proposition depend exclusively on the semantic considerations about the conditions for legal validity coming together with the meaning of each formulation considered independently. Surely, the truth or falsity of these propositions is also conditional on more fundamental semantic conventions about the meaning of 'law'.

25 See Bix (1993, 33). Hart (1994, 128) considers the relative indeterminacy of purpose as a source of linguistic indeterminacy. It is worth noting the relevance conferred by Hartian positivism to linguistic indeterminacy as a source of normative indeterminacy and, hence, as a source of judicial discretion. On the different types of legal indeterminacy, see Coleman and Leiter (1995, 212-218). On the relationship between semantic and legal indeterminacy in Hart, see Ruíz Manero (1990, 184-189).

26 On Hartian positivism as a semantic theory see, for instance, Coleman and Leiter (1995, 35-36). The above consideration, however, does not seek to reduce Hartian positivism to a semantic theory of law. It wishes to highlight the relationship between the semantic considerations set forth above, and the truth of

meaning underlying the law-communication view of law? Investigating the answer to this question will shed some light on the constraints imposed by language upon the possibility of judicial discretion.

2.4.2 Hartian semantics

It is widely accepted that Hartian positivism assumes antirealist semantics[27]. This follows from the premises that law is a matter of social conventions, and that some legal propositions have no truth-value[28]. It can thus be concluded that the truth conditions of legal propositions and the conditions for recognising their truth are not independent of one another[29]. If the meaning of statements about law is reducible to what the majority of the members of a given legal community normally understands by these statements, their meaning does not transcend the epistemic abilities of the speakers. Moreover, discarding the principle of bivalence, i.e. that all propositions are either true or false, implies denying semantic realism[30].

It is worth considering whether the thesis of partial indeterminacy as advocated by Hartian positivism just contends that propositions about law may be true, false, or, have no truth-value because of the open texture of language. Hartian positivism assumes that there are easy cases in which legal propositions are either true or false. Thus, although our concepts may admittedly be indeterminate because there are always dubitable instances of application, it is claimed that some applications of the concept will always be unquestionable. Partial indeterminacy is a reply to radical indeterminacy, the view that holds that no legal proposition has truth-value. Taking the law-communication view as a starting point, positivism claims that there will always be true and false legal

---

judgements about what is legally the thing to do. In addition, it does not imply that the thesis on the social sources of law is merely a semantic one. Raz (1979, 37-40) specifies that the thesis on the social sources of law seeks not only to explain the substratum of the meaning of normative statements, but also their normative force. The normative force of law is linked to the idea of internal point of view proposed by Hart. This is the standpoint adopted by the participants in a social practice that is subject to rules, and not just to habits of conduct. Participants view legal rules as providing guidelines to their own conduct and standards for assessing that of their peers. On the notion of normativity and the internal point of view, see Hart (1994, 82-91, 116-117). See also Raz (1990, 154-177).

27 Note that both realism and antirealism maintain a semantic theory based on the conditions for truth of legal propositions. The difference between them is, precisely, what they understand these conditions to be, i.e. what are the specific conditions that make a proposition true. See Patterson (1996, 18).

28 See, for instance, Marmor (1992, 87-90).

29 Marmor (1992, 90)

30 See Dummet (1978, 164-165). Marmor (1992, 88) observes that the relationship between realism and the principle of bivalence is not symmetrical: realism implies bivalence, but the converse is not true.

propositions[31]. The question is: what does the truth-value of non-vague propositions depend on? In order to provide an answer to this question, it appears essential to investigate when is a particular meaning ascription to a legal term or expression right or wrong according to Hartian positivism. This will in turn allow us to study the relationship between antirealist semantics and the positivist postulate of the social sources of law.

Meaning as settled use: easy cases

Hartian positivism advocates that there exist easy cases as far as the ascription of meaning to legal terms and expressions is concerned. This suggests that there must exist certain normative-semantic criteria (semantic rules) determining the extent to which a given ascription is correct[32]. Only when it is the case that semantic rules are indeterminate is the interpreter granted the freedom to choose between open alternatives. In these instances, making a decision requires stipulating new meanings for normative formulations in such a way that the final conclusion does not result from following pre-established rules.

According to a Hartian view of law, the criterion determining whether a certain meaning ascription is correct is the use of language in the community. Semantic rules govern meaning, and they are dependent on the existence of a settled convention about the use of language to report about certain phenomena, events, or objects[33]. Although Hartian positivism favours the plain or literal meaning of terms as a criterion to determine the semantic contents of normative texts, it does not understand meaning as something entirely atemporal and acontextual[34]. Literal meaning is not simply the meaning of a given expression in terms of the semantic rules of language regardless of the context in which it occurs: along the lines of Searle's theory of meaning, Hartian positivism argues that literality needs to be supported by a background of social practices[35]. Furthermore, Hartian positivism considers that the public dimension of language and meaning restricts, for the sake of communication, the possible uses of a term in the context of the particular speech act. For this reason, Hartian positivism

---

[31] Regarding this point, Hart (1994, 126) asserts that 'general terms would be useless to us as a medium of communication unless there were such familiar, generally unchallenged cases'. See also Marmor (1992, 134-135).

[32] Marmor (1992, 30) claims that the meaning of expressions, unlike what is actually meant by them, is essentially determined by rules and conventions.

[33] See Hart (1994, 126-127; 1983, 106), Schauer (1991, 56) and Bix (1993, 63-70, 73-76).

[34] See Bix (1993, 73-74), Marmor (1992, Ch. II) and Schauer (1991, 53-62).

[35] See Searle (1983, 141-148).

assumes that the language in a normative text restricts the communicative intention of the legislator[36]. Moreover, it claims that the correctness of a certain meaning ascription is independent of the interpreter's beliefs about the inter-subjective use of terms. Whether a certain ascription is right or not is not in any way conditioned by the epistemic abilities of the interpreter - the interpreter may fail to describe correctly the general use of language, or even mistake it for her own.

These preliminary considerations show that there is a clear difference between the positivist theory of meaning as settled use, and other semantic theories such as intentionalist or referencialist semantics.

Particular and social contexts of use

According to Hartian semantics, grasping the meaning of an expression is not merely grasping its illocutionary force, i.e. the communicative intention of an speech act[37]. The meaning does not depend on each particular context of use, on the state of mind, or on the intention of the speaker[38]. A distinction is made between the meaning of an expression (*meaning of*), and what a speaker means by it (*meaning that*)[39]. From this point of view, knowing the contents of law in fact requires understanding the meaning

---

36 See Hart (1994, 127-128). Schauer (1991, 55) points out that the meaning is not reducible to the purpose for which the language is being used on a particular occasion. Language is semantically independent of the communicative intentions of its users. Fuller (1958, 662-669) criticises the position that posits that the inter-subjective use of a word or sentence is central to its meaning. He thinks it pointless to attempt to dissociate the meaning of an utterance from its particular context of use and the communicative intentions of the speaker.

37 When uttering a statement, language can be used for different purposes. The illocutionary force of a speech act is the intention or communicative purpose that drove its production. On the distinction between illocutionary, locutionary and pre-locutionary acts, see Austin (1976, 94-120) and Searle (1969, 22-53).

38 See Schauer (1991, 55) and Bix (1993, 75). Hart claims that assigning meaning to a legal expression does not entail describing a psychological fact. See Hart (1983, 33).

39 On the definition and distinction between *meaning of* and *meaning that*, see Marmor (1992, 15, 30). Schauer (1991, 53-58) claims that this distinction is necessary to differentiate the meaning of general rules from their justification. Rules are instances of further rules that account for their justification. If the meaning of these instances is limited to the intentions of the agent who enacted them, their meaning is simply the justification as applied to the case at hand. Hence, it would obtain that the meaning of the instance and its justification collapse into one and the same thing, that is, they become coextensive. Grice distinguished between the sentence meaning on the one hand, and the utterer's meaning, on the other. But it should be noted that Grice, in contrast to what is being presented here, tried to reduce the sentence meaning to the utterer's meaning. See Grice (1989, 86-137). See also Searle (1969, 42-50).

of certain linguistic formulations. For this reason, positivism affirms the autonomy of legal language with respect to particular contexts of use[40].

However, as mentioned above, Hartian positivism is not supportive of an idea of meaning that disregards the moment in time and the context in which an utterance is found. In this respect, Schauer points out that the meaning of a normative statement is only partly acontextual[41]. He further notes that the semantic autonomy of legal language does not necessarily imply dissociating legal language from its public dimension or from linguistic practice. At this point, it is interesting to distinguish between two different contextual levels with different implications as far as the ascription of meaning to legal terms and expressions is concerned: on the one hand, there is the context of a linguistic community in which speakers in a non reflective manner attribute a unique meaning to legal terms[42]. This community may include certain sub-communities that use words differently. If this is the case, the sub-community becomes itself a specific social context of linguistic use[43]. In both cases the meaning is socially established, i.e. it is the result of the public, inter-subjective use of language. On the other hand, there is the particular context in which an utterance occurs. Here no semantic rule necessarily governs the use of language: the meaning of a term or expression could depend on the intention of the speaker, on the circumstances surrounding the speech act, on the linguistic agreement between speaker and listener, or on all of the above[44].

Hartian positivism claims that reducing meaning to the communicative intention in each particular context is tantamount to reducing meaning to something private or particularistic and would not provide an explanation to the public and conventional dimension of language. It is precisely the public dimension of language that this theory is most interested in. Regarding this point, Schauer writes:

> 'Much of the particular context embellishes and enriches the process of communication, making it possible for speakers to communicate far more effectively than they would if their discourse were restricted

---

[40] On the semantic autonomy of meaning see, for instance, Davidson (1984b, 164-166).

[41] Schauer (1991, 55-56).

[42] Bix (1993, 75).

[43] These sub-communities of use have specific jargons and dialects: the literal meaning of words differs from one context to another. On this point see Bix (1993, 73-76) and Marmor (1992, 26-27). For criticism on a variety of fronts of the idea of sub-communities, see Coleman and Leiter (1995, 260-263).

[44] The claim that the literal meaning of a word, unlike its pragmatic meaning, is determined by linguistic rules and conventions is defended by Marmor who, along the lines of Wittgenstein's considerations on rule-following, distinguishes between understanding the meaning of an expression, and interpreting it. Understanding the meaning of an expression relies on its literal meaning, whereas its interpretation is linked to its pragmatic meaning. See Marmor (1992, 22-30, Ch. VII).

to literal or acontextual meaning. Still, the phenomenon of literal or plain meaning remains the foundation of linguistic communication, and a totally particularist theory of meaning [...] cannot explain how it is that communication is possible. If the meaning of an utterance were entirely a function of how it was *then* used (as opposed to how the word is used within a language), it would be impossible to explain how meaning is conveyed, and why it is that we pick one word rather than another to serve a particular communicative task.'[45]

This passage sheds light on the implications of accepting literal meaning as partly acontextual. The fact that the social context is what determines the linguistic competence and the correct use of terms deserves some attention. Notwithstanding that literal or plain meaning may change over time, its public and conventional nature endow it with a degree of stability and permanence that is nowhere to be found in pragmatic meaning[46].

Along similar lines, Raz argues that intentionalist semantics prove useful only to verify that law is the product of certain intentional acts of a normative authority. In his opinion, the legislator produces an utterance which has the illocutionary force to prescribe something, and in fact does so: '*A* being an agent who has the legal authority to make a law that *p*, legislates (i.e. makes it the law) that *p* [...] by performing an action which expresses the intention that *p* become the law in virtue of that intention being manifestly expressed'[47]. However, the relationship between intention and meaning can be taken no further. The propositional contents of these normative acts cannot be read in terms of the intentions of those who perform them[48]. The meaning of the resulting

---

45 Schauer (1991, 58). See also Marmor (1992, 24-28). Searle (1969, 48-49) contends that communication between speaker and listener is made possible by the public dimension of language, i.e. by the fact that both share the same language. His idea is illustrated by the following example: '1. Understanding the sentence "Hello" is knowing its meaning. 2. The meaning of "Hello" is determined by semantic rules, which specify both its conditions of utterance and what the utterance counts as. The rules specify that under certain conditions an utterance of "Hello" count as a greeting of the hearer by the speaker. 3. Uttering "Hello" and meaning it is a matter of (a) intending to get the hearer to recognize that he is being greeted, (b) intending to get him to recognize that he is being greeted by means of getting him to recognize one's intention to greet him, (c) intending to get him to recognize one's intention to greet him in virtue of his knowledge of the meaning of the sentence "Hello". 4. The sentence "Hello" then provides a conventional means of greeting people'.

46 In connection with this issue, see Marmor's thesis that literal meaning is governed by rules whereas pragmatic meaning is beyond the control of semantic rules.

47 Raz (1996, 266).

48 Raz (1996, 262-266) draws attention to the fact that legislators are often not acquainted with the details of the legislation they vote, or only to a very limited extent.

normative texts depends on the linguistic and cultural conventions of the community in which the legislative acts occur[49].

As can be easily observed, literal meaning as something partially acontextual appears to be the fundamental component of the positivist theory of easy cases. It offers a useful criterion to distinguish those cases that clearly fall within the core of plain meaning of a term or outside it, from those which belong to the penumbral zone[50]. Moreover, this criterion provides a justification to the thesis of partial indeterminacy of law (as a response to radical indeterminacy) by asserting that linguistic conventions, although they predetermine the meaning of terms, are not omnicomprehensive.

Nevertheless, the nature of the semantic criterion of positivism as well as its consequences remain to be investigated. We shall have later to consider them. For instance, Schauer's claim that the meaning of a term or expression depends on its use in the community is insufficient to determine how the relationship between inter-subjective use and the correct meaning ascription to legal texts is to be established. To my mind, clarifying this point appears crucial to elucidating the extent to which this positivist view presupposes antirealist semantics. We shall address these questions in sections to come. Hitherto we have explored the differences between a theory of meaning as settled use and intentionalist semantics. Let us next investigate how the theory of meaning as settled use differs from a further kind of semantics, namely referencialist semantics.

Indexicality and social conventions

An additional feature of Hartian positivism is its denial of the idea that the meaning of legal expressions and of the term 'law' is determined by the reference of our concepts. Here, the reference stands for the object or state of affairs that we designate by means of words[51]. Contemporary referencialist theories such as Kripke's and Putnam's claim that the meaning of indexical terms, i.e. terms designating natural classes of entities, cannot be fully grasped if the knowledge of their meaning is considered to be just a matter of being in a certain psychological state, be it individual or collective[52]. States of mind do

---

49 See Raz (1996, 267-268). This standpoint entitles Raz to maintain the thesis that law is the product of acts of institutional authorities without having to assume strong intentionalism, the view that identifying the contents of the texts that have been elaborated by institutional authorities requires elucidating their state of mind and real intentions at the time of writing.

50 Raz claims that the plain or conventional meaning of a text is the only factor restricting the possible interpretations of the legislative intention. Unless one adheres to plain meaning, even a Shakespearean interpretation of the Constitution is imaginable. See Raz (1986, 1103-1119; 1995, 161-162).

51 On reference, see Frege (1993, 24-28).

52 Indexical terms operate as rigid designators for they refer to the same object in every possible world. Kripke (1980, 106-155) has used this approach to account primarily for the meaning of proper names.

not constitute the reference of these terms. Only the very object or substance can account for the meaning of the words that name it[53].

One of the chief differences between Hartian and referencialist semantics is that the former advocates the non-indexicality of legal terms and of the term 'law' itself while the latter does not[54]. Law is a social phenomenon and, unlike natural phenomena, it is a product of human activity. The existence and contents of law cannot be dissociated from shared conceptions and linguistic practices. The concepts of contract and property, for instance, refer to a function, a social way of assigning consequences to specific acts - they do not just refer to objects or states of affairs entirely independent of human activity[55]. Hart claims that the meaning of legal terms and expressions can be understood by simply specifying their truth conditions and showing how they are used to obtain normative conclusions in particular cases. These terms, unlike most ordinary terms, do not have an empirical counterpart. Consequently, grasping their meaning does not simply consist in describing the existence of certain objects or material or psychological facts. Thus, although Hart admits that there may be some relationship

---

Putnam (1975, 229-235, 245-247) extended this approach to any term referring to classes of objects whose existence does not result from mere human intervention and intellectual ability. In fact, it could be argued that Putnam's extension is far more ambitious, for it wishes to extend this view of meaning to most terms, regardless of whether they designate artefacts, or, classes of objects that come into existence only as a consequence of the structure of the world.

53 For this reason, referencialist theories claim that a whole community of speakers may misidentify the meaning of the words it uses. See Putnam (1975, 223-227, 245-247; 1981, 22-25) and Kripke (1980, 121-139). The most recent attempt to show the indexicality of the term 'law' is due to Michael Moore (1985, 277-398).

54 Marmor (1992, 96-97) stresses that the assertion that 'law' is indexical is in contradiction with the antirealist position that, in his opinion, characterises positivism. No positivist would agree that the whole of a legal community may be mistaken on the extension of the term 'law'. The reason for this lies in the fact that positivists, unlike natural theorists, consider that the extension of this term is reducible to social rules, practices and conventions.

55 Searle (1995, 14) writes that functions are not inherent in objects - functions are assigned to or imposed upon objects by conscious users. Hence, functions are always observer-relative. See Searle's theory on institutional facts, and MacCormick and Weinberger's further development and extension of this theory to the legal context. The truth or falsity of statements about institutional facts, unlike those referring to brute facts, does not depend on the structure of the world and the causal relationships among its elements. The existence of institutional facts presupposes human institutions and social rules. Thus, statements about institutional facts are true on account of an interpretation of events that is intrinsically bound to human practices and normative rules. See MacCormick and Weinberger (1986, 49-55) and Searle (1969, 50-53; 1995, 27-29).

between legal terms and material facts, in his opinion this relationship is complex and clearly indirect[56].

Hart's approach to legal ontology as a social construct causes Hartian positivism to deviate from semantic views such as that which Michael Moore advocates for law. According to Moore, legal terms are indexical[57]. They refer to natural classes of objects whose relation to the words used to name them is not arbitrary, as assumed by conventionalism[58]. In Moore's view, assigning meaning to legal expressions is simply discovering the structure of the world[59]. Hence, Moore argues, judges should ignore the conventional use of a legal term when, in their view, it does not reflect the very nature of its reference[60].

A direct consequence of Hartian semantics seems to be the rejection of semantic realism, particularly if the paradigm of realism to be borne in mind is a referencialist theory of meaning along the lines of Moore's[61]. As pointed out by Stavropoulos, Hartian semantics do not fit the semantics of natural classes. He asserts that positivism does not claim that the restrictions that judgements about the applicability of legal concepts are subject to are natural properties awaiting discovery. Law is a social construct and hence the restrictions on judgements about law cannot transcend our epistemic abilities[62]. Coleman and Leiter assert that semantic realism entails strong semantic objectivism. Accordingly, realism assumes that 'the meaning of a sentence never depends on what any speaker or community of speakers takes it to mean'[63]. They attribute to positivism minimal semantic objectivism, which significantly differs from strong objectivism. For

---

56 On this point, see Hart (1983, 23, 31-35). For a similar articulation of this idea, see Moreso (1996, 113) and Carnap (1971, 308).

57 Moore claims that, whether consciously or unconsciously, we think of words as indexicals. See Moore (1985, 331).

58 See Moore (1985, 294-301; 995, 3-6). Note that the problem we are considering here is not whether the terms we use are conventional or not, but whether objects carry their own identifying labels or whether the differentiation between objects is essentially conventional. On this point see Coleman (1995, 41 footnote 8).

59 Moore (1985, 338).

60 Moore (1985, 287) points out that legal definitions of terms and the conventions about their use can only be viewed as an agreed summary of the real meaning of words. Such legal definitions may misidentify the reference and lead to absurd conclusions about the meaning of terms. See Moore (1985, 329-331).

61 Note that Putnam's referencialist theory is hard to redirect towards a realist approach to semantics, for the latter presupposes a correspondentist theory of truth. On this point, see Putnam's argument in favour of what he calls 'internal realism', and which he put forward in response to truth as correspondence, Putnam (1981, 1-74).

62 See Stavropoulos (1996, 76) and Bix (1995, 138-141).

63 Coleman and Leiter (1995, 252).

minimal objectivism, the correctness of a meaning ascription is independent of the epistemic abilities of a particular interpreter, but not of those of the community of speakers as a whole. The collective practices and what the majority of the speakers understands by a certain term determine its meaning[64].

The idea of minimal objectivism yields a criterion to determine the correctness of a meaning ascription to a legal text. The existence of easy cases and of right answers is thus preserved. The latter elements are essential to the thesis of the partial indeterminacy of law[65]. Nevertheless, it should be borne in mind that semantic realism posits that the meaning of normative texts depends on states of affairs whose existence is independent of our ability to identify them. Nothing but the reference determines the truth or falsity of the propositions about law. The question of whether the social character of legal ontology is sufficient to reject semantic realism remains yet to be answered.

Positing that the substratum of meaning rests on social facts such as contextual practices and linguistic behaviour implies rejecting that legal terms be indexical. Such terms do not designate natural classes of objects. However, this does not imply that legal terms have no reference, but only that the reference is a social construct[66]. Thus, denying the indexicality of legal terms is insufficient in my mind to conclude that Hartian positivism maintains an antirealist semantic theory[67]. Within this line of argument, Brink observes that the artificial nature of social institutions and practices means that they are a causal product of the beliefs, wishes and mental states of individuals. They are therefore causally dependent on human mind. But this causal relation does not imply that they be dependent on human knowledge, that is, that they be constituted by the evidence available to us about their existence. Social facts could thus still be separable from their conventional descriptions. From this point of view, accounting for these artefacts is not incompatible with holding a realist semantic view. Brink indicates that practices and institutions could be understood as facts independent of people's conceptions about them in the following senses: a) these social phenomena

---

64 Coleman and Leiter (1995, 253) point out that positivism displays antirealist features such as the rejection of the epistemic transcendence of meaning and legal ontology. Moreover, they claim positivism holds an objectivist position because it rejects the idea that the social world may depend only on how a particular individual perceives it.

65 See Hart (1994, 126-127, 131-132) for further consideration of this point.

66 Schauer (1991, 55), for example, claims that the basis for the semantic autonomy of language with respect to particular instances of use can be explained in terms of a socially established reference.

67 Moore elaborates a detailed criticism of positivism that develops along similar lines. He argues that asserting that legal terms are not in correspondence with natural classes of objects but with functional classes is compatible with semantic realism. Hence, no additional theory of language is needed to account for legal terms. See Moore (1992, 206-208). Brink (1989, 183-185) presents a similar argument.

are the object of individuals' beliefs and therefore they precede their conceptions; b) the community may share mistaken conceptions about these facts; c) people's conceptions about these phenomena are right insofar as they correctly describe the nature of these phenomena[68]. In a similar sense, Coleman and Leiter claim that accepting that chairs and tables are human products does not imply holding an antirealist position[69]. According to these authors, we usually accept this to be the case, but we are nevertheless realist in holding that chairs and tables exist independly of our beliefs and abilities to identify them. Thus, realism does not only claim that these objects are causally independent of human activity, but that they are epistemically and structurally independent of human mind.

Hence, none of what has been presented so far seems to be in contradiction with the claim that, from a Hartian point of view, an agent's assignation of meaning to a normative text is correct when it is the case that there is a linguistic use in his or her community, and he or she succeeds in describing this social fact that occurs at a particular point in space and time[70]. To assign meaning would thus become an empirical task and the truth-value of legal propositions would then depend on their correspondence to certain facts that transcend the epistemic abilities of the specific interpreter. It could also be argued that the shared linguistic use is a datum independent of the epistemic abilities of the community of speakers as a whole, or of the majority of its members, to verify it. This conclusion can be reached provided the shared use of terms is differentiated from widespread knowledge that this use is shared. It may be the case that all, some, or even none of the members of the linguistic community are aware of the fact that a linguistic use is shared. Notwithstanding, it may still be true that a shared use exists[71]. In my opinion, Hartian positivism ought to concede that the

---

68 Brink (1989, 184).

69 Coleman and Leiter (1995, 249).

70 In his analysis of the social sources thesis, Joseph Raz (1979, 39-40) asserts that 'a jurisprudential theory is acceptable only if its tests for identifying the content of the law and determining its existence depend exclusively on facts of human behaviour capable of being described in value-neutral terms [...]'. This idea clearly suggests a preference for a correspondentist position about the truth conditions of legal propositions, and for an explanation of mistakes in the identification of law in terms of erroneous descriptions of certain facts.

71 With regard to this point, it may be interesting to consider Marmor's criticism of Lewis's thesis that the very existence of a convention requires that its existence be widely known. Following Burge, Marmor points out that people may be mistaken about the conventional nature of the rules they follow. Moreover, it may be the case that people believe to be following a convention when in fact they are not. In effect, whether or not something is a convention is not a matter of convention. A community may follow a convention even if it does not possess the concept of convention. Marmor's main objection to Lewis is that the he leaves no room for the controversies about the conventionality of any dimension of human

meaning is determined when a linguistic use is not only shared, but also known to be so if it is to be identifiable with antirealist semantics. Only then does Hartian semantics conform to the antirealist idea that the truth conditions of legal propositions do not transcend our epistemic abilities to verify them.

For the time being, I would like to point out that assuming a social ontology as the basis for meaning of legal terms and expressions seems insufficient to reject realist semantics. For this reason, the foundations of Hartian antirealism should be sought elsewhere.

I would like to stress that addressing the question about the meaning of normative texts is relevant to a study of a restrictive theory of strong discretion insofar that it permits an analysis of the constrains placed by language upon the very possibility of existence of discretion. Hartian positivism argues that linguistic constraints transcend the epistemic abilities of individual judges. This enables positivists to claim that judges may be mistaken when identifying the contents of law. The origin of their mistakes lies in wrong descriptions of the shared use of language. However, we cannot readily conclude that Hart's theory of truth for legal statements is closer to assertability than to correspondence. Given that the aim of legal theory is to provide useful criteria to distinguish the understanding of norms from their invention, we are urged to investigate whether the theory of truth conditions proposed by Hartian positivism relates to assertability or to correspondence. The main difficulty is how to reconcile the following two ideas: on the one hand, that truth conditions for legal statements are independent of the specific interpreter; on the other, that these truth conditions are nevertheless not independent of conceptual schemes, as the notion of truth as assertability seems to suggest. Moreover, there remains the open question how to avoid the thesis of 'anything goes', which asserts that there is no genuine restriction acting on judgements about law. To avoid this conclusion, it is imperative to justify the existence of objective constraints

---

conduct. This type of controversies is possible and intelligible because it involves matters of facts which are not necessarily matters of common knowledge. In spite of assuming Burge's criticism to Lewis, Marmor indicates that this criticism is of limited applicability. It can only be taken into consideration in connection with the question about when is it that we face a convention. In Marmor's opinion, accepting that there could be a general misunderstanding of the contents of a rule is a far more delicate question. Nevertheless, the only reason put forward not to extend this idea is that it is inconsistent to maintain simultaneously an antirealist position for a certain kind of statements, and to accept the possibility of general mistake about the truth of such statements. Marmor (1996, 354-355). Regardless of how Burge's criticism affects Marmor's position about linguistic conventions in the determination of the propositional contents of legal rules, this criticism proves useful to illustrate the possibility to distinguish between shared use, and widespread knowledge of this shared use.

to what can be said about the contents of law and to do so without resort to semantic realism.

Current Hartian positivism has devoted much attention to this problem, particularly to clarifying the foundations of its semantic antirealism and of its views on partial indeterminacy beyond the rejection of the indexical nature of legal terms and expressions. Firstly, Hartian positivism presents an interpretation of Wittgenstein's considerations on rule-following and on the normativity of meaning that seems incompatible with semantic realism. Secondly, this theory rejects Kripke's sceptical reading of Wittgenstein's remarks on rule-following. Finally, positivists assume that the open texture of language leads to the conclusion that there are instances in which legal propositions have no truth-value. As a result, the bivalent structure for propositions about law breaks down. According to Dummet, this amounts to adopting antirealist semantics[72]. These arguments are vital for the viability of Hartian semantics and will therefore be carefully considered in the next two sections. The idea of a shared use of language and what it is from a Hartian point of view that determines such a use will be further explored. In addition, we will examine the question what is it the members of a community need to comprehend to conclude that the meaning of a linguistic formulation is a specific one, and not any other.

Rule-following

In *The Concept of Law*, Hart sets forth a theory of meaning as use that is half way between a criteriological and a paradigmatic theory[73]. On the one hand, Hart stresses that the existence of a shared use is determined by the existence of a general agreement about the applicability of legal terms to obvious or paradigmatic cases[74]. In addition, he insists that sharing a use in fact means sharing criteria about the applicability of classifying terms[75]. In my view, Hart appears to suggest that the existence of paradigmatic cases allows for an inductive identification of general criteria of use. For this reason, these paradigmatic cases provide minimal necessary (but not sufficient because of the open texture of language) conditions for the correct use of terms.

---

[72] Dummet (1978, 162-165) claims that rejecting bivalence necessarily implies antirealist semantics and, hence, a theory of truth as assertability. See also Marmor (1972, 86-93) and Moreso (1998, 49-51).

[73] Bix (1993, 9).

[74] Hart (1994, 126-130).

[75] Hart (1994, 129). This explains why, in spite of acknowledging a relevant analogy between the language of rules and that of precedents, Hart points to an important difference between them, namely that the language of rules reflects general criteria of use in far more stable and permanent a way than the case-to-case language of precedents does.

Bix draws an interesting distinction within paradigmatic cases: strong paradigmatic cases and absolute paradigmatic cases. This distinction may be useful to grasp Hart's perspective. Strong paradigmatic cases are those which are thought to embody clear examples of use of the general criterion in question. We could say, for example, that if there is such a thing as law, traffic rules are certainly part of it. Bix claims that the most important feature of strong paradigmatic cases are the general criteria that can be inferred from them, and not the paradigms themselves. Hence, it may be the case that traffic rules cease to be a clear example of legal norms. It could be argued that strong paradigms are no more than specific realisations of general criteria about which there is consensus. Paradigms, then, exist only insofar as there is general consensus about the concept. In contrast, absolute paradigmatic cases actually define a term. In Bix's terms, 'the paradigm could never be understood as not exemplifying the concept and any change in belief about the paradigm would result in a change in belief about the concept'[76]. Bix suggests as an example of this the religious claim that living a good life consists in living as much as possible like Jesus. A change in belief about how Jesus lived his life will immediately result in a change of our concept of what it is to live a good life[77]. Hart's notion of paradigmatic case is closer to that of strong paradigm. He argues that paradigmatic cases are important because they reflect the existence of consensus about the criteria of use of classifying terms. He thus distances himself from the formalist view that in order to know the meaning of legal terms we ought to establish the necessary and sufficient conditions of applicability. Paradigmatic cases allow to extract necessary conditions (minimal criteria of use), but not the sufficient ones. He thus also distances himself from scepticism for he supports the idea that some instances can be seen to fall into the zone of certainty of the concept[78].

Yet, Hart does not explain how paradigmatic cases, which are just samples of shared general criteria of use, actually establish the literal or plain meaning of legal terms. Therefore, he does not answer the question how their existence justifies the presence of right legal answers. It is interesting to consider this question because the link between consensus and meaning may raise philosophical difficulties in justifying a deterministic thesis, in particular a deterministic answer to the problem of rule-following. Since the question of rule-following is central to the problem of judicial discretion, it will be carefully investigated in what follows.

---

[76] Bix (1993, 56).

[77] See Bix (1993, 56-59) and Baker (1988, 31, 34, 49).

[78] See Hart (1994, 129-131).

Wittgenstein's considerations about the normativity of meaning yielded fruitful philosophical discussion on the question when is it plausible to claim, if at all, that a semantic rule is being used correctly. There is room for two different interpretations of the rule-following problem in connection with the question of semantic determination, and for several readings of the heading 'meaning as use'[79]. The first one is a sceptical interpretation based on Kripke's interpretation of Wittgenstein's remarks[80]. Its starting point is the claim that there is no-thing in the rule itself, or in facts such as its previous use or the intentions of those who used it in the past, determining whether or not a present conduct conforms to the rule[81]. Such a position rests on Wittgenstein's idea that every act can be seen as following a rule in the light of some interpretation[82]. Wittgenstein illustrates this point by appealing to the continuation of an arithmetic series, for example, that which arises from the rule 'n+2'. Let us assume that a numerical sequence such as: 1000, 1002, 1004, 1008 is obtained by applying the rule called 'n+2'. It can be argued that this sequence follows the rule n+2 incorrectly. However, this series could also be viewed as the correct application of the following interpretation of the rule 'n+2': add 2 up to 1004 and thereafter add 4[83]. The aim of this example is to show that it is always possible to offer an interpretation of a rule that views the case as an instance of the rule. Rules themselves do not tell us how we ought to use them. On the grounds of these reflections, Kripke concludes that 'anything goes'. Thus, rule-following is not possible because every act can be interpreted as following and as breaking the rule[84]. In other words, Kripke maintains that it is impossible to *a priori* assert such things as the correct use of a word, or that a proceeding conforms to a rule. The meaning of a term

---

[79] See Schauer (1991, 226). Understanding the meaning of a linguistic formulation seems to be very closely related to following a rule or acting in accordance with it. Given that rules are expressed by means of language, the range of conducts that constitute acts of rule-following will be specified insofar as the meaning of normative formulations is determined. For this reason, 'the correct use of a term' and 'following a rule' will be considered synonymous henceforth. On this synonymy, see Bix (1993, 43, 47-49).

[80] See Kripke (1982). For a sceptical interpretation of rule-following in the legal context see Yablon (1987, 629-636).

[81] According to Kripke (1982, 13-22, 53-54), rule-following is not determined by platonic entities nor by any past event such as external behaviours or states of mind.

[82] See Wittgenstein (1953, secs. 186-188) and Kripke (1982, 7-13).

[83] See Wittgenstein (1953, secs. 185-201).

[84] Kripke (1982, 55) and Wittgenstein (1953, Sec. 201). Kripke draws attention to the fact that this is not merely an epistemological problem. The sceptic position does not claim that there is no way of knowing when an agent has complied with a rule or contravened it. On the contrary, any past event taken to be a criterion of meaning is compatible with either conclusion and hence, nothing can establish the meaning of a term or expression. Kripke (1982, 21).

can only be determined *a posteriori* of its use. Only insofar as an alleged act of use gives rise to general agreement, are we entitled to assert that words have been used correctly. Thus, the correct application of terms is not governed by rules available to the agent when attempting to use the language[85]. To the sceptic, the interpreter's act will be no more than a leap in the dark based on her interpretation of the contents of the rule[86]. In short, Kripke's theory does not reject the existence of easy cases with respect to the meaning of words[87]. His argument turns on the idea that the factor determining whether or not a case is an easy case, and whether or not a particular assignation of meaning is correct, is not the rule itself nor the language in which it is expressed, but the degree of general consensus generated by every alleged rule-following act. Moreover, according to sceptics, the degree of *a posteriori* consensus strongly depends on ideological and political factors, whence their slogan: 'law is politics'[88].

However, there is an alternative non sceptical interpretation of the rule-following paradox which Hacker and Baker carefully explain, and which has been adopted by Hartian positivism[89]. This view stresses that Wittgenstein's considerations cannot be seen to support the thesis of 'anything goes' nor to deny the existence of easy cases as something prior to the application of a rule and with respect to which the rule is therefore determined. Rather, their aim is to show that interpretation, as the substitution of one rule for another (or of a sign for another), cannot be the intermediary between rules and their instances of use. To know a rule cannot merely consist in offering an interpretation of its contents because it is always possible to offer an interpretation that regards a certain conduct as an act that conforms to the rule. The key point of the non sceptical position is another one of Wittgenstein's remarks[90], specifically that 'there is a way of grasping a rule which is not interpretation, but which is exhibited in what we call "obeying a rule" and "going against it" in actual cases'[91]. This remark suggests that there is no intermediary between the rule and the instances of its use which fixes its meaning[92]. The meaning rests on the internal connection between the rule and the acts arising from the practice of using or following the rule as a standard of correctness, and

85 See Kripke (1982, 111-112, particularly footnote 87) and Yablon (1987, 632-636).

86 Kripke (1982, 55).

87 On this point, see Bix (1993, 37).

88 Yablon (1987, 632-636).

89 Baker and Hacker (1994, 82-262). See also Marmor (1992, 146-154), Bix (1993, Ch. II), Schauer (1992, 225-230) and Greenawalt (1992, 68-69).

90 Wittgenstein (1953, sec. 201).

91 Wittgenstein (1953, sec. 201). See also Dummet (1978, 224-225).

92 Baker and Hacker (1994, 98-105).

the explanations and justifications we offer or give of these acts in connection with the rule[93].

This thesis has been adopted by Hartian positivism to support two chief postulates of this theory that conflict with the theory of radical indeterminacy. The first one is that some cases are easy cases as far as the application of classifying terms is concerned. In accordance with this, rules are partially determined. The second refers to the distinction between understanding and interpreting a normative formulation. To know the meaning of a term or expression is to understand it. To understand is the ability to use language correctly, in other words, it is the ability to specify the conditions for the use of language. From this point of view, this is all it takes to understand the meaning of normative texts[94]. Interpretation, by contrast, becomes necessary when an instance is neither included in nor excluded from the literal meaning of a certain term or expression, that is, when interpreters are unable to specify the conditions of use in a particular instance[95]. In such cases, the linguistic formulation of the rule needs to be replaced with some other formulation that frees it of its indeterminacy.

As was already pointed out, the foundation of these two positivist theses lies in the idea that there is no intermediary between the rule and its instances of use that determines its meaning. No past event can be determinant of the meaning because any event can be reconstructed in multiple ways[96]. Neither can interpretation be regarded as a valid mediator. The contents of the rule is fixed by the rule itself or, more precisely, by the internal relationship between the rule and its acts of application[97].

---

[93] Baker and Hacker (1994, 102, 171-172).

[94] Opponents of scepticism claim that the search for mediators between the rule and its instances of use is what in fact leads to the thesis of 'anything goes'. Taking interpretation as such a mediator yields the sceptical conclusion. See Marmor (1992, 149) and Bix (1993, 39, 74).

[95] In line with Dummet, Marmor advocates the thesis of the exceptionality of interpretation. Interpretation is required only when a rule cannot possibly be followed, that is, when it is dubitable whether or not a specific action complies with the rule. In this case, we need some interpretation of the rule imposing meaning to it on the basis of somebody's understanding of what its meaning is, be it the interpreter or the author of the linguistic formulation himself. According to Marmor, this activity is no longer governed by rules and conventions, but guided by paradigms. However, interpretation is an exceptional kind of understanding for it is parasitic on understanding. Thus, every interpretation requires a previous understanding of the instances embraced by the literal meaning of the formulation of the rule. See Marmor (1992, 21-24) and Dummet (1993, 464-472).

[96] Hartian positivism acknowledges the importance of the problem identified by Wittgenstein and pointed to by scepticism, but considers that Wittgenstein does not (and need not) offer a sceptical answer to it. See Bix (1993, 38-41).

[97] Marmor (1992, 148-152).

Current versions of Hartian positivism favour both this non sceptical interpretation of Wittgenstein's considerations and the idea of consensus about the use of legal terms as a key point to meaning. To my mind, these two views are in conflict with one another: if Hartian positivism seeks to distance itself from Kripke's interpretation of Wittgenstein, it should maintain a thesis about the relationship between consensus and meaning significantly different from both the one criticised and the one embraced by scepticism. This relationship ought not to be that consensus permits to determine *a priori* when is it the case that a particular assignation of meaning is correct, for this is precisely the problem that scepticism points out to: that taking a past event as a semantic criterion does not in any way determine the meaning of normative texts because we can reconstruct past events in a multiplicity of ways. Nor is it plausible to argue that the relationship between consensus and meaning is, specifically, that consensus determines only *a posteriori* whether or not a word or sentence has been used correctly. To accept this conclusion would lead to a Kripkean understanding of Wittgenstein, that is, to the conclusion that law is indeterminate. The point is whether Hartian positivism succeeds in tendering a different relationship between consensus and meaning.

Marmor, Schauer and Bix, to name but a few, have proposed an alternative relationship between consensus and meaning. They take as a starting point the second interpretation of rule-following, i.e. that the meaning of terms lies in the internal relationship between the rule and the acts of use. The rule determines its own use, but not as a metaphysical entity. What is relevant here is the grammatical relationship (internal to the language game of following standards) between the rule and its instances of application[98]. Nevertheless, their starting point seems to be their end point too. For although they exclude interpretation as the means to grasp rules, their explanation on how this internal relationship determines the meaning virtually reduces to Hacker and Baker's idea on Wittgenstein: that agreement on definitions and judgements, as a sign of a shared form of life, is what makes possible the existence of rules, and the very idea of following rules[99]. Notwithstanding, it is not agreement what enables us to ascertain that

---

98 See Bix (1993, 41), Marmor (1992, 153) and Baker and Hacker (1994, 259-262).

99 According to Hacker and Baker, agreement on judgements consists in interpersonal consensus about the truth or falsity of empirical propositions, which, in fact, is just a consensus on how we describe the world. Agreement on definitions, by contrast, is consensus on how we use words, which implies that we use the same words to refer to the same objects. We shall have later to consider the relationship between these two kinds of agreement. On this distinction, see Baker and Hacker (1994, 258-262), Hurley (1989, 30-33), Stavropoulos (1996, 125-128) and Bix (1993, 53-59).

an act conforms to the rule. In order to make such an assertion we need to examine what criteria has been applied and how the concept of correctness has been used[100].

This idea is liable to two interpretations. It can be argued, on the one hand, that resorting to use as the semantic criterion is virtually the same as measuring each particular act of use against the shared linguistic behaviour as a reflection of more fundamental agreements on the form of life. This interpretation eventually requires accepting one of the characterisations of the relationship between consensus and meaning set out above. On the other hand, resorting to use as the semantic criterion may appear to imply that the question whether an act is in accordance with a rule can only be answered under the light of the circumstances surrounding the instant act of use and the particular point of view shared by the individuals involved[101]. According to this second interpretation, correctly using a term or following a rule is the ability to formulate the rule and to apply or follow it in practice. In other words, it requires the mastery of a specific technique and of certain criteria of use. This is only indirectly indicative that individuals participate in a shared linguistic practice[102]. Thus, an agent may understand

---

[100] Baker and Hacker (1994, 170-174) and Bix (1993, 41).

[101] This, however, does not imply that the meaning is ultimately reduced to the particular intention of the speaker, that is, the communicative purpose with which language is used in a particular instance. It seeks to stress that the meaning of an expression is not independent of the epistemic abilities of the individuals applying the semantic rules, nor of the interpreter that evaluates the correctness of somebody else's application of the rule according to her own understanding of it. Hacker and Baker assert that only two requirements must be satisfied to ascertain that a rule has been followed. Firstly, the agent ought to have rules of an appropriate class, and an awareness of the rule that she claims to be following. Secondly, her conduct ought to exhibit a sufficient degree of complexity to demonstrate the intention and ability that are essential to following a rule. It should be borne in mind that Hacker and Baker think these two conditions to be independent of the existence of either a shared use or a community of speakers. An isolated individual could follow a rule even if there is no community. Similarly, an agent can follow a rule even if there is no general consensus about its use. This is so because, although following a rule requires the existence of a technique or a practice (a criterion of correctness), this practice need not be social. Claiming that there is an internal relationship between the rule and its instance of application amounts to asserting that the agent does not act arbitrarily but in accordance with some criterion of correctness that allows her to distinguish between compliance and violation of the rule she claims to be following. See Baker and Hacker (1994, 170-179).

[102] Baker and Hacker (1994, 259). Agreement on the form of life accounts for the similarity of the answers given by different individuals, but does not justify the claim that they are following a rule. On the contrary, answers may coincide but they may not result from following a rule. As pointed out by Hacker and Baker, the only factor that permits the distinction between rule-following and the mere appearance that a rule is being followed is the mastery of a particular technique - the ability to provide an answer to which is the rule that is allegedly being followed, and which acts are required to follow it correctly. See Baker and Hacker (1994, 176-179). Along similar lines, McDowell (1981, 149) states that 'there is nothing that keeps our practices in line except the reactions and responses we learn in learning them'.

a rule because she shares a social practice and has internalised a shared technique. (This is, by the way, the standard situation). However, she may also understand a rule and internalise a technique when there is neither general consensus nor a social practice of use.

Hacker and Baker identify the foregoing ambiguity in the thesis that in order to be able to assert that someone is following a rule, one must appeal to the act of use. According to these authors, this ambiguity is due to a rather common misinterpretation of Wittgenstein's emphasis on the social dimension of language as a human activity. Thus, it is claimed that, in the same way that the very possibility of language as a means of communication relies on the existence of an agreement among the speakers about the definitions and judgements, so the distinction between believing that one is following a rule and actually following it can only be made by comparing the particular act to the general conduct of the social group in question. Accordingly, agreement or shared practices is considered to be what settles the meaning of rules[103]. Hacker and Baker contend that this interpretation of Wittgenstein is wrong on several fronts. Firstly, they assert that rule-following is compatible with the possibility that the community as a whole may, at times, erroneously apply its own rules. The rule establishes a standard of correctness not only for the answers provided by an individual, but also for those provided by the group[104]. Secondly, they argue, Wittgenstein's position does not assume that an isolated individual, such as Robinson Crusoe, is not in a position to follow a rule. All that such an individual needs in order to follow a rule is to be immersed in a practice of following rules. This entails having a criterion of correctness, but not necessarily being immersed in a social practice, as pointed out above[105]. With regard to this point,

---

103 Baker and Hacker (1994, 170 171, 233, 243-251).

104 In this sense, Hacker and Baker argue that agreement in behaviour can only be taken as an explanation to what is correct if the idea of an internal relationship between a rule and its instances of use is dismissed. See Baker and Hacker (1994, 172).
Note that the claim that a community may be wrong about the contents of its own rules does not inevitably lead to support realist semantics. The community may be mistaken because the rule is the criterion to evaluate conduct. Here rules are understood as the object of debate, and not as metaphysical entities. Hence, a semantic judgement that dissents from the opinion of the majority still makes sense (and may even be right) insofar as it rests on a better characterisation of the standard of conduct than other judgements do. Thus, the debate about the contents of the rule is not descriptive of shared linguistic conventions, but dialectic.

105 Baker and Hacker (1994, 173-179, 243-251). In a similar sense, see Pears (1991, 280) and McGinn (1984, 77-84). According to Stavropoulos, Wittgenstein's project seeks to maintain a negative thesis. The distinction between the correct and the incorrect application of a rule rests neither in a pattern hidden in a secret book, nor in a particular interpretation, view of the world, or anything we agree on.

McGinn suggested that the very possibility of following rules requires that there be more than one occasion of use, that is, regular use[106]. But Wittgenstein's idea of custom or practice refers to a multiplicity of rule-following acts rather than a multiplicity of users. Hence, interpersonal agreement is not required for an assignation of meaning to be correct.

Hartian positivism seems to implicitly adopt the interpretation of Wittgenstein's emphasis on the public dimension of language to which Hacker and Baker clearly object. Schauer, for instance, claims that the meaning of terms depends on their use in a community of speakers in addition to the conventions and shared habits governing the use of words[107]. Bix, on the other hand, relates the problem about how to guarantee that a rule is followed correctly to the agreements on the form of life[108]. However, if semantic determinacy is conditional on more fundamental agreements, but nevertheless agreements, these fundamental agreements do not solve the paradox of rule-following because they operate as mediators between rules and acts. Similarly, Marmor points out that the claim that linguistic use is governed by rules relies on the social and conventional dimension of language[109].

These authors' remarks suggest the semantic view objected to by Hacker and Baker. The clearest exponent of this view is Hart himself. He asserts that 'the clear cases are those in which there is general agreement that they fall within the scope of a rule'[110]. Furthermore, he writes:

> General terms would be useless to us as a medium of communication unless there were such familiar, unchallenged cases. But the variants on the familiar also call for classification under the general terms [...]. Here something in the nature of a crisis in communication is precipitated: there are reasons both for and against our use of a general term, and no firm convention or general agreement dictates its use, or, on the other hand, its rejection by the person concerned to classify'[111].

Wittgenstein's thesis implies denying that the normativity in the application of concepts may be reduced to something simpler. See Stavropoulos (1996, 154-155).

106 McGinn (1984, 78, 89-91).

107 Schauer (1991, 56 footnote 5, 58-59). See also Bix (1993, 65, 71).

108 Bix (1993, 62, 179). Consensus on the form of life as the criterion for meaning invalidates the thesis of an internal relationship between the rule and its instances of use. This, in turn, leads to the sceptical problem. The situation would be different if resort to this consensus were with a view to explaining why we follow the same rules, rather than to identifying when is it the case that we are following them correctly.

109 Marmor (1992, 19).

110 Hart (1983, 106). See also Hart (1994, 126).

111 Hart (1994, 126-127).

Therefore, Hartian positivism defends three ideas that seem to conflict with the claim that the criterion for semantic determinacy is to be sought in the internal relationship between the rule and its acts of use. These three tenets are the following: a) meaning is conventional in nature; b) rule-following necessarily requires that there be social practices[112]; and c) the truth-value of legal propositions transcends the individual epistemic abilities, but not those of the linguistic community as a whole[113]. Hartian positivism, in contrast with Hacker and Baker, would not accept that the community as a whole may occasionally be mistaken about the correct application of its own rules because widespread misunderstanding may only be conceived of if rule-following is dissociated from social agreement. Finally, positivism thinks it meaningless to talk about rule-following when there is no community of speakers to develop a social practice. Thus, Hartian semantics seem to be oblivious of the fact that the existence of social consensus and of a shared form of life does not in itself permit to distinguish the situation in which the rule is apparently followed from that in which it is actually followed. Nor does it allow to decide when a given act is in accord or in conflict with a rule. The existence of social consensus and of a shared form of life provides, of course, an explanation as to why the members in a community follow the same rules. But social consensus is not a mediator between rules and acts. The propositions about rules are not reducible to propositions about shared linguistic conduct.

It could be argued, as in fact Bayón does, that one of the shortcomings of contemporary positivist positions, and in particular Marmor's, is that, in spite of their emphasis on the internal relationship between rules and acts, and on the fact that not every rule-following act presupposes an interpretation, positivists do not specify the nature of the relationship between the rule and the instance of use any further[114]. This is the question to be investigated in order to establish a link between consensus and meaning without resorting to a theory of social reference - in my view, a mild version of semantic realism[115] - or to the thesis of radical indeterminacy. If this question is

112 In this sense, positivism seems to approach Kripke's idea on the impossibility of private language. Kripke rejects the plausibility of accounting for rule-following in terms of an analysis of either the circumstances or the standpoint of the acting agent without referring to her membership of some community, Kripke (1982, 108-110).

113 On this point see, among others, Bix (1993, 64-65) and Coleman and Leiter (1995, 253).

114 Bayón claims that Marmor's version of rule-following does not overcome the problem about how to link meaning and consensus because it does not supply sceptics with an explanation on how this internal relationship comes about. See Bayón (1996, 16, 17). It could thus be argued that positivism does not explicitly reject consensus as the mediator between a rule and its instances of use.

115 I already pointed out in previous sections that the idea of a social reference as the determining factor of meaning only introduces a change in the ontology to be identified to grasp meaning. Although it is not

neglected, the theory of easy cases becomes meaningless because it does not warrant that rules are partially determined.

Nevertheless, none of what has been set out so far explains how should the idea of an internal relationship be articulated to avoid both the sceptical challenge and a solipsist or subjectivist position. Chapter 6 will address this issue once the theory of weak discretion and its epistemological consequences have been analysed. For the time being, I would just like to point out that Hartian positivism does not offer such an explanation. Moreover, the conventionalist semantics positivism assumes seem to push this theory away from the thesis of the internal relationship.

Let us return to Shiner's exposition of the differences between simple and sophisticated positivism. It has been shown that one of the possible arguments to support the antirealist nature of sophisticated positivism - namely, a non-sceptical interpretation of rule-following - has not been adequately developed. A theory of truth as assertability for legal statements cannot be attributed to Hartian positivism on the grounds of this argument because this argument is flawed. Thus, Shiner's distinction between simple and sophisticated positivism remains unclear given that the distinction itself rests on the assumption that simple positivism deems the truth conditions of legal propositions to be conditional on the occurrence of certain past events, whereas sophisticated positivism does not[116]. But Hartian positivism has submitted further arguments to advocate the antirealist nature of its semantics. Specifically, that some legal propositions have no truth-value, i.e. that law is not entirely determined and that there exist hard cases for which law does not dispose of the dispute. In those cases law provides no right answer.

2.4.3 No right answer: hard cases

The thesis of the partial indeterminacy of law entails a specific approach to hard cases and to the consequences of their existence as far as normative adjudication is concerned. Most positivists relate the idea of hard cases to that of absence of right answer or normative indeterminacy[117]. Thus, the settlement of the dispute requires exercising strong judicial discretion[118]. The thesis of law as communication regards semantic

---

assumed that legal terms are indexical (they do not designate natural classes of objects), their reference is based on social facts which are reducible to collective linguistic behaviour.

116 Shiner (1992b, 89-90).

117 On this point, see Hart (1983, 105), Kress (1989, 296-297), Barak (1989, 40-41), Conklin (1981, 231), Schauer (1985, 415) and Parent (1980, 99).

118 It is a common assumption within positivism that the need for discretion is the counterpart of the absence of right answer. See Bix (1993, 26) and Schauer (1991, 222).

indeterminacy as an important source of normative indeterminacy. This section will therefore concentrate on semantic indeterminacy. Positivism neither denies nor neglects the existence of other sources of legal indeterminacy and factors generating difficulties in the solution of cases. However, a positivist theory of law typically justifies the partial indeterminacy of law on the grounds of semantic considerations such as the open texture of language. Moreover, it draws a clear distinction between those cases whose solution is difficult and complex, and those for which there is no right legal answer. Only the latter require discretion. In order to grasp this point, it will be useful to distinguish a few different senses of 'hard case':

1.- Normatively hard cases. These are cases for which law provides no answer and for which the conduct is consequently not deontically qualified. If this is the case, propositions about law are assumed to have no truth-value. As pointed out in Chapter 1, normative indeterminacy is often related to legal gaps, contradiction, and semantic indeterminacy. Semantic indeterminacy has attracted Hartian positivists' attention who understand what we shall call 'semantically hard cases' to be a subclass of 'normatively hard cases'[119]. Semantically hard cases are those situations in which a legal proposition is neither true nor false because it can neither be asserted that the case falls under the scope of the classifying term nor that it is excluded from it.

2.- Epistemically hard cases. Although law provides a legal answer to these instances, identifying what this answer is requires a sophisticated intellectual process. Here, it is important to distinguish between objective and subjective epistemic difficulties. While the former arise from the way in which a domain of conduct is regulated, the latter refer to the fact that the interpreter may not be endowed with the

119 It should be noted, as indeed Schauer does, that a case may be normatively determined, that is, it may be an easy case, and yet its inclusion in the semantic contents of a rule may be indeterminate. Hence, in order to link normative indeterminacy to semantic indeterminacy a notion of rule that goes beyond a simple canonical formulation is needed. Sometimes a rule may be a combination of a formulation and a first order justification. Then, semantic indeterminacy arises when the contents of both of these elements is undetermined, Schauer (1991, 210-212). See also Hart's and Raz's reflections on the role of principles and rules of interpretation as factors reducing the semantic indeterminacy of rules, Raz (1972, 846) and Hart (1994, 126). Note that these observations simply intend to point out that normative indeterminacy does not result from the semantic indeterminacy of a rule as an isolated entity, but from the semantic indeterminacy of law in general with respect to some specific case.

necessary epistemic abilities (she may lack experience or have too little information) to realise the corresponding right legal answer[120].

3.- Pragmatically hard cases. These are disputes whose resolution is surrounded by immediate circumstances that transcend the legal aspects of the judicial decision. The political impact of a judicial decision and the reaction of the public opinion to the solution of certain social conflicts are examples of this kind of circumstances.

4.- Factually hard cases. The difficulty in these cases arises in connection with assessing the sufficiency of evidence to warrant that particular normatively relevant events took place[121].

5.- Morally hard cases. These are situations in which the answer provided by the law leads to an unjust outcome. In other words, the legal answer has no moral justification[122].

I would like to highlight that normative problems in general, and semantic ones in particular, lie at the heart of the positivist interest in the limits of law[123]. The reason for this lies in the consideration that only in case of normatively hard cases can we speak of no right answer and invoke strong judicial discretion. It is typical of Hartian positivism to ignore epistemic, pragmatic and moral difficulties as sources of legal indeterminacy. Epistemic difficulties are excluded on account of the claim that the existence of a right answer transcends the epistemic abilities of the interpreter. In this sense Marmor asserts that the relevant difficulty of a case is unrelated to either epistemic difficulties or to individual epistemic abilities[124]. Hartian positivism also discards pragmatic difficulties as a source of legal indeterminacy because, unlike sceptical movements such as

---

120 It was already pointed out in the previous chapter that these are 'intermediate' cases according to Barak's terminology. They are thus distinguished both from those for which a legal answer is readily available to the interpreter, and from those for which there is no right legal answer, Barak (1989, 39-40).

121 In connection with this point, see MacCormick (1978, 86-93).

122 It is typical of positivism to reject this notion of 'hard case' as a source of relevant difficulty to the knowledge and application of law. Schauer, for instance, argues that if the difficulties in a case depend on a rule leading to unjust results, then the notion of rule itself eventually collapses with that of its justification. For Schauer this does not imply that there are no legal mechanisms to overcome this problem. Most legal orders include what Schauer calls 'rule avoiding norms'. These norms allow the judge to reduce the rigidity of the rules in the event of unjust or absurd results. Nevertheless, both, this type of norms and the rules that justify further rules, are of a legal nature. See Schauer (1988, 515-520; 1991, 53-56, 211). For the positivist thesis on the differentiation between law and morality, see Hart (1983, 49-87; 1994, 185-212) and Raz (1979, 37-52; 1990, 162-170).

123 I will not elaborate any further on factually hard cases because my interest here is in the knowledge of law.

124 See Marmor (1992, 127) and Waluchow (1983, 335-336).

American legal realism, positivism does not adopt a factual perspective of the legal phenomenon. Hence, positivism assumes legal correctness to be independent of the psychological factors playing part in judicial decisions. Finally, moral difficulties are not envisaged because in accordance with the positivist view that the legal context can be taken into consideration independently of other normative contexts, the question on the existence of a right legal answer is separated from the moral evaluation of that answer[125].

Hard cases and legal interpretation

There is a single predominant view among Hartian positivists as to when a case is to be rated a semantically hard case. Given that the meaning of normative texts depends on linguistic practices, disagreement and absence of settled conventions lead to hard cases. The contents of law is indeterminate with regard to these cases and hence, there is no rule to follow. Here, legal propositions have no truth-value because there is no rule including in or excluding from its scope of applicability the case under consideration.

In such a context, adjudication is discretionary, and making a judicial decision requires interpretation, i.e. the substitution of one formulation of the rule for another. A new meaning is thus assigned to a normative formulation by means of some plausible reconstruction of its contents. According to Marmor, this reconstruction is neither subject to rules nor conditional on linguistic conventions. However, he stresses that an interpretation may be controlled by or judged in terms of interpretative paradigms embodying criteria of acceptability within the community[126]. Thus, although interpretation requires the exercise of strong discretion, it does not imply that 'anything goes'. Marmor contends that interpretation should be differentiated from both understanding and invention. However, he does not specify clear criteria to draw this distinction[127]. He claims that interpreting a legal text is substantially different from

[125] The reader is surely familiar with the fact that this is one of the most controversial points in legal positivism. It could be argued that the thesis of the social sources does not prevent moral criteria from being part of a rule of recognition. Nevertheless, positivism does not accept that the legal validity of a specific normative act should necessarily depend on its moral justification. Hence, the existence of a right legal answer is independent of its moral evaluation. As pointed out in a previous footnote, this does not exclude the possibility that the legal system may itself contain mechanisms to diminish the morally unacceptable consequences to which the application of legal rules may lead. See Waluchow's account of inclusive positivism, Waluchow (1994, 80-140).

[126] Marmor claims that, unlike rules, paradigms cannot be misunderstood or followed incorrectly. The paradigm may be respected or not, but not respecting it does not presume a lack of understanding. See Marmor (1992, 21-22).

[127] See Endicott (1994, 22).

understanding its meaning. Interpretation as a reformulation process entails imposing meaning within the limits of a reasonable reconstruction of the counterfactual intent of the normative authority. Invention, by contrast, involves a genuine substitution of one sign for another. In short, from this standpoint, every interpretation is a weak form of invention because it results in a new answer to the legal question[128]. Nevertheless, the new answer, unlike in the case of pure invention, belongs strictly to the zone of legal reasonableness[129]. This point will be given full consideration in Chapter 4.

Marmor's perspective as set out above draws a clear distinction between the domain of legal understanding and that of legal interpretation. The former relies on literal meaning and thus on the existence of a right legal answer. Legal interpretation, in contrast, comes into play when literal meaning is not sufficient to associate the case to a legal concept but a plausible reconstruction of its contents can nevertheless be devised. Thus, the truth conditions of legal propositions seem to be regarded as quite distinct from the conditions of admissibility or reasonableness. The interesting question at this point is to what extent does positivism assume a correspondentist theory of the truth conditions of legal propositions in easy cases, and offers, on the grounds of restricted strong discretion, mere standards of acceptability for interpretation in hard cases. It was noted in the foregoing section that the thesis of the social sources of law is insufficient to dismiss correspondentist or realist semantics[130]. However, it remains to be investigated whether a theory that rejects the principle of bivalence for legal propositions in hard cases must inevitably assume antirealist semantics.

Antirealism and semantic indeterminacy

Dummet establishes a dichotomy between semantic realism and semantic antirealism on the basis of whether they accept or reject the principle of bivalence[131]. Realism argues that the meaning of statements is conditional on states of affairs whose existence is independent of our epistemic abilities for verification[132]. For this reason, propositions referring to those facts are always either true or false according to the presence or

---

128 Endicott (1994, 22-23).

129 See Chapter 1 for a detailed description of the zone of reasonableness.

130 Shiner's assertion that sophisticated positivism assumes a theory of truth as assertability in hard cases is wrong for such a claim would presume that this theory regards the possibility of discussing even these cases in terms of right legal answer, that is, that the truth value of propositions is preserved in hard cases. Let us refer the reader to the link between the notions of hard case, absence of right answer and limited strong discretion pointed to by Bix (1993, 26-27) among others. See also Hart (1994, 131-132).

131 Dummet (1978, xxi-xxiii, 14-15, 162-165, 175-176, 275-276, 315-316).

132 Dummet (1978, 146).

absence of such facts. It can be thus concluded that despite knowledge of reality being limited, the truth-value of propositions is always fixed. Realism requires accepting the principle of bivalence. Therefore, rejecting bivalence leads to antirealist semantics. In other words, antirealism advocates that the truth-value of propositions does not transcend our epistemic abilities. To assume that some propositions have no truth-value implies assuming that the truth or falsity of propositions relies on what we count as evidence to assert or to deny them. Nevertheless, antirealism is compatible with both a rejection and an unrestricted acceptance of the principle of bivalence[133]. Thus, the denial of bivalence only implies that the semantic theory embraced is not realist - it is not one that assumes truth to transcend our means of knowing it.

Dummet's dichotomy is widely accepted and considered to be a cornerstone of modern epistemology. Questioning it is clearly beyond the scope of this text. I simply wish to point out that objections to Dummet's distinction have occasionally been pressed. Crispin Wright claims that Dummet's analysis of the relationship between realism and bivalence is superficial because it does not justify why should realism accept the principle of bivalence[134]. It remains to be shown that the acceptance of bivalence for a certain type of statements follows from the fact that their truth-value is independent of our epistemic abilities. Wright, unlike Dummet, considers these to be two independent postulates[135]. In addition, Wright argues that realist semantics may deem a vague proposition to be one with no truth-value. Hence, realism could claim that every statement of a certain type is determinately true or false except when it is vague or ambiguous[136].

---

133 Recall that it is on these grounds that Marmor claims the relationship between realism and bivalence to be asymmetric. It is possible to hold an antirealist position and accept the principle of bivalence. Marmor writes that it is plausible to envisage an artificial language which respects bivalence without assuming realism. Thus, even though in this language the truth-value of statements will be fixed, their truth or falsity will not be conditional on the existence of an objective reality independent of our knowledge. Marmor (1992, 88; 1995, 186-188). It will be shown in later chapters that the assumption of antirealist semantics without abandoning bivalence can be found in Ronald Dworkin's theory of law.

134 Wright (1993, 433-434).

135 Wright (1993, 434-436, 458-465). Similarly, McDowell distinguishes classical realism from bare realism. While the former maintains the principle of bivalence for statements transcending verification, the latter only claims that the assertion that the truth or falsity of these propositions may transcend our epistemic abilities is plausible. In McDowell's opinion, these forms of realism are independent of one another, and hence bare realism need not accept bivalence for those statements that transcend verification. See McDowell (1993, 42-66) and Wright (1993, 85, 434).

136 For this reason, Wright claims that the principle of bivalence as a substratum to realism should be understood in the sense that any statement that is neither vague nor ambiguous is necessarily either true or false, Wright (1993, 458, 464). Similarly, Putnam (1995b, 76) argues that if the principle of bivalence

This issue will not be addressed in this work. We will merely point out that Wright's idea appears to imply the existence of a third state of affairs quite independent of our knowledge, and which is different from the state which makes a certain proposition true, or that which makes it false.

Let us return to the positivist postulate of the open texture of language. It claims that every proposition may be vague. A proposition is vague when we refer to borderline cases, i.e., those cases placed in the penumbra of the scope of a concept. Vague propositions have no truth-value and hence vagueness points to a semantic problem. Recall that Hart's theory of partial indeterminacy claims that some legal propositions are true and some are false. In other words, although every legal proposition is potentially vague, whenever concepts are actually applied, vagueness will occur only occasionally.

What is the origin of this semantic indeterminacy? A positivist approach to this issue yields two different answers to this question: widespread uncertainty about whether a case is clearly included in or excluded from a concept; and, disagreement about its inclusion or exclusion, that is, disagreement as to the use of terms. The former refers to a shared psychological state of uncertainty about the applicability of a term. In spite of there being shared criteria regulating its use, confusion arises as to whether or not the case accords with the criteria. If the meaning of legal terms and expressions relies on shared certainty, a lack of such certainty necessarily implies that the legal proposition at stake has no truth-value. This, in turn, raises ontological problems if we assume a notion of truth as assertability. The reference of the term or expression will be indeterminate because there is insufficient evidence to assert or deny that the state of affairs is a particular one. Hence, indeterminacy in the truth-value of a proposition results from indeterminacy in our social ontology. Nevertheless, it should be borne in mind that the lack of truth-value cannot be claimed on the grounds of uncertainty only, for the occurrence of widespread doubt is compatible with a realist position in what regards vague concepts, and thus, following Dummet, with preserving the principle of bivalence[137]. It should be stressed that the notion of uncertainty becomes equivalent to that of indeterminacy only as a result of assuming antirealist semantics. The principle of bivalence is thus breached for these propositions.

---

needs to be abandoned simply because the situation encountered has no right answer, e.g. there is no right answer to the question of which of two children is taller if it is the case that both of them are the same height, then the principle of bivalence could never have been accepted as a logical principle in the first place.

137 See, for instance, Redondo (1997, 189-191).

The second reason accounting for semantic indeterminacy is disagreement on the use of terms. Disagreement does not presume a shared psychological state of uncertainty. It is compatible with the fact that no member in the community doubts or is uncertain about the applicability of a term to a certain case. Speakers simply support different views as far as the use of a term to the situation under consideration is concerned. In this situation, indeterminacy does not derive from uncertainty nor from a lack of criteria of use, but from disagreement about what these criteria are. From the standpoint of antirealist semantics, if consensus about criteria is a factor determining the meaning of legal texts, these situations entail vagueness, and thus, semantic indeterminacy. This is so because we have insufficient evidence to assert that a case falls within the zone of certainty or outside it.

In his exposition of the open texture of language, Hart does not specify whether the cause of vagueness is shared doubt, or disagreement on the criteria of use. A careful analysis of Hart's considerations reveals that reference to disagreement and controversy about the applicability of classifying terms as the source of vagueness is not infrequent[138]. Nonetheless, Hart also relates vagueness to widespread doubt. New circumstances for the use of a term that had never been imagined before give way to collective doubt[139]. It may be worth noting that Hart's remarks on disagreement and conflict in his dissertation about the open texture of language relate to widespread uncertainty. When there is such uncertainty, it is impossible to prove that a concept covers or excludes the instant case and therefore there arises legally irresolvable conflict.

From this standpoint, criteriological disagreement embodies a different source of semantic indeterminacy. It does not generate vagueness because vagueness presumes consensus about the criteria of use and thus the discussion concerns marginal cases. When diverging opinions about the application of a term to a certain case are unrelated to uncertainty, the problem is simply that of irresolvable ambiguity of legal terms and expressions. If this were the case, different speakers in the reference community would be using different concepts - they would have different things in mind. As we shall discuss in future chapters, when disagreement refer to fundamental aspects of social life it is thought to indicate that individuals do not participate in the same linguistic practice, cultural substratum, or social context. In short, such a disagreement suggests that there is no shared form of life concerning that particular aspect[140]. If there is criteriological

138 See Hart (1994, 126-134).

139 Hart (1994, 122-123, 128-132).

140 On this claim, see Bix (1993, 53-59, 62) and Blackburn (1981, 172-174).

disagreement and the meaning of texts is dependent upon a consensus about the criteria, then law is indeterminate. In those cases it is meaningless to refer to the differing opinions as correct or incorrect - there is no room for communication. Here, legal ontology is indeterminate because individuals refer to different objects even though none of them is uncertain about the term's use.

It can be concluded that Hartian positivism establishes two factors determining the semantic contents of linguistic formulations dictated by a normative authority: absence of ambiguity, and absence of vagueness. The former refers to a shared perception about the usual instances of application of a term; the latter to widespread certainty that these instances of use clearly fall within the scope of applicability of the rule. The occurrence of either ambiguity or of vagueness causes rules to be indeterminate.

2.5 FINAL REMARKS

Given that problems such as vagueness and ambiguity are presented as proof for the lack of sufficient evidence to guarantee the truth-value of a legal proposition, it seems plausible to claim that the positivist theory of meaning as use advocates antirealist semantics on the basis of a theory of truth as assertability. Legal ontology can thus be understood as a fictional ontology. This can be shown to be so by means of an analogy with literary objects[141]: the contents of a literary work depends on our perception of the fictional world presented in it. The answer to any question we may formulate about a character such as Lady Macbeth is conditional on Shakespeare's particular imagination and, ultimately, on our understanding of the character and of the intention of its creator. Any claim about Macbeth which cannot be backed up with evidence is neither true nor false because both the character and its environment are a product of our perceptions. From this point of view, it is pointless to claim that there is a collective misconception about the life of Macbeth. A statement about this character is only true if, as readers, we imagine it to be so. Thus, it seems that a shift in our opinion about the character (either because our shared beliefs are no longer as firm, or because diverging perceptions occur) leads to a new story about Lady Macbeth.

The comparison drawn illustrates the take on social phenomena adopted by antirealism and constructivism. However, it poses some problems for Hartian positivism as a constructivist theory based on the idea of social convention. Firstly, the conventionalist character of Hartian positivism could lead to conclusions such as if there never was a shared perception on Macbeth or consensus about Shakespeare's intentions

---

[141] For discussion, see Dworkin (1985, 133-139) and Moreso (1998, 48-51).

in the writing of the play, then it could be argued that the character never existed in the fictional world. Any statement about the play would be mere interpretation, a substitution of one sign for another, which, as pointed out above, leads to scepticism and to 'anything goes' (which is tantamount to claiming 'nothing goes'). However, this conclusion, which to my mind seems to follow from Hartian positivism, is highly counter-intuitive. It would not be easily accepted by Hartian positivism itself insofar as this theory supports the thesis that law is the product of the actions of normative authorities. Secondly, the question about what it is that an agent should know in order to grasp correctly the fictional ontology on which there is a shared perception remains unanswered. Should the agent share this perception? Should she simply be able to describe correctly the perception shared by the community, i.e. the psychological states of the community of speakers?

As has been shown, the idea that understanding the meaning of words amounts to identifying correctly their instances of use is ambiguous. If it is assumed that 'understanding' means being able to identify somebody else's beliefs and perceptions, and distinguishing between one's beliefs and what is inter-subjectively believed to be correct, such a notion of understanding is compatible with realist semantics. Brink claims that the conflict between realist and antirealist semantics arises also when speaking of psychological states[142]. If, however, 'understanding' means sharing perceptions, beliefs and criteria, the interesting questions to be addressed by positivism is how to separate the correctness of an assignation of meaning from the epistemic abilities of the interpreter, and how to respond to the sceptical challenge of voluntarism.

Hartian positivism seeks to set forth arguments against scepticism, but its strategy proves unsuccessful, as was already suggested with regard to the question of rule-following. It remains to be shown what is the epistemic mistake of an agent who dissents from the majority of users when identifying the contents of law[143]. In my view, an antirealist position ought to answer these questions in the context of legal statements, if it is to survive as a semantic theory.

We will return to this issue in later chapters. Nevertheless, I would like to highlight that, although Hartian positivism may be consistent with a theory of truth as assertability when there is agreement (i.e., in easy cases), it does not defend such a theory of truth in hard cases. On these grounds, Shiner's argument in favour of assimilating Dworkin's

---

142 Brink (1989, 183).

143 A number of authors have directed their criticism of Hartian positivism against its inability to account for legal disagreement on the truth-value of legal propositions without having to assume an absence of right answer for these cases. In this sense, see Dworkin (1986, 45-46), Brink (1988, 14-116; 1989, 181-191) and McDowell (1981, 150-155).

theory on hard cases to sophisticated positivism, to my mind, seems wrong[144]. The distinguishing feature of Hartian positivism is that hard cases are characterised by an absence of right answer. They thus involve strong discretion, for the judge is expected to make a choice between open alternatives. In this context, discretionary activity is regulated by standards such as admissibility and reasonableness. These standards legally guide and control the judges' role as interstitial legislators and not as agents applying the law.

In the next chapter, an alternative approach to law and to the role of adjudication will be presented: the 'weak discretion model'. Some of its features are close to positivism, whereas others strongly deviate from it. The weak discretion model, mainly defended by Ronald Dworkin, seeks to overcome realism and avoid falling into scepticism in the process. Its strategy, however, is rather dissimilar to the positivist one: its starting point is the rejection of the thesis of the social sources and of semantic conventionalism; in addition, the weak discretion model seeks to maintain an optimistic thesis on the existence of right answers.

It was concluded in the first chapter that the concept of weak discretion within a theory of truth as assertability seems to hint at something more than the mere need for good judgement in the identification of the course of action prescribed by the law. For a legal approach such as Dworkin's, this seems to affect the nature of propositions about the contents of law. His characterisation of weak discretion is to be considered in the wider context of his interpretive theory of law. In the model he defends, weak discretion plays a central role as a means to gain legal knowledge, and comes into play both in easy and in controversial or hard cases.

---

144 On this association, see Shiner (1992b, 90, footnote 56).

CHAPTER 3

THE WEAK DISCRETION MODEL

3.1 INTRODUCTION

Weak discretion was introduced in Chapter 1 as one of the possible uses of 'judicial discretion'. It was broadly defined as the need for reasonableness and good judgement in identifying the course of action prescribed by the law when there exists a right legal answer. The different approaches to weak discretion arise in connection with what the nature of the link between right answer and the epistemic abilities of interpreters is taken to be: if the right legal answer is assumed independent of interpreters' considerations, difficulties in identifying it lead to a need for weak discretion; by contrast, if the right legal answer is considered to be dependent on the epistemic abilities of the interpreting agents, weak discretion merely embodies the implementation of a particular theory or conception of law. Before embarking on a full analysis of what I will call 'the weak discretion model', I would like to stress that these are the two approaches underlying the debate on the existence and the extent of weak discretion in legal adjudication.

One of the most controversial points between Hartian positivism and Dworkin's theory of law has traditionally been the settlement of hard cases. Dworkin has often insisted that disagreement about the contents of law creates a need for weak discretion merely, and that weak discretion is necessary in every act of adjudication[1]. Both positivists and sceptics have pressed numerous objections to this position[2]. Positivists claim that the existence of a single right answer in hard cases can only be defended either from the point of view of natural law theory, or realist semantics. Sceptics such as Fish, on the other hand, believe that Dworkin does not succeed in overcoming legal positivism without falling into semantic realism. Hence, they claim, his approach to law

[1] See Dworkin (1977, 68-71; 1986, 353-354, 400; 1985, 119, 146-148).

[2] See Raz's, Mackie's, MacCormick's, Greenawalt's and Woozley's papers in Cohen (1991).

does not reflect a new way to tackle the determination of the truth conditions of legal propositions[3].

Over the years, Dworkin has maintained his thesis of a single right legal answer in hard cases and denied the need for strong judicial discretion in these cases. With a view to justifying his position, he has developed a sophisticated approach to law, the so-called interpretive theory of law, which challenges both the chief postulates of positivism and sceptics' thesis of indeterminacy. Dworkin's theory seeks to offer a new approach to law and to construct arguments in favour of the existence of a unique right answer in hard cases. However, these are two distinct matters and should be considered separately. Several aspects of Dworkin's theory are question begging: to what extent is it a distinct theory that offers a new perspective of law? Does it provide good reasons for a general dismissal of positivism and scepticism, and does it avoid falling into natural law theory? Are its arguments to advocate the existence of a unique right answer and the relationship it implies between weak discretion and hard cases convincing?

The next two chapters will aim at providing answers to these questions by giving careful consideration to the main aspects of Dworkin's interpretive theory of law. Our characterisation of Dworkin's approach will turn on three headings: the link between legal theory and adjudication of norms; the view of law as interpretation; and, finally, the idea of law as integrity. These three issues are interconnected and dependent on one another for, as we shall see, Dworkin argues that legal theory is merely the most general part of adjudication; that adjudication requires interpretation, that is, it requires offering the best possible perspective of the phenomenon in hand; and that the best perspective of law is one adopting the ideal of integrity as the descriptive-justifying criterion for legal practice.

3.2 LEGAL THEORY AND NORMATIVE ADJUDICATION

One of the distinguishing features of Dworkin's approach to law is his claim that there is no clear or qualitative distinction between legal theory and legal practice. He writes:

> So no firm line divides jurisprudence from adjudication or any other aspect of legal practice. Legal philosophers debate about the general part, the interpretive foundation any legal argument must have. We may turn that coin over. Any practical legal argument, no matter how detailed and limited, assumes the kind of abstract foundation jurisprudence offers, and when rival foundations compete, a legal argument assumes one and rejects others. So any judge's opinion is itself a piece of legal philosophy [...]. Jurisprudence is the

---

[3] See Fish (1982,551-567) and Mackie (1991, 161-169).

general part of adjudication, silent prologue to any decision at Law. [4]

Dworkin thus challenges two very well-settled theses of positivism: a) that it is possible to draw a clear distinction between the analysis of the concept of law, and, what the law prescribes in each particular case; and b) that legal theory is merely descriptive even though legal practice may be understood as having an interpretive character[5]. Full consideration will be given to this discussion in the next section. Note that if, in fact, there is no clear distinction between legal theory and legal practice, proving the interpretive character of legal practice suffices to show the interpretive character of legal theory[6].

Dworkin advocates a link between the analysis of the concept of law and the identification of what the law prescribes in each instant case (a connection between theory and practice) based on the distinction between two types of statements: those referring to what the participants in the practice think, and those referring to the legal practice. If it is a theory's concern to describe what people think, believe and accept that law is, then it does not produce statements about law, but about the states of mind and attitudes of people[7]. By contrast, when a theory attempts to answer the question what is law[8], it spells out its understanding of the legal practice from some particular point of view and, hence, it advocates a view that competes with that defended by any other internal user of law. Therefore, as far as their legal methodology and the character of their statements about law is concerned, there will be no difference whatsoever between

---

4 Dworkin (1986, 90; 1986, 412). Although Dworkin always associates adjudication to the judicial application of norms, he occasionally argues that the link between theory and practice goes beyond the relationship between theory and judicial adjudication. According to Dworkin, the arguments of citizens and jurists (in other words, the statements of any participant) are also to be considered part of legal practice, Dworkin (1986, 413).

5 See, for instance, Hart (1983, 88-98; 1994, 239-254) and Raz (1979, 37-52).

6 Dworkin (1994, 2-4).

7 Dworkin (1986, 63) writes:

> A social practice creates and assumes a crucial distinction between interpreting the acts and thoughts of participants one by one, [...] and interpreting the practice itself, that is, interpreting what they do collectively. It assumes that distinction because the claims and arguments participants make, licensed and encouraged by the practice, are about what it means, not what they mean.

On this point see also Dworkin (1986, 54, 62-65; 1985, 158-160).

8 A statement such as 'Law is what the legislator dictated intentionally' is what Dworkin has in mind at this point. This statement differs from 'judges think that law is what has been intentionally dictated by the legislator'. Dworkin claims that legal theory is concerned with the first kind of statements. On this point, see his response to Hart and to Hart's view that legal theory describes what the legal community in general calls 'law', Dworkin (1994, 2-8). See also Hart (1994, 239-244).

the user and the theoretician[9]. According to Dworkin, the difference is only a matter of the degree of abstraction of their legal arguments[10]. This is a crucial point to Dworkin's project because his interpretive understanding of law presumes that participants' statements are internal to the practice and that, because there is no difference between the positioning of a user and that of a theoretician, statements about the concept of law are internal to the practice too[11].

As a result of this reductionist premise, Dworkin constructs a theory of law in which judicial reasoning embodies the paradigmatic case of legal interpretation as a means to knowledge[12]. This epistemic approach, which turns on the adjudication of norms, throughout his work appears in conjunction with a political thesis, namely that judges should play a pre-eminent role in the determination of what is demanded by the law in each particular case[13]. This position rests on the liberal conception that the judicial body acts as a protector of individual rights *vis à vis* the state, and that law does not only depend on the legislative will but also on the justification of state coercion. Dworkin claims that judges can, by means of their interpretive decisions, help to present legal practice from a point of view that reflects an equilibrium between authoritative acts on the one hand, and the justification of these acts on the grounds of individual legal rights on the other[14].

In the main, this work will not deal with Dworkin's political position because it is not a necessary consequence of his epistemic approach to legal knowledge. In my opinion, these two aspects of Dworkin's theory of law can be investigated separately. Henceforth, we will devote our attention to the interpretive theory of law as a view on legal knowledge because this is the approach that relates to the problem of the technical need for discretion in normative adjudication.

---

[9] Dworkin, (1986, 64).

[10] On this point see Marmor's (1992, 47) and Coleman's (1995, 53) considerations on Dworkin's legal theory.

[11] See Dworkin (1991b, 360-366; 1996, 94-99).

[12] Notwithstanding, his methodological proposal seeks to have implications on all aspects of an approach to law, and not just on the structure of judicial reasoning. See Dworkin (1986, 12, 413).

[13] This standpoint is clearly reflected in the controversy between Dworkin and originalism, which has mainly turned on what is the correct reading of the American Constitution. While originalism argues that a constitution should be understood as a collection of standards with a specific contents primarily determined by the intentions of its founders, Dworkin insists that a constitution is in fact a collection of abstract principles that reflect an abstract legislative intention to be interpreted under the light of a theory about the rights and obligations of the citizens, i.e. a theory that offers the best possible justification for state coercion. See Dworkin (1993, Ch. 5; 1986, 179-181, 355-379).

[14] Murphy (1990, 90) has objected to the possibility of adopting such a political conception in continental law.

3.3 LAW AS INTERPRETATION

One of Dworkin's chief contributions to legal thought is the idea that law does not merely consist of a collection of patterns of behaviour which are identifiable on the grounds of a pre-established rule of recognition. Law is a specific social practice whose distinguishing feature is its argumentative character[15]. He thus asserts that 'every actor in the practice understands that what it permits or requires depends on the truth of certain propositions that are given sense only by and within the practice; the practice consists in large part in deploying and arguing about these propositions', and what is demanded by it 'cannot be discovered except by noticing how they ground and defend these claims'[16]. From Dworkin's standpoint, establishing the truth conditions of legal propositions is arguing and holding a position as participant 'of what counts as a good or bad argument within the practice'[17].

This idea suggests a tendency to identify the legal practice with the legal arguments offered by its participants. Dworkin can thus formulate a global conception about what is law, and about what is the most fruitful method to grasp it as an argumentative social phenomenon. His conception of law turns on three ideas: the semantic sting, constructive interpretation, and the chain novel. The next three sections will be devoted to analysing each one of these theses.

3.3.1 The semantic sting

The thesis of the semantic sting can be thought of primarily as a negative one for it aims at rejecting the widespread view that law is determined on the basis of linguistic conventions. Nevertheless, this thesis is addressed mainly against a particular kind of semantic theory, namely that which assumes the existence of certain past events to be the conventional criterion establishing the existence and the contents of law. Dworkin calls this particular kind of semantic theory *The Plain Fact Theory* and associates it to Hartian positivism[18]. Regardless of whether this association is appropriate, it is interesting to analyse Dworkin's critique of it. According to Dworkin, *The Plain Fact*

---

15 See Dworkin (1986, 6-15, 413). 'Practice' is to be understood as regularity in behaviour or human interaction, assessable in terms of its adequacy to the purpose or value justifying its existence.

16 Dworkin (1986, 13).

17 Dworkin (1986, 14).

18 See Dworkin (1986, 6-15, 31-33, 37; 1985, 131). Although we shall not concern ourselves with a detailed analysis of Dworkin's main argument against *Plain Fact Theory*, let us just indicate that it turns against the assumption that the facts conventionally associated with the existence of law are 'brute facts', i.e. facts whose existence and meaning is independent of any conceptual construct and which therefore carry their own identifying labels, Dworkin (1986, 7, 66; 1985, 137-138, 167-168).

Theory claims that there can be no genuine disagreement about the contents and sources of law among the members of a legal community because the very existence of a legal order depends on certain past events that are conventionally thought to be necessary and sufficient conditions for the existence of the legal order[19]. It is precisely the shared linguistic criteria or conventions what links these facts with the existence of law, and what determines the truth conditions of legal propositions. Hence, only to the extent that such a general convention or shared practice exists, do legal propositions have truth-value. From this point of view, criteriological disagreement is meaningless because it implies that there no longer is a shared social practice to identify and discuss: law is indeterminate. In this context, speakers use language to refer to different things - there is no genuine disagreement[20]. *Plain Fact Theory* only envisages disagreement on the facts referred to by the conventional criterion, that is, empirical disagreement about whether events actually took place. Criteriological disagreements only happen in penumbral cases, in which legal propositions have no truth-value. Therefore, they will not constitute disagreement about the contents of law, but merely about what law should be like with regard to the particular point at stake. Here, every decision stipulates a meaning and creates new legal norms by means of strong judicial discretion.

The thesis of the semantic sting challenges the conceptual link between social conventions and the existence of law. To suffer from the semantic sting means to persist in the attempt to find shared criteria that make legal propositions true or false assuming that only the existence of such shared criteria make it possible to speak of one and the same legal practice[21]. Dworkin esteems that the most relevant discussions within the legal context are not those arising in connection with penumbral cases, but those concerning theoretical disagreements about central cases[22]. These are not empirical disagreements. Theoretical disagreements occur, but they do not suffice to claim that

---

19 Dworkin (1986, 31-33). Dworkin considers that positivism has traditionally defended this general conception in spite of important divergences about what the conventional criterion is. Austin, for instance, takes the existence of commands of a sovereign to whom obedience is customarily paid as the conventional criterion. For others, Hart among them, the conventional criterion is the social acceptance of a rule of recognition defining the validity criteria for legal norms. On this point, see Dworkin (1986, 33-34). As was pointed out in the previous chapter, it should be borne in mind that Hart's semantic theory does not accord with a semantic theory based on the notion of necessary and sufficient conditions. Notwithstanding, it can be considered a conventionalist semantic theory. See Hart (1994, 124-136; 1983, 89-98).

20 Dworkin (1986, 45-46).

21 Dworkin claims that it is a mistake to think that we identify legal institutions by means of a shared definition of what a legal system should necessarily be like. See Dworkin (1986, 45, 46, 91; 1987, 10).

22 Dworkin (1986, 43-46).

speakers are referring to different practices. In his opinion, they represent competing versions of one and the same social phenomenon.

To illustrate this point, Dworkin addresses the question whether photography is a form of art[23]. This question can be approached in two different ways. It can be argued that photography is a penumbral case with respect to the concept of art. In that case, whether we decide to include or exclude photography from those activities that qualify as art is a matter of stipulation. Here, it is meaningless to ask what the correct answer is because there is no right answer to this question. Dworkin suggests that we tackle this question in terms of theoretical disagreement. This alternative approach assumes that a correct answer exists since both those who agree that photography is a form of art, and those who agree that it is not, understand the problem of photography to be central to the concept of art. When discussing this issue, advocates of either opinion put forward different competing versions of what art really is or, what turns out to be equivalent in Dworkin's view, what is the best way to conceive of art within a specific aesthetic practice. To assert, for instance, that photography belongs to the core of the concept of art implies that our version of art is more attractive if photography is taken to fall within its aesthetic parameters.

Dworkin uses the expression 'theoretical disagreement' to refer to a kind of discrepancies that other authors have called 'substantive disagreement'. Substantive or theoretical disagreement is in opposition to conceptual disagreement. It is difficult to establish a clear-cut distinction between these two kinds of disagreement because such a distinction could be viewed as a mere matter of degree about the scope and outreach of the divergences within a group of individuals. Notwithstanding, it will be useful to draw a tentative differentiation between the two. In that sense, Stavropoulos writes:

> Substantive disagreement consists in there being disagreement over whether something is X, which turns on different views of what it is for something to be X, so that different views are mutually incompatible. For instance, we may disagree over whether some state of affairs is a contract, despite agreeing on all relevant facts identifying the state of affairs (short of its being a contract or not), because we disagree over what is required for there to be a contract.[24]

These disagreements reflect differences in the way we describe the world and hence relate to our judgements and beliefs[25]. By contrast, conceptual disagreements arise when speakers use the same language to refer to different states of affairs. If, for

[23] Dworkin (1986, 41-43).

[24] Stavropoulos (1996, 125).

[25] On the idea of substantial disagreement as a disagreement in judgements see Baker and Hacker (1994, 258-262).

instance, several individuals discuss the importance of preserving the Roman Catholic Church, and some have a religious building and its aesthetic value in mind, whereas others believe to be discussing the continuity of the Catholic religion, although they speak the same words, they are referring to two completely different and distinct things. The debate between these individuals becomes meaningless. As Hurley and Bix point out, this kind of controversies conceal no genuine disagreement since the positions involved are not really in conflict with one another[26].

The notion of conceptual disagreement has been extensively used to reflect diverging social practices and forms of life when conceptual divergences occur in connection with basic aspects of a culture or social context. By contrast, 'substantive disagreement' refers to differences within the same social practice and form of life. Hurley asserts that 'it may be correct to regard some apparent disagreements [...] as differences in form of life, and our opponents as different sorts of being from us, with whom we do not stand in substantive disagreement because they do not have the concepts necessary for them to stand in disagreement with us'[27]. From this point of view, substantive disagreement presupposes a basis of agreement, at least on the paradigmatic cases for the use of the concept, or on judgements about some basic aspects of the issue in question. This shared framework allows us to speak of a shared practice[28]. Without this more basic agreement, differences are conceptual and, therefore, speakers refer to different things. Communication then becomes impossible and discussion unintelligible[29].

Dworkin affirms the plausibility of substantive disagreements in the legal context and asserts that they can only occur if there is some basic agreement. But Dworkin insists that these disagreements are not of a semantic nature - they are more closely connected with judgements about how law is than with the meaning of terms[30]. They lead to interpretive controversies, that is, differences with regard to what is the best way to develop a common idea within a particular social practice[31].

---

[26] See Hurley (1989, 30-33) and Bix (1993, 57-59). See also Stavropoulos (1996, 125-126).

[27] Hurley (1989, 32).

[28] See Hurley (1989, 38, 52), Bix (1993, 58) and Stavropoulos (1996, 125-127). On the contention that a common ground of agreement is necessary for disagreement to be significant, see Davidson (1984b, 194-198).

[29] Hurley (1989, 51-52).

[30] Dworkin (1986, 5-6). Similarly, Hurley (1989, 34) observes that substantive disagreement, unlike conceptual disagreement, arises in connection with beliefs, and not meaning.

[31] Dworkin (1986, 45-48).

Thus, Dworkin's main criticism to *The Plain Fact Theory* as a semantic theory is that it only leaves room for conceptual disagreement, and that it renders the truth-value of legal propositions dependent on the existence of a linguistic convention. This is why *The Plain Fact Theory* concludes that in case of disagreement, law is indeterminate. It is not straightforward to determine the extent to which Dworkin distances himself from a semantic position when he uses the notion of theoretical disagreement. He might be just proposing non-conventionalist semantics. However, we will not concern ourselves with this issue for now[32]. This section intended to highlight the negative character of the semantic sting thesis. It has been pointed out that this thesis challenges the feasibility of a conventional theory of meaning for legal statements and, indirectly, the assumption that these conventions are based on factual criteria. However, it is important to analyse the positive or constructive thesis of Dworkin's position in order to fully grasp the implications of these two pieces of negative criticism. A link between the notion of theoretical disagreement and the view of law as interpretation should be established bearing in mind the distinction between agreement by convention and agreement of conviction, and, moreover, that between concept and conception.

3.3.2 Constructive interpretation

The thesis of the semantic sting denies that the truth-value of legal propositions depends on facts fixed by conventions. As pointed out earlier, Dworkin claims that a legal proposition is true if it is the case that it fits better than any other with the set of propositions that offer the best interpretation or version of the social practice under consideration. For this reason, Dworkin insists that law is a matter of interpretation[33].

Interpretation as an epistemic method is, together with the assumption that the best interpretation is what determines the truth conditions of legal propositions, the cornerstone of Dworkin's approach to law. His theory includes a distinct understanding of the notion of interpretation that will be investigated in more detail in the next chapter.

---

[32] It may be worth noting that Dworkin's position appears to be very close to referencialist semantic theories such as Putnam's or Kripke's. It will be shown in later chapters that Dworkin does nevertheless not assume a causal theory of reference. (Note that it is not straightforward to present Putnam's position towards a causal theory of reference, mostly because of his acceptance of the thesis of internal realism). Dworkin maintains that the reference is never a brute fact, but an interpretive object or state of affairs. As such, it is the product of the best theory about what a social institution is like. Thus, although the truth-value of a proposition depends on the reference rather than on a convention, the reference is limited to a coherent set of convictions about how things are. On the latter point, see Dworkin (1983, 292-303; 1985, 169-174; 1984, 275-278; 1991b, 360-365; 1996, 87-94).

[33] Dworkin (1985, 138, 146-149).

From his point of view, the meaning of statements about law depends on the truth conditions of the propositions they express. These conditions are dependent on the best theory about the reference of these propositions, that is, the best theory about what is actually meant by those propositions. Thus, although interpretation is an activity that aims at assigning meaning, there is also an epistemic dimension to it - it is a means of gaining knowledge[34]. Dworkin's idea, then, contrasts with the widespread thought that interpretation is purely a semantic phenomenon, or, in other words, a mere linguistic matter[35]. In his view, legal interpretation is a form of constructive interpretation to be distinguished from what he calls 'conversational interpretation'. The latter refers to the activity carried out by the recipient of a linguistic message who analyses the purposes and state of mind of the speaker at the time of the utterance in order to identify his or her intentions. The framework of this kind of interpretation is the face-to-face communication process in which the speaker uses language with a specific intention[36]. Constructive interpretation, by contrast, 'is a matter of imposing purpose on an object or practice in order to make of it the best possible example of the form or genre to which it is taken to belong'[37]. Clearly, constructive interpretation places much more emphasis on the intentions of the interpreter than on those of the speaker [38]. Constructive interpretation deals with objects created by individuals but as something distinguishable from the individuals themselves. Hence, Dworkin assumes that offering an interpretation of a social practice is, in fact, offering a version (the best version) of the global result of the interactions in a group of persons. It is not a version of their thoughts and beliefs. In order to carry out interpretation, the interpreter ought to have some idea as to the global sense of the practice. This entails an understanding of the practice that competes with that of other participants. Dworkin concedes that the distinction between

---

[34] Dworkin (1985, 138, 158-160).

[35] Aarnio (1987, 218) shares the position of Dworkin on this point. He stresses, referring to those who take interpretation to be a mere linguistic matter, that 'those who have this view have misunderstood the concept of language. If language, as a semantic category, is seen together with the form of life, and the action element in language is picked out, the analysis of language can specifically be said to be the analysis of matters. The analysis of language is the analysis of the form of life. Through it we can specifically understand our life, the acts of which our form of life is composed'.

[36] Dworkin (1986, 49-50; 1985, 148-150).

[37] Dworkin (1986, 52).

[38] Dworkin (1986, 50). Note that Dworkin distinguishes these two types of interpretation and establishes a hierarchy between them: constructive interpretation takes conceptual priority over conversational interpretation because the latter can be reconstructed as a form of constructive interpretation. We will defer further consideration to this point till later chapters. However, note that this consideration suggests a tendency to view constructive interpretation as the general way of assigning meaning to any phenomenon or object. See Dworkin (1986, 53) and Marmor (1992, 48).

what the participants think and what the social practice actually requires might be irrelevant if participants always agree on the contents of their practice. The dichotomy becomes interesting when controversy arises between participants. Precisely at this point the question what is being interpreted becomes relevant[39].

Dworkin applies the notion of constructive interpretation to social practices that like the legal practice are argumentative. Although individuals may participate in one and the same practice, they may hold different competing views with regard to its meaning. Thus, 'the participants do have reasons for preferring one proposition to another, or at least they think they do, and even when they disagree, each of them thinks he can distinguish cases when his opponents have genuine reasons on their side from cases when they do not'[40].

In order for this thesis to be granted some plausibility, it need be proven that participants are able to distinguish between a situation in which they face substantive disagreement from that which involves conceptual divergences. Dworkin's proposal can only be meaningful if interpretation takes place in a right-wrong context where differences between participants are commensurable because they are alternative reconstructions of a single phenomenon. Here, participants discuss which interpretation is the correct reconstruction of the practice they all participate in[41]. With a view to accounting for this point Dworkin argues that the very idea of participating in a legal practice requires that participants be aware of the distinction between interpretation and invention when they produce statements about law. Only if this distinction is incorporated into their schemes of beliefs do we have a legal practice in which meaningful discussion about its contents can take place.[42].

The dichotomy invention-interpretation is a much-debated one and will be analysed in detail in Chapter 4. Yet, it is worth noting that in order to conclude that interpretation is taking place, we are urged to assume that there is a social phenomenon to be identified and that such a social phenomenon can only exist if certain ideas and basic attitudes are common to participants in the practice. Dworkin explains this idea by means of a further distinction, namely that between concept and conception[43].

---

[39] Dworkin (1986, 63).

[40] Dworkin (1985, 139).

[41] See Dworkin (1983, 289-290).

[42] Dworkin (1986, 66-67; 1985, 167-169; 1983, 289-291).

[43] For a classical discussion of the distinction between concept and conception, see Rawls (1971, 5) and Hart (1994, 246 footnote 26). This question had already been addressed by Gallie (1956, 167-180) though he used a different terminology. It is worth noting that Dworkin uses the same terminology as Rawls and

Concept and conception

One of the distinguishing features of the interpretive theory is that participating in a practice entails holding a position about what such a practice demands. It is important to stress that Dworkin's interpretive theory is concerned with social practices as something clearly distinguishable from private ones[44]. Dworkin therefore insists that in order to avoid indeterminacy and for disagreement to be substantive, participants must share certain ideas and attitudes: the 'interpretive concepts'[45].

The interpretive concept

We can begin the characterisation of Dworkin's notion of interpretive concept by indicating what, in his view, the concept *is not*. The concept is not the intension of a term, that is, it is not the set of necessary and sufficient conditions for its application. Neither does the concept refer to necessary conditions for use. Dworkin does not link the interpretive concept to the conventional meaning of a term, but to the purpose of a social practice or institution. An individual whose understanding of the interpretive concept differs from that of the majority of speakers in the community is not necessarily contradicting himself, nor is he necessarily unfamiliar with the use of a certain word. Notwithstanding, 'what he says marks him as outside the community of useful or at least ordinary discourse about the institution'[46].

From this viewpoint, the concept is not semantic but interpretive in character. It could be defined as the most abstract idea or judgement about the best way to present a social phenomenon. Moreover, its appropriateness or truth is uncontroversial in a particular discursive context and moment in time[47]. Anyone objecting to the truth of this basic judgement ceases to be a participant in the practice in which it occurs. However, his exclusion from the practice is not due to his wrongly defining the terms involved. Rather, he is left out because his opinion and beliefs about what the actual object of interpretation is deviate to too great an extent from those of other participants, to whom such a position appears no less than absurd. His view, then, does not qualify as an opinion on the same phenomenon.

Hart, but understands this distinction in a peculiar way: it is not reducible to a mere differentiation between the meaning of a term and the criteria for its application.

44 The possibility of a private practice of rule-following was discussed in the previous chapter with reference to the conditions that would enable Robinson Crusoe to claim to be following a rule. See Baker and Hacker (1994, 170-179).

45 Dworkin (1986, 63).

46 Dworkin (1986, 71, 90-91).

47 Dworkin (1986, 70-72).

In line with this, every argument within the practice should be based on the concept, which assigns a general purpose to the interactions among the participants. The correctness of the concept is not subject to debate because a justificatory discussion on this point is not conceivable. Participants can only provide an explanatory reason for the concepts they possess and share[48]. The ultimate explanation for the beliefs they hold rests on a shared form of life and a unitary perception of the world.

It is urged that Dworkin draws a clear distinction between what is uncontroversial in general, and what is uncontroversial at a particular moment in time. The concept is assumed uncontroversial. However, due to its interpretive nature, it may become controverted; in other words, the interpretive attitude that generates a specific social practice may turn into a critical one and cast doubt on the very concept that unifies the practice[49]. This is an important point of Dworkin's position that we shall discuss in detail later on. Let us just stress that, for Dworkin, the existence of a social practice requires both at least and at most an agreement on the interpretive concept. For normative practices (in which there is a tendency towards convergence about how conduct is to be guided)[50], the nature of this minimal agreement can be clarified by distinguishing between agreements of convention and agreements of conviction[51]. Dworkin actually resorts to this distinction to analyse the character and the necessary

---

[48] Dworkin (1986, 63-64) refers to Wittgenstein's notion of form of life as a condition for a social practice to be shared in the following way:

> They must share a vocabulary: they must have in mind much the same thing when they mention hats or requirements. They must understand the world in sufficiently similar ways and have interests and convictions sufficiently similar to recognize the sense in each other's claims, to treat these as claims rather than just noises. That means not just using the same dictionary, bur sharing what Wittgenstein called a form of life sufficiently concrete so that the one can recognize sense and purpose in what the other says and does, see what sort of beliefs and motives would make sense of this diction, gesture, tone, and so forth.

Note that this idea coincides with Davidson's charity principle for translation. Davidson (1984b, 195-198) argues that other speakers' discourse is only intelligible if the listener can assume the speaker both to have beliefs and interests similar to his own, and to behave consistently with his beliefs

[49] See Dworkin (1986, 48-49) for an exposition of his views on how the interpretive attitude in a social practice such as courtesy may raise doubts about the very concept that endorses it, namely that courtesy is a matter of respect.

[50] Although it is commonplace to consider that legal practice is normative, to my mind this does not distinguish it from any other practice. Every social practice, and even every private practice, is normative because it is defined on the basis of rules of conduct and standards of correct behaviour. The distinction between aesthetic, courtesy, ludic, and moral practices is merely the kind of conduct sought to be regulated. The idea of practice advocated here is that which understands a practice to be a set of actions and interactions justified and sustained by a criterion of correctness. This is common to every language game. See Baker and Hacker (1994, 161-164).

[51] Dworkin (1986, 136; 1991b 371).

level of consensus among the participants in a normative practice such as the legal practice.

The minimal agreement among participants may be either an agreement of convention or one of conviction. Agreement of convention arises when participants concede that a proposition is true by convention, that is to say, when they accept its truth because they believe that any other participant will accept it as true. In this case, the existence of a convention is the only reason accounting for the truth of the proposition. Participants do not have any substantive reason to accept its truth - they accept it only on the grounds that other participants do so. In contrast, agreement of conviction occurs when all participants accept that a proposition is true because they all consider there to be good enough reasons to believe it so. Thus, agreement of conviction does not arise on the grounds of convention but because every participant genuinely believes that the proposition is undoubtedly true. Thus, shared substantive reasons generate agreement of conviction. In the case of agreement of convention, no substantive objection against the truth of a proposition makes sense because this type of agreement does not rest on substantive reasons; dissidence embodies neither a genuine attack on the agreement, nor a mistaken conception of reality[52]. Diverging opinions are thought to reflect a misuse of words. In case of agreement of conviction, by contrast, dissident opinions may appear absurd, but at any rate are clearly considered mistaken positions or erroneous beliefs about the object of discussion. For Dworkin, the idea of participating in a practice and sharing the concept is conditional on the existence of agreement of conviction, and hence, on a certain uniformity of beliefs and abstract judgements.

Nevertheless, or so Dworkin seems to argue, agreements of conviction may affect matters other than the concept. On some occasions he refers to consensus about paradigmatic cases as something distinct from agreement on the concept, that is to say, as distinct from the abstract judgements and shared interpretations about the global meaning of the practice. For this reason, it seems appropriate to refer to this point before initiating a detailed analysis of conceptions.

Dworkin points out that in order for the legal practice to exist, in addition to shared judgements that derive from a shared form of life, it is essential that certain particular examples be undisputedly accepted as part of the practice[53]. Every interpretation of the contents of the social practice should be able to account for these examples as part of what is being interpreted. These paradigmatic cases, Dworkin claims, are of an

---

[52] In this sense, the only significant deviating view would be that which argues that the truth of a proposition is to be rejected because there exists no convention.

[53] Dworkin (1986, 72-76, 92).

interpretive nature and not of a semantic one[54]. For this reason, not to mention these examples is not just a verbal neglection, but a fundamental mistake about the object of interpretation[55].

In order to gain further insight into Dworkin's approach to paradigmatic cases, it may be useful to return to the distinction between strong paradigmatic cases and absolute paradigmatic cases, this time under an interpretive light[56]. Strong paradigmatic cases are clear examples of the contents of the social practice or institution. In this sense it can be argued that, if there is such thing as law, traffic rules are surely part of it[57]. Here, the general judgement we derive from, or associate with, these cases is more important than the cases themselves. Paradigms will exists as long as there exists an agreement on the idea they embody, and hence, may cease to be considered paradigmatic cases when a better interpretation of the practice proves that other situations constitute clearer examples[58]. Absolute paradigmatic cases, by contrast, define the concept. Thus, they cannot be said to cease to embody a clear example of the concept because the concept reduces to these paradigms[59].

Dworkin envisages the possibility that paradigms cease to be undisputed examples of the practice. This is why he appeals to the notion of strong paradigmatic case when

---

54 For this reason, although the idea of paradigmatic cases could virtually draw Dworkin's position closer to Hartian semantics, a significant difference in approach seems to persist. Hart tackles paradigms from the standpoint of conventional semantics. He seems to suggest that the semantic view on the necessary and sufficient conditions is to be overcome, and that certain necessary (though not sufficient) criteria together with consensus about paradigmatic cases determine the convention establishing the truth conditions of legal propositions. Nevertheless, these elements are not interpretive but belong to the convention determining the meaning. For discussion, see Hart (1983, 89-92; 1994, 244-248, 255-259).

55 Dworkin urges to distinguish paradigms of interpretive truth from analytic truths. He does not claim that statements about these paradigms be true by definition, as it is often said to be the case about the statement that 'single individuals are those who are not married' in connection with the concept of single. See Dworkin (1986, 72, 92). Dworkin's position on paradigmatic cases does not imply accepting the distinction between synthetic and analytic truths. On the contrary, his general perspective develops along the lines of those who try to blur this distinction. With regard to this point, see Quine's criticism to empiricism in Quine (1953, 20 46).

56 Bix (1993, 56-59).

57 Dworkin (1986, 92).

58 Although a new radical interpretation may appear absurd at a specific moment in time, it may eventually prevail as the best way of understanding the social institution in question. See Dworkin (1986, 72, 89).

59 The notion of absolute paradigmatic cases can be exemplified with the term 'game'. It can be argued that the only reasonable way to explain the meaning of 'game' is by means of paradigmatic cases that define the concept. Although Wittgenstein's idea of game seems to develop along this line, he proposes family resemblance as the connection among the members of a family. This connection could also be viewed as the search for a minimal conceptual link between the paradigms, however remote and weak. This would distance him from the strict notion of absolute paradigmatic case. See Wittgenstein (1953, secs. 65-77).

he refers to the examples that should be shared if a social practice is to exist. Here, sharing the concept and sharing the paradigm may be regarded as one and the same thing. Sharing a strong paradigmatic case, unlike sharing an absolute paradigmatic case, is merely a consequence of sharing the interpretive concept it embodies, that is, it is the result of convergence in certain abstract convictions about the contents of the practice. Due to the dependence between interpretive concepts and strong paradigms, an analysis of the latter inevitably takes us to an investigation of the former. Indubitably, when we inquire into strong paradigmatic cases we are in fact inquiring into the interpretive concepts or uncontroversial abstract judgements they embody.

Conceptions of the concept

It was pointed out in the foregoing section that a social practice requires both at least and at most sharing the interpretive concept. For this reason, the survival of the practice does not depend on the participants reaching the same conclusions as to how to develop the most general ideas they share. The interpretation of a social phenomenon may present different degrees of abstraction, and it may be possible to identify sub-interpretations or implementations of more general judgements: the conceptions of the concept[60]. A conception is a position or theory on how to specify an omnicomprehensive interpretation of the practice. Conceptions aim at developing arguments that seek to determine the best way to implement the concept in each particular case, and which compete with those produced by other conceptions[61]. Thus, while the concept tends to be uncontroversial, Dworkin claims that conceptions are essentially controversial, at least as far as legal practice is concerned[62]. Notwithstanding, the social practice is not indeterminate when there is disagreement between rival conceptions because this disagreement is substantive. The different positions represent alternative interpretations of the same social institution. Participants perceive these positions as commensurable because they seek to account for the same shared idea. Moreover, they assume that some interpretations are better than others.

Dworkin bases his approach to law on the notions of concept and conception, and the two different levels of abstraction they entail. His interpretive concept of law can in his view be undisputedly assumed: law is a means of justifying state coercion. The conception of law that in his opinion presents this concept under its best light is what he calls 'law as integrity'.

---

60 Dworkin (1986, 71).

61 Dworkin (1986, 71, 75-76, 94, 98-101).

62 Dworkin (1986, 99).

In addition to the distinction between concept and conception as substratum to any interpretation, Dworkin's theory includes a general picture of interpretive dynamics in the legal context. He splits up the interpretive process into several stages on the basis of which participants reach a conclusion about what is demanded by the practice.

Stages of constructive interpretation

In order to structure interpretation as a means to knowledge, Dworkin suggests that we break up this process into three stages. Participants articulate their legal judgements as they advance through these stages. The first of them is known as the pre-interpretative stage. At this point, agents provisionally identify the object and the context of interpretation. This provisional identification allows them to single out legal practice from other sorts of social practices on the basis of external data that are considered to be indicative of a distinct type of conduct (e.g. regularity in conduct, legal texts, normative decisions)[63]. Moreover, Dworkin observes, every participant should be able to acquire and share 'a preinterpretive sense of the rough boundaries of the practice on which our imagination must be trained'[64]. This first stage demands that there be a shared perception of the context in which an answer to the question what is law is discussed and developed. This, however, does not presume an agreement on what is the right approach to the social phenomenon under consideration. In the first stage, it is only urged that legal arguments, regardless of whether they are right or wrong, be distinguishable from other kinds of argument (e.g. aesthetic arguments). Dworkin contends that even the first stage is interpretive in character. The particular provisional ontology on which every meaningful legal judgement rests depends on a contextual theory that may be subject to controversy[65]. Nonetheless, the formal and contextual beliefs that shape the ontological framework need be shared at a particular moment in time (at least, participants should assume so) for interpretation to be possible[66]. Pre-interpretive data thus constitute the first constraint to any attempt to interpret the social

---

[63] Dworkin (1986, 65, 91-92). The beliefs about these data do not determine the truth conditions of legal propositions. For Dworkin they do not constitute the legal ontology but pre-conditions for a meaningful discussion on the truth conditions. The legal ontology will be conditional on the meaning assigned to these data by means of interpretation.

[64] Dworkin (1986, 75).

[65] In the context of literary interpretation, Dworkin considers that this contextual theory is the theory that determines what the literary work is. Thus, interpreters' convictions should enable them to recognise that their interpretation turns on a specific literary work and hence, although this judgement may be controversial, their discussion will only be meaningful if they share one and the same contextual theory. For discussion see Dworkin (1986, 66; 1985, 150-151, 167-168).

[66] Dworkin (1985, 169-171; 1991b, 292-297; 1986, 67).

practice[67]. An interpretation that takes as its object something other than these data cannot be understood by the rest of participants as a possible version of the legal practice. Nevertheless, the pre-interpretive stage is compatible with several reconstructions of the legal practice, and at a later stage every interpreter shall have to develop her own view with regard to the global meaning of the phenomenon under consideration.

Next comes the interpretive stage[68]. Participants attempt to attach meaning to the interactions identified in the pre-interpretive phase by considering the data under the light of some purpose or general justificatory reason. To this end, interpreters need to devise a general reason for the existence of such interactions. Although Dworkin elaborates no further on this point, it should be noted that at its most abstract level, the participants should share this justificatory reason precisely because the several competing conceptions will turn on the interpretive concept. Moreover, in order to distinguish between interpretation and invention, every reconstruction of the practice should appear as an omnicomprehensive reading of the pre-interpretive data[69]. Dworkin refers to this constraint as the *dimension of fit*. Thus, every interpreter should possess and share the conviction of the extent to which 'the justification he proposes at the interpretive stage must fit the standing features of the practice to count as an interpretation of it rather than the invention of something new'[70]. This dimension restricts the range of possible general justifications or abstract purposes to be ascribed to the practice. Notwithstanding, once the test of fit has been passed, each participant may develop her own (controverted) perspective regarding which arguments about the contents of the practice are correct, that is to say, which arguments show it under its best light. According to Dworkin, this leads to a subsequent step to discriminating which arguments actually refer to the practice, namely the post-interpretive stage[71].

As long as participants can imagine different ways of passing the test of fit, deciding which interpretation portrays the practice in its best light requires a further step. Each participant articulates a position on how to develop the general justification of the practice that presents it under its best light. Each of them is compelled to defend a substantive conception about what it is the practice requires in every specific case to

[67] Dworkin (1986, 66-67, 75). See also Marmor (1992, 71-73).

[68] Dworkin (1986, 54, 92-93).

[69] This, however, does not imply that a given interpretation should account for all pre-interpretive data, but only that it should have some general criterion facilitating the choice of sufficient relevant data to reconstruct the practice as a whole. See Dworkin (1986, 66, 230).

[70] Dworkin (1986, 67).

[71] Dworkin (1986, 66-67).

represent the best possible example of its justification, purpose or general value. This substantive conception need not coincide with that of other participants. Eventually, which is the right interpretation will depend on which arguments best withstand what Dworkin calls the *dimension of value*, in other words, on what is the best way to assign a general purpose to the relevant data of the practice[72]. Dworkin observes that argumentative controversy may change the participant's conception about some of the pre-interpretive elements of the practice. This will require the participant to be persuaded that the version that reconstructs the practice best is different from her own[73].

The dynamic structuring of constructive interpretation in three stages enables Dworkin to show when is agreement necessary and when is controversy possible without causing the practice to be indeterminate. This also illuminates his view about the character of participants' judgements. Every judgement depends on a theory, i.e. on a set of beliefs and convictions that, as a whole, constitute a coherent vision of the object of interpretation. These stages show that participants need hold beliefs of various kinds, some more formal, some more substantial, some shared, some controversial. Insiders should be able to distinguish these different kinds of convictions in their conceptual schemes[74]. The model of constructive interpretation seems to require no further conditions to assert the existence of a single right answer within the legal practice. But it is obvious that accepting Dworkin's epistemic theory does not solve the problem of legal indeterminacy. We ought to examine the extent to which interpretive theory guarantees objectivity and a single right answer for hard or controverted cases. With a view to answering this question, we will devote some attention to the implications and nuances of Dworkin's epistemic and ontological position in Chapter 4. This should be done most carefully for this author seeks to reconcile premises which have traditionally been considered irreconcilable, namely that legal judgements be simultaneously theory-dependent or interpretive and objectively right or wrong.

Before we undertake this analysis I would like to give some consideration to two further aspects of Dworkin's theory of law. Firstly, I shall explore his answer to how

---

72 Dworkin (1986, 52-53; 231). Recall that the relevant data are those that can be part of a plausible reconstruction of the practice as a whole. Which one of the possible interpretations of the practice best reflects its general justification is, precisely, the object of discussion at the post-interpretive stage.

73 Dworkin appeals to courtesy for an example on this point. Although it may be agreed that courtesy is a way of showing respect and deference, the debate about how best to demonstrate respect may influence what is perceived as a sign of respect in interactions between participants. Thus, removing one's hat when saluting a woman may initially be taken as a paradigmatic case. At a different moment in time, however, in the light of a more powerful interpretation of the general justification, this case may no longer qualify as a paradigmatic case of courtesy. On this point, see Dworkin (1986, 48-49, 66).

74 Dworkin (1986, 67-68; 1985, 167-171; 1983, 287-297).

constructive interpretation may account for a social phenomenon that takes place over time and whose participants change, each one of them with their own individual beliefs and convictions. Dworkin asserts that constructive interpretation is helpful to grasp a dynamic phenomenon such as law (whose past history projects itself onto the future) provided it is regarded as similar to a chain novel. To explain this metaphor, Dworkin resorts to an analogy between legal and literary interpretation. Secondly, I shall examine the approach to law that in his view shows it under its best light: the model of integrity.

3.3.3 The chain novel

Dworkin compares judicial interpretation within legal practice to the task of a novelist who is asked to write a chapter for a chain novel, the previous chapters of which have been written by several other authors. Her contribution is to be added to the novel and passed down to the next author. The task of each one of the writers is not to produce a new novel that conforms to her own literary criteria, but to continue the work in progress and to interpret its plot according to her artistic convictions. Each author should find a unitary sense to the work of her predecessors as a whole under the assumption that it is possible to identify the general argument of the novel[75]. To this end, each chain novelist should read the previous chapters as if the different authors had intended to write a single story, and the various chapters had been inspired by a general purpose that transcends each individual chapter[76]. Thus, each novelist will accept as true propositions about the novel those that best fit what she perceives to be the global plot of the novel[77]. Furthermore, her contribution is not limited to a chapter. It is assumed that she thereby presents the novel in its best light. In other words, it is her duty to produce a good literary work, the best possible work on the basis of the text passed down to her. It is precisely at this point that her task becomes creative and where she will be expected to prove that her aesthetic convictions lead to the best interpretation of the novel. For this reason, a given chain novelist will only take into account what has been said by her predecessors to the extent that doing so contributes towards a better

[75] This assumption is needed for the interpreter to view herself as an author in a chain novel rather than the creator of a new literary work. Not allowing for this possibility because of conceptual reasons is equivalent to denying her very role. This is, according to Dworkin, the position defended by internal scepticism, the theory that claims that the best reconstruction of a practice is that which asserts that no such practice exists. This discussion shall be pursued further and the distinction between internal and external scepticism addressed again in later chapters. For discussion, see Dworkin (1986, 78-85, 266-267; 1985, 175-177).

[76] Dworkin (1986, 228-229).

[77] Dworkin (1985, 136-140, 149-154).

perspective of the novel within its genre. Thus, Dworkin claims, the writer will be expected to develop her formal convictions to identify the text, and her aesthetic convictions to reach a conclusion as to the plot and contents of the novel[78].

From Dworkin's point of view, the task of the chain novelist is similar to that of the art critic, and unlike that of the artist. The artist interprets while she creates, whereas the critic creates while she interprets[79]. If the artist intends to create something, she shall possess some criterion to distinguish art from other contexts, and a certain notion of the genre to which she wants her work to belong. Moreover, she ought to be able to justify her choice of materials and her preference for one style. The critic, by contrast, has an object to interpret. This object constrains the character and contents of her judgements. She will be unable to offer a good criticism (or not even a criticism) if she does not understand that her judgements refer to the particular object she is interpreting and assessing. But the critic ought to decide which is the best way to look at the piece of art to evaluate its aesthetic value[80].

The chain novel is a metaphor to illustrate an interpretive activity governed by the criterion of textual coherence or narrative consistency, more so than by the identification of the thoughts and beliefs of participants[81]. The aim is to extend this activity to legal interpretation as a way to better grasp this social phenomenon. The most immediate consequence of this approach is that more importance is granted to the global coherence of a normative system than to the legislative or institutional will in the determination of what law is[82]. The institutional will is in fact dependent on the best legal argument. None of the participants in the practice have privileged epistemic abilities. Each one of them, be it a legislator or a judicial body, is just one link in the chain, one link in the legal history that the judge interprets and prolongs by means of her actual decisions. In each act of adjudication, it is the judge's responsibility to decide what the general plot of the legal history is[83]. Here, only the best arguments, those that cannot be dissociated from the formal and substantive convictions of those arguing in their favour, can set a genuine restriction to legal judgements.

---

78 Dworkin (1986, 230-231; 1985, 159; 1983, 303-307).

79 Dworkin (1985, 158; 1986, 229).

80 This is according to Dworkin the only way to construct a genuine criticism of a work of art. The critic should aim at showing the subject of her interpretation under its best light because by being fair to it, she will be able to evaluate the aesthetic richness of the piece of art to its fullest extent.

81 Dworkin (1985, 136-137).

82 For criticism to this approach, see Raz (1992, 309-321).

83 Dworkin (1986, 410).

This imaginary picture of law has its advantages and its drawbacks. On the one hand, it seems to offer all the participants the chance to argue about what is law and to discuss what is the best argument to account for the practice they participate in and conform by means of their interactions. Hence, any participant, whether judge or legislator, may be mistaken as far as the contents of law is concerned. This is an appealing conclusion. On the other hand, it challenges the widespread perception that law is the product of normative acts of institutional authorities. This contravenes a well-settled principle in our understanding of law: legal certainty. However, it may be unfair to attribute to Dworkin a view that is so far from institutional will and so close to the empire of argument. A detailed study of his conception of law as integrity may provide further insight into his interpretive theory of law as an attempt to create balance between these two extremes and to establish what he calls 'Law's Empire'.

3.4 LAW AS INTEGRITY

It has already been mentioned that Dworkin proposes an interpretive concept of legal practice: law is a means of justifying state coercion as the preservation of individual rights recognised by institutional decisions in the past with the intent to control state power[84]. Different conceptions can be constructed on this interpretive concept, but they should all be able to account for the relevant data of the practice. For Dworkin, no position can ignore that legislative acts and judicial precedent are part of the social practice[85]. This is so because of well-settled formal convictions that constitute the very object of discussion[86]. However, a conception seeks to show why and how institutional decisions conform to the interpretive concept. In order to achieve this, the conception should reconstruct these data as the best example of the general justification provided

---

[84] Dworkin (1986, 93).

[85] Dworkin (1986, 99)

[86] It is important at this point to highlight the difference between something being the object of discussion, and it being its result. Assuming an interpretive theory ultimately implies accepting that the contents of law is the result and not the object of interpretation. Quite often the term '*prima facie* law' is used to refer to the object of interpretation. This expression is nevertheless misleading for it may appear to suggest that '*prima facie* law' is, in fact, the law; thus, the arguments that aim at reconstructing these provisional data can be viewed to fall outside the legal context. They embody proposals about what law should be like in terms of parameters that belong to quite a distinct discursive context. This way of understanding '*prima facie* law' directly implies dismissing the interpretive theory *ab initio*. In the context of interpretive theory, *prima facie* law is the provisional data that, if not interpreted, are meaningless. Some authors consider that Hartian positivism, unlike Dworkin's theory of law, views law as a social phenomenon consisting of *prima facie* law solely. For discussion on this point, see Gavison (1987, 29-33) and Guest (1992, 30).

for the practice as a whole[87].

In *Law's Empire* Dworkin seeks to show that the conception of law that portrays it under the best light is that which takes integrity as the truth criterion for legal propositions. However, this model is circumscribed in a controversial arena where different conceptions claim to offer the best answer to the question what is law. This author analyses two interpretive conceptions that present an alternative reconstruction to his own: conventionalism and pragmatism. Conventionalism understands that the best way to reconstruct the legal practice as a justified exercise of state coercion is by considering the explicit prescriptions of conventionally established institutions, or by analysing what can be derived from their explicit statements by conventionally established methods of meaning ascription[88]. For conventionalist interpretive theory, the practice is a way to respect and express the conventions that arise from majority will. The predictability and legal certainty needed to justify state coercion are thus ensured[89]. Nevertheless, these conventions are not exhaustive and there remain open questions, which the convention itself cannot provide an answer for. Thus, the best reconstruction of the practice requires admitting the absence of right answer in certain cases.

According to pragmatism, on the other hand, the best version of law is that which does not take into account past institutional decisions for the justification of state coercion[90]. Instead, state coercion is justified in terms of the virtues of the judicial decision (e.g. fairness, efficiency) in each particular case and set of circumstances. Thus, judges must provide the best argument without taking into account previous legal history[91]. In this sense, the reconstruction of the practice that shows it under its best light is that which portrays judges as on every occasion reaching a new decision based

---

87 As was already pointed out, the interpreter need not account for every pre-interpretive datum but only for those essential to achieve an omnicomprehensive view of the legal practice. In this sense, Dworkin states that a particular conception of law may exclude data such as old-fashioned legislative decisions on the grounds that they no longer conform to a global reconstruction of the practice. See Dworkin (1986, 99, 154).

88 Dworkin (1986, 95, 114-117).

89 Predictability and legal certainty demand that every citizen be able to know his or her legal rights and duties prior to his or her actions. See, for instance, Aarnio (1987, 3-5).

90 Dworkin agrees that pragmatism could be reconstructed as a position that rejects the interpretive concept of law outlined above. In this case, pragmatism would embody a radical form of scepticism about the existence of law and about the very idea of justification of state coercion. Nonetheless, it could also be portrayed as an interpretive conception provided it uses the language of legal rights and duties, at least at the formal level. Pragmatism as an interpretive theory posits that the contents of these rights and duties is fully contained in the convictions of every judge when she makes the actual decision. See Dworkin (1986, 94-95, 151-155).

91 Dworkin (1986, 151-154).

on their individual will and beliefs about what is the most appropriate way to dispose of the dispute taken to court.

Law as integrity presents itself as an alternative to these two conceptions. Its first assumption is that the best interpretation of the legal practice is half way between conventionalism and pragmatism: it seeks to reach a balance between the importance granted to past decisions and that granted to the best argument. Nevertheless, the fact that it aims at an equilibrium between these two conceptions does not imply that in Dworkin's view the best theory is that which reaches a compromise between convention on the one hand, and justice applied to the instant case on the other. His proposal dismisses on the one hand, a conventional perception of past decisions; on the other, that the notion of best argument depend on the will and beliefs of the decision-maker about the instant case[92]. Dworkin's alternative proposal is based on the principle of integrity.

3.4.1 Integrity as a legal virtue

Dworkin makes use of the idea of integrity to extend the criterion of narrative coherence of the chain novel to the domain of law. His premise is that participants in the legal practice commit themselves to integrity as a legal virtue[93]. This value can broadly speaking be defined horizontally as the balance or coherence between principles underlying the justification of normative acts, and vertically as the coherence of these acts with the set of principles that justify them[94].

For Dworkin, in addition to presuming a specific normative attitude, integrity acts as a methodological or procedural requirement. Integrity may be relevant in two different spheres: that of legislation, where it requires that the law created by the legislator be coherent with the scheme of principles that justify the existence of the legal practice; and that of adjudication, where it demands that the bodies in charge of identifying what is prescribed by the law in each particular case understand law as a coherent whole[95]. This entails specifically that judges assume an omnicomprehensive view of law that can account for the entirety of the practice and not just for individual

---

[92] On this point, see Dworkin (1986, 147-150, 171-175).

[93] Dworkin (1986, 178).

[94] In a later chapter the notion of integrity as coherence will be thoroughly discussed within the analysis of the epistemology of interpretive theory.

[95] Dworkin (1986, 167). In Chapter 5 we shall analyse the concept of coherence and differentiate it from derivability and logical consistency. See MacCormick's (1984, 235-236) for an illuminating discussion of this point.

isolated decisions[96]. Dworkin's main focus of attention in what concerns integrity is in the context of adjudication because he understands adjudication to be the most general paradigm of legal knowledge. Nevertheless, some of the elements in his theory are also applicable to other decision-making processes.

His explanation of the notion of integrity develops from the justification of individual acts. An agent acts with integrity if her particular decisions conform to the scheme of general principles she accepts. This scheme reflects a homogenous form of life[97]. That an individual be integral presumes that she does not act capriciously. Dworkin seeks to extend this idea to the social context by devising a view of the community based on integrity. Integrity affects the interpreter-participant's perception of the legal phenomenon.

With a view to gaining insight into this issue, it is worth devoting some attention to three values or principles that Dworkin deems relevant to every legal community[98].

a) Fairness. This principle dictates that every citizen should have equal opportunities to influence public decisions within his or her community. This value places more emphasis on procedures than on the final outcome of collective decisions. Fairness demands from the judge respect for what has been decided by the majority in the community by means of its representative bodies.

b) Justice. This value refers to the result of institutional decisions. Every resolution should distribute the available resources and protect individual rights in the morally most acceptable way.

c) Due process. This demands that the established procedures be respected both when a new norm is created and when law is applied to particular cases. This value is the manifestation of the principle of legality and legal certainty[99].

---

[96] Strong objections to this perspective have been pressed by positivists. Raz, for instance, claims that this view is a gross distortion of legal practice. For Raz, global coherence does not accurately describe the reality of law nor can it be seen as an ideal to be pursued. According to this author, law is conditional on the existence of a normative authority and the ideal of coherence is incompatible with the assumption of an institutional authority which, regardless of whether coherently or not, guarantees social co-ordination. See Raz (1992, 290-297, 309-314). As will be discussed later on, Raz's objections are misleading because Dworkin's argument, along the lines of Davidson's principle of charity, does not claim that an interpreting agent has a choice between a perspective according to which law is a coherent whole, and one for which this is not the case. Dworkin argues that an interpreter cannot fully grasp the practice in which she participates and which she attempts to interpret unless she attributes to it a homogenous structure.

[97] Dworkin (1986, 166).

[98] Dworkin (1986, 164-167).

[99] For discussion see Calsamiglia (1992, 164).

In Dworkin's view, integrity is a virtue clearly distinguishable from the previous three[100]. It is of a dual nature, methodological and substantive. It is methodological because it serves as a criterion to identify and render meaningful the contents of the practice; it is substantive because it presents the legal practice under a more attractive light as the justification to state coercion. Integrity is proposed as the restriction to, and balance among, the three above-mentioned principles as the best reconstruction of the practice.

In order to illustrate the role and interest of this value, Dworkin claims as a platitude for a legal community the unacceptability of 'checkerboard solutions', that is, different solutions to identical cases (i.e. lack of unitary criteria)[101]. Each one of these diversified decisions may be the fairest and most equitative, but from Dworkin's point of view, compromise based on contradicting principles is politically defective in the context of a truly political community. In what he refers to as 'fraternal community', public action is not justified by morally acceptable results nor by the will of the majority of its members[102]. Justice and fairness are subject to the coherence of principles. For Dworkin, this global coherence is meaningful only if the community is imagined as a moral agent (a personification of the community) who can include integrity as one of its

---

100 Dworkin (1986, 165-167, 176-178).

101 Dworkin (1986, 178-184). The following may prove a useful example to illustrate the problem of checkerboard or diversified solutions. Let us assume that diverging opinions about whether the consumption of drugs should be allowed occur within a community. Let us further assume that the different opinions occur in distinct geographical areas, e.g. those in the north would permit consumption, whereas those in the south would not. It may be the case that the most equitable decision turns out to be the diversified one, i.e. that which makes consumption legal in the north and illegal in the south. It is thus ensured that the majority of the citizens have similar opportunities to influence public decisions. Moreover, the diversified solution may be preferable, in terms of justice, to a unitary one. Those who are of the opinion that permitting drug consumption is a moral mistake will find it fairer that consumption be allowed in the northern strip only rather than in the entire geographical area. Integrity, by contrast, requires that the same solution be adopted throughout the territory because it does not contemplate the possibility to differentiate between similar cases. In this case, global coherence overrules fairness and justice.

102 Dworkin distinguishes three different models of community: circumstantial community, community of statute, and fraternal community. Circumstantial communities are those whose members perceive their association as a *de facto* matter, accidental, because they understand there to be no further connection among themselves. In communities of statute, members reach an agreement to establish a convention about how to guide conduct. In fraternal communities, members do not only accept a certain convention to guide conduct, but also share the following beliefs: a) the community is to be governed by shared principles (agreement of conviction); b) each participant is individually responsible for respecting these principles; c) the community speaks with a single voice and hence diversified solutions are unacceptable. Dworkin (1986, 206-216).

qualities[103]. This perspective generates a duty in the bodies of adjudication: they should read their practice as though it were derived from a collective agent as something distinct from its individual members. This collective agent is to be held liable for its acts and expected to be consistent with its convictions. Moreover, it may review its own ideals and values[104]. It speaks with a single voice and is consistent with its own principles in each and every one of its acts. Such a view of the community renders integrity a basic requirement for adjudication. A judge-participant who undertakes the application of law needs to reconstruct legislative decisions and legal precedents as manifestations of the unitary will of the community[105]. This is reflected in the pre-eminence of the principle of universality and that of formal equality as criteria to identify and apply the law[106].

To sum up, integrity emerges as an appealing legal value provided we adopt a specific understanding of the political community and a distinctive way of participating in this community. From this standpoint, the interpreting agents may only understand law and justify its existence if they impose upon every single institutional action, as well as upon themselves when they interpret the practice, a global intention to speak with a single voice.

3.5 FINAL REMARKS

So far, we have explored the main features of the interpretive theory of law and of the model of integrity. The interpretive attitude is presented not only as an essential feature

---

103 See Dworkin (1986, 167-175).

104 Dworkin (1986, 167-175, 186-190, 225-228).

105 In this sense, Dworkin distinguishes between two types of integrity relevant to adjudication: inclusive integrity, and pure integrity. The former demands that the judge reach some balance between the three above-mentioned virtues - justice, fairness, and legality. By contrast, pure integrity is achieved by favouring justice over the other two values. Dworkin points out that pure integrity is only possible in an ideal world in which justice would offer the best justification of law. In the real world, however, only inclusive integrity can be achieved. See Dworkin (1986, 405-406).

106 Alexy, for instance, introduces the requirement of universality in legal reasoning on the basis of the following rule: a speaker is allowed to assert those judgements of value and duty that he or she would assert in any situation that he or she considers to be identical in all relevant aspects to the one under consideration. See Alexy (1989, 190-191, 275-278). The principle of universality may be realised in two demands, one addressed to the legislator and one to the judge. The former is the principle of material equality. It prescribes that the (choice of) scope of applicability of a norm should be justifiable in order to avoid discrimination. The latter is formal equality, which requires judges to give the same legal solution to all cases that they consider equal in all relevant aspects. See Alexy (1993) and Dworkin (1986, 219-224).

of the legal practice, but also as a necessary assumption for a theory to be a theory of law. For Dworkin, every statement about a social phenomenon depends on an omnicomprehensive theory of the object of interpretation, and hence, on a view as to what is admitted as a good or a bad argument within the practice. The model of integrity, in contrast, emerges as a possible way to present the legal practice. According to Dworkin, this view of the legal practice yields better descriptive-justifying results than either conventionalism or pragmatism. Nonetheless, integrity as a value is extremely ambiguous. It can simply be regarded as an attempt to invoke the narrative coherence needed to grasp the legal phenomenon. In this sense, adopting the interpretive theory would necessarily imply taking this value into account. Here, integrity would continue to be of a dual character - descriptive and justificatory - because participants' judgements are interpretive. But adopting integrity would be essential to answer the question how to approach law rather than what is law. To assert that every reconstruction of the practice requires it to be perceived as a coherent whole does not answer the question of what this whole is, or what it is like. Integrity is merely a contingent equilibrium between justice, fairness and legality. Which values are to be adjusted for the sake of integrity depends on the participants' perception of their own practice. It may be the case that the best interpretation is that which takes into account these three values. However, whether or not this is the best option will not depend on the principle of integrity itself, but on the participants' conviction that these values lie at the heart of the justification of their legal institutions.

As interpretive theories, pragmatism and conventionalism display a strongly monist criterion of coherence because of their assumption that an omnicomprehensive reconstruction of the practice will show it as the realisation of a single value - either justice or fairness[107]. Dworkin observes that these interpretations fall short of being omnicomprehensive because they do not account for the practice as a whole. He argues that the best reconstruction should take into consideration all three values - justice, fairness and legality - and aim at a balance amongst the three. Notwithstanding, Dworkin points out that the best reconstruction of the legal practice is the one that presents the community as speaking in a single voice. This last remark of Dworkin's is question-begging. Does 'speaking with a single voice' mean adopting a strongly monist criterion of coherence and, hence, presenting a fourth criterion which is in competition

[107] This terminology is Raz's, who defines strongly monist coherence as the criterion of adequacy or fit into a set of principles, which are reducible to a single one. By contrast, a weaker form of monist coherence would be adequacy to a small number of principles that are not reducible to a more general one. See Raz (1992, 286) and Kress (1996, 542-546).

with the previous three, or one to which these three can be reduced? Integrity does not seem to be of such character. Justice, fairness, and legality do not appear reducible to integrity because integrity represents precisely a balance between these three values. Neither is it a value that competes with the above values, given that it does not exclude them in the same way pragmatism, for example, excludes every value other than justice applied to the instant case. Integrity is not even an instrument to select one of these virtues as a criterion of truth for legal statements in the event of irreducible conflict between the three values.

If integrity is understood as narrative coherence, the debate between conventionalism, pragmatism, and Dworkin does not turn on the question what is the extent to which adopting the principle of integrity allows for a better reconstruction of the legal practice, since each one of these interpretive theories would adopt this criterion. Rather, the discussion focuses on which conception is most integral and, hence, which is the best approximation. From this standpoint, how does Dworkin's proposal differ from that of conventionalism and pragmatism? His substantive proposal cannot rest on integrity as narrative coherence, for all three theories accept this postulate; neither can it be that the most coherent interpretation is the most coherent one, because this is merely a tautology. The question to be addressed is, precisely, what is the theory that best coheres with the practice as a whole. Dworkin's answer is conciliatory: the theory that best coheres with the legal practice as a whole is that which takes into account all three values, and not just one of them. Hence his argument in favour of equilibrium between these three standards. Equilibrium does not lead to a different value, integrity, but to coherence applied to more than one value[108]. If Dworkin had, for instance, defended as the best reconstruction of the legal practice that which justifies it in terms of a single value (as it is the case in his example of the courtesy practice), he would have assumed such an interpretation to be the most integral one, i.e. that which shows the object of interpretation under its best light.

In conclusion, the question to be addressed by Dworkin's model is whether integrity contributes anything to legal discourse beyond narrative coherence. In my opinion it does not. The argument in favour of equilibrium between the above mentioned three values does not depend on integrity, but on the genuine and substantive enquiry of any

108 It does not seem reasonable to assume that the most integral version is that which identifies a larger number of values in the practice and takes all of them into account. The problem of the best reconstruction is not a quantitative matter but a qualitative one. Regardless of the set of values or the particular value adopted, the interpretive demand is that they contribute to the global coherence of the practice as a whole.

interpretive theory of law into which values justify the existence of the legal practice and need be balanced in order to constitute a coherent whole.

It could be argued that Dworkin's conclusion of equilibrium between these three values is most appropriate because it is most omnicomprehensive and allows reproducing some important intuitions. Conventionalism denies the importance of argument, and rejects the idea that institutional authorities as well as the majority of the participants may be mistaken about the contents of law. Why is a participant denied the right to believe that, although her argument is debatable, her judgement is correct? Pragmatism, on the other hand, does not even attempt to endow law with a general contents which justifies coercion beyond the will and beliefs of decision-makers in instant cases. The legal phenomenon is thus reduced to a private practice such as that of a hypothetical Robinson Crusoe who dictates his own rules. It can even become an instantaneous private practice which, at the end of the day, does not conform to the definition of practice set forth in the previous chapter. Every new act of adjudication then entails a new criterion, and the notion of rule-following thus breaks down. This perspective is far more pessimistic than seems reasonable.

Dworkin's model is not free of unclear issues. Its main problem is how to justify an optimistic attitude towards the existence of a right legal answer just on the basis of the idea of equilibrium between the three values. Nothing in his model seems to suggest that such an optimistic approach is sustainable. As shall be discussed later, coherence does not imply completeness. Integrity is not a metacriterion capable of solving irreducible conflict between these three values. We shall see that the model of integrity is unable to overcome problems such as incommensurability and tie between interpretations.

This problem in Dworkin's theory of law affects his epistemic approach in all of its dimensions and yet, he does not seem to have put forward reasons to justify his optimistic position. As we shall see, this shortcoming does not render his model, and in particular his general epistemic approach, less attractive or unfeasible, though it may hinder an optimistic attitude towards the existence of a right answer. We shall come back to this point later.

In coming chapters we will have a chance to show some of the advantages and shortcomings of Dworkin's theory of law. Let us indicate some of the questions that shall deserve further attention. Firstly, we shall examine whether an interpretive theory is the only valid approach to the legal phenomenon. An affirmative answer to this question would lead to the conclusion that controversy about the contents of the practice does not directly imply its indeterminacy. This would suggest that disagreement in hard cases does not necessarily lead to a lack of right answer. However, in order to reach this conclusion, it is urged that the assumptions of interpretive theory be shown not to be reasonably refutable. Only then will the positivist link between hard cases and the existence of strong discretion be invalidated. Secondly, it need be investigated how can an interpretive theory guarantee objectivity in the judgements about law if they are theory-dependent. Dworkin's theory should therefore be able to overcome the sceptic challenge of 'anything goes'. Thirdly: it has already been pointed out that interpretive theory appears in response to semantic legal theories. Dworkin's conception of a semantic theory demands clarification. It will be interesting to investigate the extent to which Dworkin's criterion of truth for statements about law is fully confined to a non-conventionalist semantic theory. Lastly, we will investigate the relationship between the positivist thesis of the social sources and the pre-interpretive elements in Dworkin's theory of law. It will be interesting to examine if and where does conflict between the two models arise. Dworkin's theory challenges Hartian positivism only if endorsing interpretive theory is necessary to answer the question 'What is law?' and if interpretive theory is shown to be incompatible with the positivist formulation of the social sources thesis, even at the preinterpretive level.

CHAPTER 4

INTERPRETATION VERSUS INVENTION

4.1 INTRODUCTION

Over the last few years, the dichotomy between interpretation and invention has come within the purview of legal philosophers. The controversy about this distinction is not all that novel. It is in many respects essentially the same discussion held by legal theorists who deal with the identification and application of norms as something distinct from the creation of new norms by judges. This distinction has allowed them to define a context for, and limits to, strong discretion. Recently, the discussion has focused on a new label: 'interpretation vs. invention' that has both enhanced and broadened the scope of the debate. Such a distinction allegedly applies to any type of meaning ascription. An analogy between legal and literary or art interpretation has been drawn and often invoked to illustrate the assumptions underlying this debate, and to prove its epistemic relevance.

Ronald Dworkin introduces this terminology in *Law's Empire*[1] to render a reckoning of the convictions that an interpreter should have, and the conceptual distinctions she ought to be able to draw, to construct a successful interpretation of her practice. His position met with strong objections and generated a number of alternative approaches to this issue. But it is important to differentiate between those who oppose Dworkin's distinction and those who use the term 'interpretation' in a different sense. The latter may reach conclusions that are not necessarily in conflict with Dworkin's. Accordingly, the first aim of this chapter is to outline the different notions of interpretation. This will frame our discussion and avoid conceptual misunderstandings in the remaining of this work.

Our main interest will be to investigate Dworkin's views on the possibility of distinguishing between interpretation and invention. If Dworkin's theory of law is to succeed in presenting the legal practice as an argumentative practice, it shall have to

---

[1] See Dworkin (1986, 67-68, 229-232; 1985, 149-153, 167-177; 1983, 286-313; 1991b, 374-382).

provide a sound account of this distinction. Such an account will be essential when considering the judgements of participants in the legal practice from the point of view of weak discretion, both in particularly controversial and in non-controversial cases. For interpretive theory to be a genuine alternative to positivism, scepticism, and natural law theory, its distinction between interpretation and invention should presume no 'brute fact' as a criterion to determine the truth conditions of legal propositions. In addition, it should refute the sceptic challenge that, because no restrictions control interpretation, the contents of law can be reconstructed in infinitely many ways. Furthermore, an analysis of Dworkin's theory of interpretation will prompt us to consider certain philosophical positions that purport to offer a plausible answer to the problem of knowledge.

4.2 NOTIONS OF INTERPRETATION

Two different notions of interpretation can be found in legal philosophy. The first one assumes Wittgenstein's remarks on the interpretation of semantic rules[2]. According to this view, interpretation is the process by which one formulation of the rule is substituted for another. It is a clearly distinct process from grasping or comprehending its contents. As pointed out in the previous chapter, to know or to understand is to display an ability, namely the skill to use a rule or to specify its instances of use. When it is no longer possible to specify its instances of use, interpretation, and eventually a choice between alternative formulations, is required. This is the viewpoint of positivists such as Frederick Schauer and Andrei Marmor. For Schauer, interpretation bears on those uses of language that entail some sort of difficulty; questions relating to the interpretation of norms are thus placed in the context of hard cases[3]. Similarly, Marmor urges to avoid confusion between interpreting the meaning of a rule, and understanding it. When the meaning of a rule cannot be determined to solve a particular case there is nothing left to explain or comprehend - to settle the conflict we must interpret[4].

---

[2] See Wittgenstein (1953, secs. 198, 201). On Wittgenstein's notion of interpretation, and how interpretation differs from comprehension or knowledge, see Baker and Hacker (1994, 81-154).

[3] Schauer (1992, 207-208). On the use of the distinction between interpretation and understanding in legal theory, see Wróblewski (1988, 21-22; 1989, 113) and Prieto (1987, 58-77).

[4] See Marmor (1992, 151-154). In a similar sense, see Patterson (1996, 86-88) and Dummett (1993, 464-473). Hart (1994, 127-128) relates the need for interpretation to the open texture of language. In the zone of certainty of a concept the judge does not need to interpret to identify the right answer, whereas in cases that fall in the penumbral zone, because there is no convention as to the use of terms, the body of adjudication must make a choice between open alternatives.

On the grounds of this concept of interpretation, which we shall call the 'non-epistemic' view of interpretation, there emerge three different positions as far as the plausibility of establishing the dichotomy between interpretation and invention is concerned:

a) The first such position argues that interpretation and invention are two forms of creation. While interpretation is inspired by something pre-existent, invention is the creation of something genuinely new. This idea can be found, for instance, in Marmor, who advocates the trichotomy understanding, interpretation, and invention. He considers that, while understanding is governed by rules that determine its correctness, interpretation is not regulated and can be assessed only in terms of interpretive paradigms[5]. According to Marmor, interpretation aims at imposing or assigning meaning to expressions on the grounds of a particular reconstruction of the speaker's intentions. This only becomes necessary when literal meaning is insufficient to understand and describe the contents of a normative text, that is, when the contents of the rule does not lead to a specific result[6]. For this reason, interpretation is seen as a creative and pragmatic activity – an imposition of meaning to formulations. But this attribution of meaning is aimed at providing an answer to the question what the speaker may have meant by a particular formulation. Thus, interpretation is restricted by the interpreter's assumptions about the speaker's intention. The interpreter should be consistent with her own assumptions about the speaker's intention[7]. Invention, by contrast, entails a genuine substitution of one linguistic formulation for another - it is free of restrictions derived from the meaning of the expression or from coherence with the intention attributed to the speaker[8].

---

[5] Along Dummett's lines, Marmor claims that interpretation is an exception to understanding because interpreting requires prior understanding of language; moreover, interpretation is only necessary when there is nothing more to be understood. Understanding is guided by semantic rules and conventions that can be followed or broken. By contrast, interpretation comes into play when no rule or convention but only interpretive paradigms can be invoked. Paradigms are more flexible than rules and, although they may be respected or overlooked, they cannot be followed or broken in the same way rules can. For Marmor, departing from a paradigm, contrary to deviating from semantic rules, is not a sign of lack of understanding. Paradigms do not measure the correctness of a given interpretation but only their degree of acceptability or plausibility within a specific interpretive community. See Marmor (1992, 21).

[6] Marmor (1992, 21-24, 122, 153-154).

[7] Marmor (1992, 30-34).

[8] See Marmor (1992, 33-34). Endicott discusses Marmor's position in detail. He observes that Marmor's approach is misleading because on some occasions this author seems to defend a restrictive notion of interpretation whereas on other occasions he appears to support a much wider notion of it. Endicott points

The trichotomy understanding-interpretation-invention allows for a restrictive conception of strong judicial discretion similar to Raz's and Hart's[9]. From this point of view, conceptual reasons prevent that strong discretion be regarded as a matter of legal knowledge. Neither can it be regarded as invention in a strict sense. In hard cases the judge must make a choice between open alternatives, albeit a constrained choice. She ought to take into account general principles and criteria guiding the judicial function. Only when the judge deviates from these parameters can it be claimed that she is inventing.

b) The non-epistemic notion of interpretation also gives rise to the view that there is no significant difference between interpreting and inventing. This position nevertheless concedes that it is possible to distinguish between understanding a rule and inventing it in terms of the difference between grasping a pre-existing rule and creating a new one. Endicott's critique of Marmor, as well as his reading of Wittgenstein's conception of interpretation as a genuine substitution develops along these lines[10]. Simple positivism also adheres to this view. It was mentioned before that in cases of no right answer, this theory assumes that bodies of adjudication are unconstrained to create new norms. Thus, when knowledge is no longer possible, invention becomes necessary[11].

c) Finally, Kripke's sceptical approach to rule-following embodies the third non-epistemic position we will consider concerning the plausibility of the distinction between interpretation and invention. Neither a dichotomy nor a trichotomy is acceptable from a sceptical point of view. Any attempt to grasp the meaning of a rule is a leap in the dark and, consequently, unrestricted individual invention[12]. Thus, both interpretation as a form of creation inspired by some pre-existing object, and knowledge are spurned by sceptics.

---

to a further problem of Marmor's distinction between interpretation and invention: although Marmor assumes Wittgenstein's notion of interpretation as an activity significantly distinct from the ability to understand, he does not accept that interpretation is a reformulation rather than a reconstruction - that is, he does not agree that interpretation is about a genuine substitution of one linguistic formulation for another. According to Endicott, Marmor's position on the distinction between interpretation and invention pushes him away from a wittgensteinian notion of interpretation. See Endicott (1994, 10-24).

9 See, for instance, Hart (1980, 9) and Raz (1972, 847-848).

10 Endicott (1994, 21-29).

11 Shiner (1992b, 30-40).

12 Kripke (1982, 55, 84-95).

The second notion of interpretation associates interpretation to knowledge and understanding. Interpretation here is a means to knowledge, i.e. a way to grasp or understand something, or to produce true judgements[13]. Dworkin and some of his critics defend this concept of interpretation, which we shall call 'epistemic'[14].

An epistemic concept of interpretation leads to two diverging views about the plausibility of the distinction between interpretation and invention. The first one contends that these are two genuinely different activities. The second, by contrast, defends a sceptical thesis as far as this dichotomy is concerned, and views interpretation as a form of invention.

In the main, this chapter will be devoted to answering the question of how to draw a genuine distinction between interpretation and invention on the grounds of an epistemic notion of interpretation. Occasional reference will be made to the non-epistemic idea of interpretation, but I will avoid merely verbal questions such as whether it is preferable to use the word 'interpretation' or 'knowledge' to refer to the process of grasping something or producing true judgements. These words will be considered to be interchangeable from an epistemic point of view of interpretation. I will turn to the non-epistemic notion of interpretation insofar as interpretation as reconstructive substitution is thought to be a form of creation distinguishable from invention.

---

13 I am of the opinion that associating interpretation to knowledge does not necessarily imply denying the possibility of grasping something without translation or substitution; that is, without making a choice between possible reconstructions when none can be claimed to be the correct one. Viewing interpretation as a way to gain knowledge often implies a notion of interpretation unrelated to substitution or translation. Instead, 'interpretation' is held interchangeable with 'knowledge' regardless of the particular epistemological position defended. For this reason, assuming interchangeability appears to be a mere verbal question and, hence, does not necessarily require adopting an approach such as Davidson's. Against Wittgenstein's idea that it is possible to understand without translating, Davidson replies that in order to know what other speakers mean by their utterances we should be able to translate their statements into our own conceptual schemes. For Davidson, knowledge is only possible when different conceptual schemes (that is, different languages) comprise some mechanism for translation. Nonetheless, Davidson does not only consider the problem of understanding languages different from our own, but also that of understanding every other speaker, even that speaker who uses our own language. He (1984b, 125) thus writes that 'all understanding of the speech of another involves radical interpretation'. Se also Davidson (1984b, 183-198)

14 Dworkin (1985, 146-149) and Fish (1983, 299-305). Raz (1996, 250-256) and Ross (1958, 115-122), for instance, also adopt this idea of interpretation. However, it is worth noting that Raz and Ross relate interpretation to 'explanation'. But they conceive 'explanation', in contrast with Hacker's view, as a manifestation or result of understanding. In spite of his claim that an interpretation is an explanation, Hacker considers that an explanation is only necessary when a statement is obscure or ambiguous. See Hacker (1988, 168). For a discussion of Hacker's position, see Patterson (1996, 86 footnote 104).

4.3 ARE WE INTERPRETING OR INVENTING?

Within an epistemic view of interpretation, the distinction between interpreting and inventing can be drawn in two ways, depending on the point of view adopted with regard to the truth conditions of legal propositions. Here, I would like to recall the distinction between realist and antirealist semantics[15]. According to our earlier characterisation of realist semantics, to interpret is to grasp an object whose existence, contents, and form are independent of our epistemic abilities. A correct interpretation leads to knowledge or understanding[16]. To invent, by contrast, is to produce a new object either because interpretation has been carried out incorrectly, or because there was initially no intention to interpret. From the standpoint of antirealist semantics, to interpret is to coherently apply an ontological theory committed with certain assumptions about what is to be interpreted, where the object of interpretation is dependent on the epistemic abilities of the interpreters. To know is to offer the best interpretation, i.e. that interpretation which best coheres with the best ontological theory. To invent, on the other hand, is to produce an object on the basis of some criterion about what one wants to create, and requires the belief that one is indeed creating something new. According to an antirealist point of view, invention does not result from misinterpretation, but from a specific attitude entirely distinguishable from the interpretive attitude.

In my opinion, Dworkin approaches this dichotomy from an antirealist point of view[17]. He contends that every interpreter participating in the legal practice should possess and be able to distinguish between the conviction about what it is to interpret, and that about what it is to invent. In order to be in a position to interpret, the interpreter must hold the belief that he is indeed participating in the social practice he wants to

---

[15] I pointed out earlier that we are assuming a very common view within semantics that relates a theory of meaning to a truth-conditions theory. We noted that this view still permits the distinction between realist and antirealist semantics in terms of what they understand the truth-value of legal propositions to depend on, and whether they assume their truth to transcend the epistemic abilities of interpreters or not. See Baker (1988, 50-51), Dummett (1978, xxi-xxiii) and Patterson (1996, 5-6). Shiner objects to this view: he claims that antirealism is a theory that rejects the very possibility of asserting the truth or falsity of judgements. In my opinion, this view is mistaken for it presumes that the term 'truth' has a single meaning. See Shiner (1992b, 210-211).

[16] On the basis of a realist position, 'to know' can be defined in terms of the coming together of three elements: a) *X* believes *p*; b) *X* is justified in believing *p*; c) *p* is true.

[17] This conclusion can be reached from Dworkin's reply to Woozley's criticism. Woozley claims that Dworkin's concept of truth is wrong. Dworkin's reply suggests a certain link between the term 'truth' and assertability. See Dworkin (1984, 275-278). We will address this issue in Chapter 5.

describe, and that some interpretations of this practice are better than others[18]. For Dworkin, the possibility of interpreting is always linked to the acceptance of a particular context of what is right and wrong. This entails, specifically, an interpretive attitude, which the agent should be able to discriminate from a genuinely creative or inventive one[19]. However, the existence of a significant distinction between these two notions requires that the objectivity of judgements be warranted, that is, that this dichotomy be not dependent on more than just individual will or preferences. Neither should a new stipulation in each particular case be required to decide whether one is interpreting or inventing. Precisely this point generates difficulties to an antirealist approach, for such an approach does not presume that objects of interpretation transcend the epistemic abilities of interpreters. (This will later be shown not to imply that interpreters cannot be mistaken when they identify the practice.) These difficulties should be overcome so as to avoid the sceptical challenge that there is no way to draw an objective distinction between interpretation and invention.

Dworkin argues that judgements about the legal practice are objective because restrictions control interpretation. However, Dworkin seeks to conciliate two postulates that at first sight appear incompatible. According to his theory, the restrictions controlling interpretation are internal to every conceptual scheme - they are agent-dependent - but still objective because they restrict the agent's will and freedom to act[20]. This position has met with numerous objections, notably from pragmatists or sceptics, who accuse Dworkin of inevitably falling into either semantic realism or scepticism[21]. Pragmatist objections are most threatening to an interpretive theory of law: if they cannot be refuted, they invalidate the basic assumptions of this theory, which can then no longer be considered to be an alternative approach to law. For this reason, Dworkin has repeatedly responded to pragmatist criticism, in particular to one of its sharpest exponents: Stanley Fish[22]. Dworkin and Fish engaged in a long controversy that involved numerous replies and counter-replies, all of which have contributed significantly towards clarifying Dworkin's views. In my opinion, Dworkin appears to

---

18 Dworkin (1983, 289-290; 1986, 67; 1994a, 469).

19 Dworkin (1983, 289-290). In this sense, see also Raz (1996, 252).

20 Dworkin (1986, 234-236; 1985, 152-154, 168; 1994, 468-470).

21 Henceforth, 'pragmatism', 'scepticism' and 'relativism' will be used interchangeably to refer to the sceptical line of thought that rejects the possibility of speaking of truth conditions for legal statements.

22 Fish has devoted a large amount of his output to criticising Dworkin's interpretive model. See Fish (1982, 551-567; 1983, 200-316; 1987, 401-419). A further reply to Dworkin from a pragmatist point of view is to be found in Knapp (1991, 323-342).

have successfully refuted global scepticism, but not so the objections pressed by partial sceptics to his thesis on the existence of a single right answer in all cases. In the next section we will have a close look at the controversy between Dworkin and Fish, particularly as far as the restrictions controlling interpretation are concerned. I will start off by exposing the contents and nature of Fish's criticism to Dworkin and then proceed to point to the reasons why I think Fish's criticism falls short of its purpose.

4.3.1 The controversy Dworkin - Fish

Fish's criticism of Ronald Dworkin focuses on Dworkin's idea of the chain novel, particularly in what regards the constraints that apply to the different participants in this shared enterprise. Fish attacks the viability of Dworkin's model as an alternative to Hartian positivism and as a reply to global scepticism. He claims Dworkin fails to warrant the objectivity of judgements about how the novel is to be continued and about how to interpret the legal practice as a dynamical phenomenon. Hence, Fish confronts Dworkin with the classical sceptical dilemma, and argues that Dworkin does not manage to escape it. In Fish's opinion, Dworkin's model is a failed attempt to claim objectivity without resort to the kind of semantic realism Fish attributes to legal positivism[23]. His criticism can be split into four arguments:

1.- Fish claims that it is only possible to establish a genuine distinction between interpretation and invention if objective restrictions constrain the range of possible ways the novel can be viewed. Objectivity only obtains insofar as the text itself as a brute fact is assumed to determine its own interpretation. In order for the text to act as a constraint to its own interpretation it need be the case that it can be grasped without resort to evaluative judgements. To this end, there should be something fixed as to its form and contents prior to any attempt to ascribe meaning to it. In other words, the object of interpretation should be self-evident, and contain its own identifying labels - it should be independent of interpreters' beliefs[24].

---

[23] In the second chapter I pointed out that Hartian positivism does not purport to assume realist semantics. However, the problems of this theory to overcome the sceptical challenge of 'anything goes' allow Hartian positivism to assume the social sources thesis, albeit at the cost of appearing to accept semantic realism or, at least, a position notably close to realism. Thus, although Fish's description of the positivist project is not entirely accurate, it seems nevertheless appropriate if we take into account positivists' failure to solve the problem of rule-following. See Fish (1983, 301, 308-312).

[24] Fish (1982, 558-561; 1983, 299-302; 1987, 403-404).

For Fish, when positivists accept the possibility of explicit or literal meaning, they advocate a non-interpretive distinction between these two notions. Consequently, they assume that, at some level, the meaning of a legal text can be grasped as something uninterpreted[25]. Dworkin's model, Fish claims, ultimately adopts a positivist position for it implicitly assumes that the text can restrict its own interpretation. Dworkin is thus virtually seen to support the position that he initially rejected[26].

2.- Fish claims that the objectivity needed to draw a genuine distinction between interpretation and invention of the chain novel does not obtain because ‘organization, style, and figure are interpretive facts –facts which, rather than setting limits to the elaboration of a reading, emerge and become established in the course of that very elaboration’[27]. He argues that the criterion that determines the point at which a change in the novel takes place is itself subject to change and interpretation. Therefore, this is no longer a helpful criterion to draw a distinction between interpretation and invention. According to Fish, then, this distinction can only be drawn 'from *within* interpretive conditions that give certain objects and shapes a real but constructed - and therefore unsettleable - stability'[28].

For Fish, objectivity makes sense only as an external restriction to interpreters' judgements. But there are no external restrictions. Only each agent's prior understanding can act as a mechanism to recognise a particular conclusion as a possible interpretation. Moreover, a particular interpretation will be regarded as a possible interpretation only once the agent views it as such[29].

3.- If an interpretive position is assumed, it should also be assumed that no restriction is independent of the restrictions set by the prior understanding of the interpreter, Fish claims. Thus, he argues that one will necessarily reach the conclusion that there is no genuine and objective difference between continuing the chain novel and striking out in a new direction, or between beginning a new chain novel and continuing the one produced so far. The same freedom for action and internal restrictions apply in both cases since it is not plausible to assume that the limit rests in the text itself. The

---

[25] Fish (1983, 301-302; 1987, 403, 409).

[26] Fish (1982, 551-553; 1983, 308-309).

[27] Fish (1983, 302). See also Fish (1987, 404-405).

[28] Fish (1983, 303).

[29] Although Fish never explicitly defines 'prior understanding', it can be argued that he thereby refers to the set of convictions the agent holds before undertaking interpretation. The agent's prior understanding endows him with a particular perspective of social reality as well as with criteria upon which to base his decisions. See Fish (1982, 554; 1983, 311-312).

agent has to decide which acts can be considered the beginning of a new novel and which ones can be viewed as its continuation given that there is nothing genuine in the text indicating the direction the novel has already taken[30].

Fish draws attention to the fact that departing from the novel (or from the legal history) is no more than a further way of continuing it. Consequently, 'an agent cannot depart from the chain even if he wants to and believes that he is doing so'[31]. Each one of his acts constitutes the very chain. In order to continue in the same direction, the agent has to decide what this direction is. Only his own definitions and stipulations limit his actions, but after every action, he must reassess what has gone so far. Accordingly, Fish concludes, no criterion allows the agent to determine whether his option is the correct one because at any given time his judgements are the criteria establishing the direction of continuation. In short, Fish seems to argue that merely mentioning that an act is being performed is enough for it to be performed[32].

4.- Finally, Fish claims that the impossibility of drawing a genuine distinction between interpretation and invention does not detract from the pragmatic usefulness of this dichotomy. However, Fish reduces this dichotomy to one between persuasive and non-persuasive interpretations. Thus, the distinction is only meaningful as an argumentative technique[33]. He points out that 'while there is, at the level of the practice, a distinction between continuing the legal history and striking out in a new direction, it is a distinction between methods of justifying arguments and not between actions whose difference is perspicuous apart from any argument whatsoever'[34]. Consequently, the distinction between interpreting and inventing is always linked to a certain normative position[35].

Fish's arguments aim at evincing the shortcomings in Dworkin's model particularly in what concerns the inevitable contradiction it seems to conceal. Specifically, that Dworkin assumes the first two arguments without giving consideration to the consequences that necessarily follow from them. On the one hand, Dworkin firstly argues that the distinction between interpretation and invention is plausible only if we accept objectivity; and that no objectivity stemming from the text itself can act as a

30 Fish (1982, 554-555; 1983, 306-307).

31 Fish (1983, 306).

32 Fish (1983, 306-307, 313-316).

33 Fish (1982, 559).

34 Fish (1983, 307-308).

35 Fish (1987, 410-414).

restriction to its own interpretation. On the other hand, Dworkin affirms a genuine distinction between interpretation and invention[36].

Let us investigate Fish's claim that an interpretive model such as Dworkin's necessarily has to either adopt semantic realism and accept that interpreters' judgements do not fix the contents of the legal practice; or else, reject semantic realism and thus deny objectivity and assume radical subjectivism[37]. Fish's criticism to my mind appears mistaken precisely because it presumes these two possibilities only. In my opinion, Dworkin supports what would appear as a third option, namely that the judgements of a participating interpreter may impose objective restrictions upon other judgements of that interpreter. Thus, in his reply to Fish, he writes:

> I said that interpreters are constrained by their own complex aesthetic judgements and by nothing more interpersonal, and I developed an argument why such constraints are nevertheless genuine. There is no trace in my essay of any claim that the identity or characterization or interpretation of a work if art is a "brute fact" (whatever that might be), or that the nature of a work of art is "independent" of the interpreter, or that the constraints of interpretation are "self-executing" [38].

Dworkin's terms seem to suggest a shift away from Fish's reply. Nevertheless, Fish's criticism can only be overruled if Dworkin's point of view holds firm. Is the third option viable? Is it plausible? In order to provide an answer to these questions it is imperative to scrutinise the idea of objectivity and the kind of restrictions that objectively control interpretation and differentiate it from pure invention. Dworkin and Fish clearly disagree on this point. As most theoreticians would concede, they too assert that in order to claim the plausibility of this distinction, it is essential to identify some restrictions to interpretation[39]. However, they disagree as to the origin of these necessary constraints. Fish only accepts as genuine restrictions those external or independent of interpreters' judgements. For this reason, only if external restrictions exist, that is, if semantic realism is assumed, does it make sense to assert that there is some objective limit to interpretation[40]. Fish's sceptical position results from denying the existence of these

---

[36] Fish (1983, 308-313).

[37] Fish (1987, 408).

[38] Dworkin (1983, 288, 289). See also his examples on how the interpreter's judgements may suffice to restrict her freedom to interpret Christmas Carol in such a way that Scrooge appears as hopelessly evil, (1986, 232-238).

[39] See, for instance, Hurley (1989, 84-95), Fiss (1982, 744-750), Raz (1996, 250-252), Dworkin (1983, 290-292) and Fish (1982, 551-556).

[40] Fish (1982, 308-309). Owen Fiss (1982, 744) holds a similar view: although he rejects the sceptical conclusion, he claims that 'objectivity implies that the interpretation can be judged by something other

constraints, which is virtually the same as denying the viability of realist semantics. Dworkin, by contrast, does not agree that only external constraints, or, constraints independent of the conceptual schemes of interpreters, control interpretive conclusions. He argues that rejecting the possibility of external restrictions does not necessarily lead to Fish's scepticism[41]. Dworkin advocates the plausibility of internal restrictions, that is, constraints resulting from the judgements and conceptual schemes of interpreters themselves. He considers these internal constraints to be objective because they restrict interpreters' freedom to act[42].

With a view to assessing whether Dworkin's position makes sense and whether it manages to escape Fish's dilemma, we are urged to examine carefully the arguments he puts forward to advocate internal objectivism. We shall see that internal objectivism shares some features with Hilary Putnam's internal realism.

4.3.2 Internal objectivity

Internal objectivity is a useful idea to avoid misunderstandings in the analysis of Dworkin's model. The success of Dworkin's approach to law greatly depends on the correctness of the assumption underlying the idea of internal objectivity, namely that adopting semantic realism is not necessary in order to warrant that judgements about the legal practice be objectively correct or incorrect. Internal objectivity rests on two assumptions: the denial of restrictions external to the interpreting agents; and that, within a given conceptual scheme, objective restrictions stemming from the very conceptual scheme control judgements and interpretation.

Let us initiate the discussion of these two assumptions by considering the general notion of objectivity. Objectivity is a mechanism to endow the evaluation of a judgement or interpretation with a certain degree of stability and rigidity. Thus, to appeal to objectivity is precisely to indicate that the correctness of a judgement, or the truth of a proposition, is beyond reasonable doubt - it is not malleable - and that is independent of individual will. Specifically the fact that objective restrictions constrain interpretation is what permits a categorical distinction between an instance of

---

than one's own notion of correctness. It imparts a notion of impersonality. The idea of an objective interpretation does not require that the interpretation is wholly determined by some source external to the judge, but only that it be constrained'. Fiss does not accept that the text as a physical object is the only relevant constraint to legal interpretation -legal rules and the community that accepts these rules and thinks them authoritative act as restrictions external to the judge too.

41 Dworkin (1983, 290-292; 1991b, 374-377, 378-381).

42 Dworkin (1991b, 376, 377; 1986, 234-235; 1985, 151-152, 167-177; 1983, 288-297).

interpretation and one of invention. However, we can identify two types of objectivity according to what we consider to be the reasons accounting for the unquestionability of the correctness of a judgement. 'External objectivity', as we shall call the first kind, understands that the very object of interpretation limits the possible interpretations of its meaning. The underlying assumption is that the object has certain properties independent of our convictions, which act as the criterion of correctness for our statements about it. External objectivity is opposed to subjectivity as long as we understand 'subjective' to mean 'dependent on the subject'. 'Internal objectivity', in contrast, regards some of the agent's judgements as the criteria to evaluate the correctness of further judgements of the same agent[43]. Internal objectivity regards objectivity as something opposed to arbitrariness, but not to subjectivity if 'subjective' means dependent on our convictions rather than our desires, will, or pragmatic interests.

In his reply to Stanley Fish, Ronald Dworkin seems to adopt internal objectivity. What we shall refer to as 'the thesis of internal objectivity' seeks to conciliate the classical distinction between objective and subjective in a similar way Davidson and Putnam reply to scepticism or relativism[44]. Dworkin observes that the pragmatic answer claiming that no restrictions apply to interpretation makes sense only if we assume that the agent is capable of identifying the instances in which the restrictions acting on her interpretation are external (derived from the structure of the world) or merely internal (stemming from his own beliefs). An interpreter can conclude that she is subject to no constraints only when she is capable of drawing this distinction and of verifying that her statements are only restricted by her own convictions[45]. Dworkin claims that if we

---

43 It is important not to mistake the above distinction between these two kinds of objectivity with the one Coleman and Leiter draw. In my view, these authors adopt external objectivity, which they then further divide into strong and minimal objectivity. Strong objectivity takes the very events or objects as the applicable external restrictions, whereas minimal objectivity presumes that external restrictions derive from the social conventions and the views of the majority of the members of the community of speakers. Coleman and Leiter argue that antirealist semantics usually assume minimal objectivity. However, it was already pointed out in a previous chapter that it is not obvious how to reach this conclusion and simultaneously overcome the sceptic challenge of rule-following. See Coleman and Leiter (1995, 252-253).

44 Davidson (1984b, 198). See also Davidson's reply to Quine, in particular to Quine's idea that meaning should be searched in the sensory stimulation that acts as a mediator between objects and beliefs. See Davidson (1993b, 313-319; 1993a, 327). See also Putnam (1981, 54-56; 1987, 16-21, 76-80).

45 Dworkin writes (1985, 174):

> This explanation supposes that we can distinguish between the game and the real world, that we can distinguish the claim that slavery is unjust, offered as a move in some collective enterprise in which such

disregard this assumption, the fact that interpreters are not constrained by anything external to their own judgements give them 'no reason to doubt or abandon the conclusions he reaches, about which interpretations fit the text well enough to count, for example, or so poorly that they must be rejected if other interpretations, otherwise less attractive, are available'[46]. From Dworkin's point of view, radical subjectivism as advocated by scepticism can be maintained only if we support external objectivity and have access to it[47]. Otherwise, the question about the objectivity of judgements becomes internal to a particular language game[48]. Accordingly, the distinction between what is subjective and what is objective depends on our convictions about what is it we are doing. We resort to this dichotomy to clarify the contents of our opinions, that is, when we seek to differentiate those opinions that refer to what the practice is like from those which express our tastes and emotions - and not when we wish to distinguish between our opinions and something external to them[49].

In short, Dworkin rejects the sceptic distinction between two discursive levels on the grounds that precisely this distinction leads to the sceptical problem. He writes:

> Rorty imagines two levels of discourse. The first is the ordinary level at which you and I live: at that level mountains exists, existed before there were people, will exist, presumably, after there are people, and would have existed, presumably, even there had never been people. If you don't agree, you don't know how to play the "mountain" language game. In addition, however, there is a second, archimedean, philosophical

---

judgements are made and debated, and the claim that slavery is really or objectively unjust in the actual world.

In a similar sense, see Ebbs's criticism of Kripke's scepticism and his metaphysical realism, Ebbs (1997, 65-67, 295-302).

46 Dworkin (1986, 236).

47 Dworkin writes (1996, 88) that external sceptics 'must assume that some of what they think (at an absolute minimum, their beliefs about good reasoning) are not just their own or their culture's invention but are true or valid –indeed "objectively" so. Otherwise they could only present their views as "subjective" displays in which we need take nothing but a biographical interest'. In a similar sense, see Dworkin (1991b, 360-361). Putnam (1990, 32), on the other hand, replies to Rorty's sceptical account that 'this very philosopher does not recognize that his picture is only a picture, but believes that in some deep pretheoretic sense his picture is the way the world is'. This line of criticism is very solid for it creates a genuine dilemma for sceptics: if the sceptic assumes that no judgement is more correct than any other judgement, he should then accept that this very judgement is no more correct than that judgement that rejects this view. It only expresses a belief. Therefore, scepticism cannot forcefully deny the position it is aiming against. It would only be sensible for scepticism to claim that no judgements are more correct than others if this claim is correct beyond the beliefs of sceptics themselves.

48 Dworkin (1991b, 364, 380-381).

49 Dworkin (1996, 98; 1985, 172-173).

level at which a different question can be raised: not whether mountains exist, but whether Reality as It Is In Itself contains mountains[50].

According to Dworkin, sceptics place themselves in the external or archimedean discourse when they affirm that the meaning of the statement 'mountains exist' (which belongs to internal discourse, that is, to the first level of discourse) differs from that of 'mountains really exist' (which is a statement of the external level of discourse)[51]. This is precisely what allows sceptics to assert that, really, there exist only beliefs, and that any judgement is as correct as any other judgement. Dworkin insists, however, that in the context of internal discourse there is no relevant difference between the claims that mountains exist and that they really exist. Furthermore, he contends, it is not possible to resort to any external discourse to draw a significant distinction between these two judgements[52].

In my opinion, Dworkin's thesis is attractive because it puts forward arguments to reject the dualism between conceptual scheme and reality. This leads to a more accessible and intelligible notion of objectivity. Advocating external objectivity as a criterion of correctness presumes that there is some kind of bridge between our beliefs and the world. It is absurd to presume so because we can never leave our conceptual scheme behind[53]. Davidson and Putnam have repeatedly insisted on this point.

---

[50] Dworkin (1996, 95-96; 1991b, 361-362, 378-381; 1983, 297-303). As we shall see, this objection to scepticism also appears in the works of Davidson and Putnam. See Davidson (1984b, 190-198) and Putnam (1981, 49-74; 1995c, 57-75).

[51] See Dworkin (1996, 96).

[52] Dworkin takes as a further example the proposition that slavery is unjust. He observes that in practical discourse there is no significant difference between claiming that slavery is unjust and claiming that it is really or objectively unjust. Insiders speak in terms of objectivity only to clarify or enhance their judgements about the practice and to differentiate them from their own tastes and preferences. This only means that they believe things to be in a particular way, and that the contrary opinion is mistaken unless convincing reasons are provided for it. Participants consider that the unjust character of slavery is not a matter of their personal opinion, but that there are compelling reasons to oppose slavery and that, moreover, everyone should share this very opinion. But including 'really' in the statement that slavery is unjust does not endow this statement with a different status and, hence, 'really' in itself does not render the correctness of this statement independent of participants' beliefs, nor does it make a statement correct or incorrect. Thus, Dworkin (1985, 172) points out that 'if some argument should persuade me that my views about slavery are not really true, then it should also persuade me to abandon my views about slavery. And if no argument could persuade me that slavery is not unjust, no argument could persuade me that it is not "really" unjust'. See also Dworkin (1986, 81-83; 1983, 299).

[53] As shall be pointed out later, this is essentially the problem of rule-following. We already observed that the idea of some internal connection between the rule and its instances of use means that no intermediary between the rule and its instances of use may function as a criterion of correctness.

Davidson replies to conceptual relativism:

> In giving up dependence on the concept of an uninterpreted reality, something outside all schemes and science, we do not relinquish the notion of objective truth –quite contrary. Given the dogma of a dualism of scheme and reality, we get conceptual relativity, and truth relative to a scheme. Without the dogma, this kind of relativity goes by the board. Of course truth of sentences remains relative to language, but that is a objective as can be. In giving up the dualism of scheme and world, we do not give up the world, but re-establish unmediated touch with the familiar objects whose antics make our sentences and opinions true or false.[54]

Along similar lines, Putnam writes:

> To pick out just one correspondence between words or mental signs and mind-independent things we would have already to have referential access to the mind-independent things. You can't single out a correspondence between two things by just squeezing one of them hard (or doing anything else to just one of them; you cannot single out a correspondence between our concepts and the supposed noumenal objects without access to the noumenal objects [55].

Davidson, Putnam and Dworkin claim that the result of rejecting the possibility of directly accessing objects is not that beliefs constitute the world and that, therefore, any interpretation is equally correct. On the contrary: for them, the consequence of this denial is the dissolution of the duality between scheme and reality. This, is turn, renders pointless the question about what, other than our beliefs, allow us to confirm whether we are mistaken in our convictions and firmest judgements[56]. Putnam asserts that, for this reason, scepticism in fact assumes, just as metaphysical realism does, an externalist perspective or 'The God's Eye view'. In his own words, 'the externalist wants to think of the world as consisting of objects that are at one and the same time mind-independent and Self-Identifying. This is what one cannot do'[57].

In order for the idea of objectivity to be preserved without having to resort to externalism, Putnam proposes internalism (or internal realism) as an alternative to scepticism. It could be argued that the differences between Putnam's internalism and Davidson's epistemic coherentism are minor. Davidson has nevertheless tried to distance himself from Putnam's position[58]. Later on we shall have the opportunity to point out some of the features of internalism as a theory of truth in contrast to the purely

---

[54] Davidson (1984b, 198).

[55] Putnam (1981, 73). See also Putnam (1987, 20-21) and Ebbs (1997, 38-39).

[56] See Putnam (1981, 54-56), Dworkin (1996, 117-118) and Davidson (1993b, 312-319).

[57] Putnam (1981, 54-55; 1987, 19-21; 1990, 27-29, 31-33).

[58] See Davidson (1993b, 309).

epistemic theory advocated by Davidson. For the time being, let us just stress that internalism shares with Dworkin its aim to reconcile a language that speaks significantly of events and objects with conceptual relativity[59].

From this point of view,

> Signs do not intrinsically correspond to objects, independently of how those signs are employed and by whom. But a sign that is actually employed in a particular way by a particular community of users can correspond to particular objects within the conceptual scheme of those users. "Objects" do not exist independently of conceptual schemes. We cut up the world into objects when we introduce one or another scheme of description. Since the objects and the signs are alike internal to the scheme of description, it is possible to say what matches what.[60]

This theory attributes genuine restrictions to interpretation as an activity distinguishable from invention. If we ignore the externalist assumption, there seems to be no reason to reject the idea that some interpretations are objectively (i.e. beyond reasonable doubt) better than others, and that some interpretations may be discarded as interpretations due to their high degree of implausibility[61]. More importantly, this view preserves the distinction between the belief that a judgement is correct only because it is believed to be correct (i.e. invoking beliefs replaces the need for justification for judgements), and the belief that a judgement is correct in spite of the impossibility of providing an absolute justification for it. Leaving externalism aside, the basis for any interpretive judgements rests on the latter belief and not on the former[62].

Nevertheless, the thesis of internal objectivity or internalism does not in itself prevent a globally nor a partially sceptical conclusion. A globally sceptical conclusion is avoided if we manage to show how an agent's conceptual scheme may impose restrictions upon her freedom to act or upon her judgements about what she is interpreting. In order to avoid the partially sceptical conclusion, by contrast, we ought to assume that the constraints imposed by a conceptual scheme always suffice to restrict the agent's freedom to act. As far as the first issue is concerned, Dworkin, Putnam and Davidson assert that a belief may only be restricted by another belief, and that this is sufficient to warrant objectivity[63]. Now the question is how can some beliefs actually

---

[59] Putnam (1987, 17-18).

[60] Putnam (1981, 52).

[61] Putnam (1987, 77) and Dworkin (1986, 235-236; 1985, 167-168).

[62] For discussion, see Dworkin (1991b, 373).

[63] See Davidson (1993b, 309-310), Putnam (1981, 55-56) and Dworkin (1983, 292-293).

function as genuine constraints to other beliefs, that is, how can some beliefs become a criterion of correctness for our judgements.

4.3.3 Constraints to interpretation: the structure of a conceptual scheme

Once we reject externalism, internal restrictions become relevant to the distinction between interpretation and invention. In order to understand the role played by these restrictions in relation to the judgements of an interpreter or a set of interpreters, we ought to imagine a conceptual scheme as a hierarchical structure of distinct beliefs or convictions that, in our case, constitute a certain perspective of the legal phenomenon[64]. Participants in this practice ought to share some of these convictions about the meaning of their interactions or, at least, they should assume that they share them[65]. Let us recall

---

64 'Belief' or 'conviction' refers to a state of mind associated to every interpretive judgement. This mental state is linked to the correctness or the truth of what is being asserted for it is, precisely, a disposition to assert that *p*. In my view, this general notion suffices to characterise 'belief'. We need not assume that a belief can only be a mental state of certainty (i.e. one of sufficient subjective evidence or unquestionability) about the truth of what is being asserted, or the contents of the belief. Such an assumption would prevent the possibility of an individual experiencing different degrees of confidence about the correctness of her judgements, and therefore the possibility that some of her beliefs be more firm or solid than others. From this more restrictive point of view, the relation between beliefs and certainty is not gradual: if an individual is certain about the truth of what she asserts, she holds a belief; if, on the contrary, she is uncertain about it, then she does not believe. Certainty, as a property relating to the agent is her highest degree of confidence about something. To my mind, however, the occurrence of a disposition to affirm *p* does not necessarily require absolute certainty about the truth of *p*. For this reason, defining a belief merely in terms of a mental state linked to truth or correctness allows for a characterisation of this concept that includes as beliefs states of mind of various degrees of confidence about the truth of their contents. The relevance of this wider definition will become clear in the next chapter. About the notion of belief, see, for instance, Cohen (1992, 367-369) and Alston (1989, 290). On certainty, see Mosterin (1987, 121-126) and Alston (1989, 257-258).

65 We stress that speakers should at least assume that they share a conceptual scheme because otherwise they are forced to accept that they cannot communicate. The very awareness that one is a participant in a social practice presumes that she can translate other participants' judgements into her own conceptual schemes; in other words, she ought to believe that she shares some basic convictions. This, in turn, allows us to identify the points at which significant disagreement occurs. Davidson's principle of charity plays specifically this role. According to this author, we need to optimise agreement in order to understand the other participants in the practice. See Davidson (1984b, 136-137, 195-198). Yet, note that the principle of charity does nevertheless not mean that in order to understand other participants' judgements one should adopt their conceptual scheme, for this is impossible. On the contrary, charity operates in exactly the opposite way: the interpreter ought to adjust the conceptual schemes of other participants as much as possible to her own. That is, she should try to maximise similarity to facilitate understanding. This, however, does not require that such similarity be real, for that would take us back to externalism - similarity is attributed only for the sake of the translatability of participants' judgements from one

that participants are those individuals who share a certain understanding of some social phenomenon. They are thus enabled to play the same language game, that is, to follow and internalise the same rules. A shared social practice can only exist if it involves different individuals that share the most fundamental features of a conceptual scheme. Consequently, the analysis of the constraints restricting the interpretation of a particular social practice turns out to be an analysis of the structure of a conceptual scheme that tends to be shared by the participants. This structure should offer an objective (non-arbitrary) relationship between judgements and the object of interpretation. As pointed out by Davidson, 'conceptual schemes (languages) either organize something, or they fit it'[66]. But the question now is how do conceptual schemes organise or adjust this object given that the object itself depends on the schemes, and, simultaneously, constrains them. The key point is the relationship between the different convictions in a body of beliefs.

The first inevitable requirement for the plausibility of internal restrictions is that interpreters be capable of distinguishing different beliefs within their own conceptual scheme. Dworkin insists that the judgements of an interpreter can restrict her own version of the legal phenomenon only insofar as she can discriminate between those opinions about what the object *is* like from those about what it *should* be like. To this end, interpreters should possess some mechanism enabling them to distinguish what embodies an interpretation from what is pure creation or invention. To draw this distinction, the interpreter should acknowledge the independence between different types of convictions[67]. For Dworkin, these independent kinds of convictions are: firstly, those referring to the formal identity of the object of interpretation; secondly, those that impose a way of showing the object in its best light; and, thirdly, those that constitute a new object, or aim at adjusting an object to the interpreter's preferences. From this point of view, if convictions cannot be viewed as independent (but necessary and interrelated), the notion of restriction eventually generates a vicious circle because agents cannot distinguish their preferences and emotions from the contents of the practice they seek to interpret[68]. Notwithstanding, independence does not suffice to warrant objectivity. A belief does not occur separately, but as part of a global scheme of

---

conceptual scheme into another. Moreover, this principle requires presupposing a high degree of consistency between the participants' acts and the beliefs they are thought to hold. On the principle of charity, see also Davidson (1984b, 136-139).

[66] Davidson (1984b, 191).

[67] Dworkin (1986, 67, 234-236; 1983, 288-290, 292-295).

[68] See Dworkin (1985, 170-171; 1983, 2922-294).

interrelated convictions[69]. Hence, the correctness of a judgement or of the contents of a belief may not be assessed independently of the remaining of convictions constituting the conceptual scheme. But a set of independent beliefs cannot act as the criterion of correctness for a particular belief if the body of beliefs is not sufficiently complex and firm, that is, if it is not structured and hierarchical[70].

One of the philosophical currents that have argued for the link between knowledge or interpretation of a phenomenon on the one hand, and the possession of a compact body of belief on the other, is epistemic holism. This view, endorsed by Quine among others, has been quite popular among philosophers. It has been adopted as a fundamental assumption for a number of theories of truth and knowledge. We shall next proceed to analyse some of its features. This shall prove useful to tackle the problem of distinguishing between interpretation and invention from an interpretive point of view.

4.4 QUINE'S EPISTEMIC HOLISM

Holism is an epistemic theory that denies the possibility of separately confronting each one of our beliefs with experience. From a holist point of view, our knowledge is a tight network of logically interrelated beliefs. Consequently, when we produce a judgement about some phenomenon we relate our entire body of beliefs to experience, and not just some part of it[71]. Although, as we shall later see, this position in itself does not escape scepticism, it is nevertheless useful to investigate the idea of internal objectivity.

Quine elaborates his response to the classical empiricist distinction between analytic statements (whose truth depends exclusively on their linguistic component: they are true by definition), and synthetic statements (which can be contrasted directly with experience: their truth is contingent) on the basis of a holistic approach[72]. He shows that this distinction is meaningless unless it is softened. Moreover, he claims, not to assume this relativisation is one of the dogmas of empiricism. In order to support this claim he argues that our knowledge is a network of interconnected beliefs about the tangible

---

[69] See Davidson (1993b, 309-310).

[70] See Dworkin (1985, 170), Putnam (1981, 55-56) and Davidson (1993b, 309-310).

[71] See Marmor (1992, 79).

[72] Quine (1953, 20-47). Quine defines 'empiricism with dogmas' as the theory that posits the two following dogmas: firstly, that there is a qualitative difference between analytic and synthetic truths; and secondly, that 'each meaningful statement is equivalent to some logical construct upon terms which refers to immediate experience'. Quine (1953, 20).

world. In his opinion, this structure meets with reality at its edges only[73]. Analytic statements tend to be positioned in the core of the network, whereas the more synthetic a statement is, the more peripheral a position it occupies within this network. The entire structure puts itself at work every time we confirm or deny a statement. Quine points out that no experience relates to any single statement within this network. He therefore contends that, because of the logical interrelationships among statements, every assertion or denial affects all the statements in the body of belief[74]. For this reason, we cannot evaluate the correctness of an isolated judgement. When we confront one of our beliefs with experience, we are measuring it against our entire epistemic structure. This may force us to reconsider the truth-value of other statements in our epistemic structure.

From this point of view, every judgement is subject to review. This prevents a qualitative differentiation between analytical and synthetic statements - the only difference between them is as to their position within the network. However, the location of a judgement within the network depends only on a pragmatic reason, namely on the likelihood that we choose to review that judgement rather than any other in the event of a negative experience[75]. Thus, Quine observes:

> It becomes folly to seek a boundary between synthetic statements, which hold contingently on experience, and analytic statements, which hold come what may. Any statement can be held true come what may, if we make drastic enough adjustments elsewhere in the system. Even a statement very close to the periphery can be held true in the face of recalcitrant experience by pleading hallucination or by amending certain statements of the kind called logical laws. [76]

Holism provides arguments for the thesis of internal objectivity because it denies the existence of a direct relationship between judgements and their reference, and relates knowledge to the interconnection of beliefs. Notwithstanding, this is insufficient both to account for internal objectivity and to overcome global scepticism. As pointed out by Marmor, epistemic holism is a theory that merely denies the possibility of separately

---

[73] Quine (1953, 42) writes in this sense that 'the totality of our so-called knowledge or beliefs, from the most causal matters of geography and history to the profoundest laws of atomic physics or even of pure mathematics and logic, is a man-made fabric which impinges on experience only along the edges'.

[74] Quine (1953, 42).

[75] Quine (1953, 43-44). Quine claims that, due to pragmatic reasons, we create myths and dogmas such as physical objects or abstract entities that have essentially an epistemic status similar to that of Homer's gods. The belief in the former is simply preferred to the belief in the latter because of their greater usefulness when dealing with experience. See Quine (1953, 44-45).

[76] Quine (1953, 42-43).

confronting each belief with experience[77]. In principle, however, it does not deny the possibility of directly confronting our entire body of beliefs with experience. Therefore, holism does not conflict with empiricism. Because Quine accepts that our epistemic structure comes into contact with the tangible world (albeit only at its edges), his theory fits into empiricist holism. The tangible world causes the sensorial stimuli that explain and justify our beliefs. Quine assumes that the assertion or denial of statements with stimulus meaning (observational statements, that is, statements at the edges of the network) is triggered and justified by sensory stimulation, mostly optical, which acts as a mediator between beliefs and reality. These stimuli determine the correctness of a particular ascription of meaning to these statements. For this reason, stimulus meanings are the only meanings that are fixed or settled [78]. Thus, Quine points out that 'our only source of information about the external world is through the impact of light rays and molecules upon our sensory surfaces' [79].

Davidson's main objection to Quine is based on claims such as the foregoing which, he argues, lead to scepticism[80]. I agree with Davidson that a confrontation of beliefs with reality, either one by one, or as a whole, is useless as a source of justification to our beliefs, for one cannot leave one's own conceptual scheme[81]. Thus, he concludes that no intermediary between convictions and reality warrants the correctness of our judgements. Our senses might be lying to us, and there is no way we can find out about it. He adds that holding that something causes our beliefs does not solve the problem of their justification, for causal intermediaries are not epistemic intermediaries, and the specific question as to the correctness of our judgements is an epistemic one[82]. Consequently, if one accepts Davidson's criticism of Quine, holism cannot offer a

---

[77] Marmor observes (1992, 79) that holism, as a negative thesis, does not necessarily lead to coherentism.

[78] Quine (1960, 32-35; 1953, 46).

[79] Quine (1975, 68).

[80] Davidson's arguments are directed primarily against Quine's advocation of empiricism. Davidson (1993b, 311-314) claims that Quine's theory leads directly to scepticism because if we assume that the mediators between convictions and the tangible world are sensorial schemes, then we must also assume that we may be completely mistaken about what we believe. Thus, Davidson (1993b, 313) observes, 'a person's sensory stimulations could be just as they are and yet the world outside very different'. See also Davidson (1984b, 190-195; 1990, 136). See also his criticism to Neurath's epistemic theory in Davidson (1993a, 320-332). This objection is important because it leads to the conclusion that Quine does not succeed in overcoming semantic realism without falling into scepticism. For this reason, some authors point out that Quine's holism eventually endorses realist semantics according to which truth always transcends evidence. See Rorty (1993, 353; 1980, 221-230).

[81] Davidson (1993b, 312).

[82] Davidson (1993b, 312; 1984b, 194-195).

satisfactory justification to the interpretation-invention dichotomy from an interpretive point of view. Nevertheless, there are other potential candidates to provide such a justification, and Davidson's theory is certainly one of them.

Davidson urges us to abandon the search for an ultimate justification to beliefs in anything other than other beliefs. Instead, he proposes that in order to determine the objective correctness of our judgements, we focus on the relationships among beliefs within a particular conceptual scheme[83]. Davidson's position embodies a form of coherentism that seeks to be compatible with a correspondentist theory of truth.

4.5 DAVIDSON'S EPISTEMIC COHERENTISM

Epistemic coherentism links the knowledge of the truth-value of propositions with the relation of fit between propositions in a particular conceptual scheme. But the question that remains to be answered by this theory is how can this relationship justify the correctness of our judgements. Davidson seeks to answer this question. He points out that:

> What is needed to answer the skeptic is to show that someone with a (more or less) coherent set of beliefs has a reason to suppose his beliefs are not mistaken in the main. What we have shown is that it is absurd to look for a justifying ground for the totality of beliefs, something outside this totality which we can use to test or compare with our beliefs. The answer to our problem must then be to find a reason for supposing most of our beliefs are true that is not a form of evidence.[84]

In *A Coherence Theory of Truth and Knowledge* Davidson sets forth his programme[85]. His starting point is a correspondence theory of truth, that is, he assumes

---

[83] Davidson (1993b, 312-314).

[84] Davidson (1993b, 314; 1993a, 331-332).

[85] In later works, Davidson renounces some of his initial assumptions, particularly those about the compatibility between coherence and a non-trivial sense of correspondence such as the one adopted in this paper. The non-trivial sense of correspondence is one which maintains that the truth of a proposition is established by means of a relationship between language and something external to both language and the speakers, be it either directly (proposition-object) or indirectly (via the principle of satisfaction). As we shall see, Davidson at first assumes Tarski's sense of truth as a non-strictly semantic one. From this standpoint, the Convention T: p is true if and only if p, as a basic definition of truth for a language, does not merely state an equivalence between the name of the sentence and the sentence itself. Tarski claims that a structured language should consist of a set of primitive, verifiable sentences (those we can state as conventions T), as well as all those statements that can be deduced from these by means of rules of inference. But Convention T as a theorem should be verifiable, as Tarski himself contends. By means of the principle of satisfaction, i.e. that a statement is true if it is satisfied by all objects that fulfil the function f (for example, if x is snow, x is white) and otherwise false, Tarski seeks to provide a non-trivial

the truth-value of a proposition to depend on how reality is arranged. A proposition is true if it corresponds with the world[86]. He notes, however, that the idea of correspondence that appears in connection with the notion of truth should be differentiated from the notion of confrontation associated to the problem of the knowledge of the truth-value of propositions. The epistemic problem is, precisely, that we do not possess mechanisms beyond our beliefs to contrast this correspondence. Davidson suggests that, in order to overcome this problem, we render the theory of truth as correspondence consistent with an epistemic theory based on coherence. This is summed up in his slogan: 'correspondence without confrontation'[87]. Correspondence relates to causality, that is, to those facts that trigger or provoke our judgements. But this does not contribute anything new as far as the possibility of confronting our beliefs with the world is concerned. We cannot know what it is that causes our beliefs because we have no referential access to it. Therefore, while correspondence is to be preserved, confrontation should be dismissed. This, in turn, implies denying the existence of intermediaries between beliefs and reality. To this end, we need to make coherence compatible with correspondence[88].

Davidson appeals to the concept of belief to support this compatibility. He claims that every belief is by definition or by nature veridical, that is, a belief exists as a state of mind only if its content is presumed true[89]. This is closely related to the fact that there is no such thing as an isolated belief. A belief always occurs in conjunction with other beliefs, and together they shape an interrelated epistemic structure. Thus, the presumption of truth that defines any belief increases or becomes more powerful if the belief coheres or fits well with the main body of beliefs[90]. Davidson argues that, for this

---

proof to the triviality enunciated by the Convention T. Thus, there emerges a non-trivial and explanatory sense of truth that connects language to something else. This sense of truth is clearly distinct from that which would arise from taking Convention T as an axiom rather than as a theorem. Tarski (1960, 115-130) and Davidson (1984b, 37-54). For Davidson's turn against a Tarskian notion of truth, see Davidson (1990, 134-137).

86 Davidson (1993b, 309; 1984, 37-54).

87 Davidson (1993b, 309-310).

88 Davidson (1993b, 309).

89 Davidson (1993b, 314-315; 1993a, 332).

90 Davidson (1993b, 319). The underlying assumption is that every agent usually knows the meaning of her statements and the contents of her beliefs. This is a crucial point for any epistemic theory. The agent does not determine her own states of mind by means of observing the causal relationships between her beliefs and reality. But she enjoys a privileged position as far as the knowledge of her own states of mind is concerned. Davidson affirms the first person authority in the knowledge of one's own beliefs because global coherence is the only evidence needed by the first person. This means that in order to gain

reason, an agent may admit that she is mistaken with regard to some of her beliefs. This will be yet another belief. But an agent cannot possibly conceive of herself being globally mistaken in all of her beliefs. If she concedes that she may be globally mistaken, she thereby admits that she does not understand her own propositional attitudes. Unlike Quine, Davidson advocates applying the principle of charity to its full extent. This affects the necessary assumptions for the understanding of one's own mental states[91]. An agent can only hope that, if her beliefs are consistent with her entire conceptual scheme, and if each belief is presumed true, most of the time she will be right in what she thinks. In short, charity applied to the first person leads to the conclusion that some descriptions of reality appear to be better than others. Coherence between beliefs is the only piece of evidence we can provide to support the claim that our judgements are objectively true.

Davidson's argument is summed up in the following passage:

> The agent has only to reflect on what a belief is to appreciate that most of his basic beliefs are true, and among his beliefs, those most securely held and that cohere with the main body of his beliefs are the most apt to be true. The question, how do I know my beliefs are generally true? Thus answers itself, simply because beliefs are by nature generally true. Rephrased and expanded, the question becomes, how can I tell whether my beliefs, which are by their nature generally true, are generally true?
>
> All beliefs are justified in this sense: they are supported by numerous other beliefs (otherwise they wouldn't be the beliefs they are), and have a presumption in favor of their truth. The presumption increases the larger and more significant the body of beliefs with which a belief coheres, and there being no such thing as an isolated belief, there is no belief without a presumption in its favor.[92]

---

knowledge of her own beliefs, an agent does not have to confirm that they are true. She need only understand what it means to hold a belief, that is, that beliefs refer to the world and are veridical. In this sense, there is a clear asymmetry between knowing one's own beliefs, and interpreting other speakers' beliefs. In order to know someone else's beliefs, the interpreter needs evidence about the causal relationship between those mental states and the world. Thus, an interpreter can only know the beliefs of the speaker if she can consider them to be by and large correct. See Davidson (1984a, 110, 11; 1993a, 332).

91 Davidson (1984b, 153). Along similar lines, Aarnio (1987, 214), quoting Wittgenstein's remarks stresses that "we can not doubt everything. 'If you tried to doubt everything you would not get as far as doubting anything. The game of doubting itself presupposes certainty'".

92 Davidson (1993b, 319). Note that the presumption of truth is not an ultimate source of evidence. Beliefs constitute this ultimate source since they incorporate, by definition, the presumption of truth of their contents. For Davidson, this presumption replaces the need to provide further evidence. This can be easily understood if we note the difference between presumption and evidence. To claim that something stands as evidence for the truth of a proposition means that it is sufficient to assert its truth. By contrast, presuming a proposition to be true consists in taking the proposition as true although, in fact, it may not be so. The presumption of truth of a proposition eliminates the requirement that sufficient evidence be provided to assert its truth. Davidson's project, then, should be regarded as an attempt to reject that the

Davidson's project has met with some opposition, in particular with regard to its aim to render coherence consistent with correspondence[93]. A careful reading of his work reveals that Davidson himself acknowledges that possessing a coherent scheme of beliefs merely implies the presumption of truth of what we believe. Coherence is not a mechanism to reach correspondence in the classical sense that Davidson still defends in *A Coherence Theory of Truth and Knowledge*, that is, a non-epistemic sense of truth[94]. Coherence only leads to the presumption of truth, not to truth as correspondence between propositions and reality. The attempt to reconcile coherence and correspondence falls short of its purpose. Davidson provides good reasons to argue that the justification to our beliefs can only lie in our own beliefs. This is all we can do; and moreover it seems sufficient if we truly communicate and interact with the world, or if we assume we do so. The presumption of truth, as pointed out earlier, only avoids having to provide further evidence to our claims. It is not a new intermediary between beliefs and the world, as Davidson himself would admit. If it is not a new mediator, Davidson's theory does little to render compatible a coherence theory of knowledge with a correspondence theory of truth. Such a theory of truth understands truth to be a non-epistemic notion. Accordingly, it establishes a clear-cut distinction between truth and

---

ultimate justification of knowledge may be linked to sufficient evidence as sufficient proof. This is a good argument on which to dismiss scepticism, for scepticism only embodies the disillusion of not being able to provide sufficient evidence, which results from relating the justification of knowledge to the notion of evidence.

93 See Davidson (1993b, 309).

94 See Davidson (1993b, 309). It has already been noted that Davidson assumes Tarski's correspondentist notion of truth even though he disagrees that it be a merely semantic concept. Davidson distinguishes between a correspondentist view such as Aristotle's, for whom words are directly linked to the world, and Tarski's, who establishes a more complex relationship between words and the world by means of the principle of satisfaction. In both views, the notion of truth plays an explanatory role. Davidson (1984b, 48) thus writes that 'the semantic concept of truth as developed by Tarski deserves to be called a correspondence theory because of the part played by the concept of satisfaction; for clearly what has been done is that the property of being true has been explained, and non-trivially, in terms of a relation between language and something else'. See also Davidson (1984b, 50-54). See also his refutation of Ramsey's theory of truth as redundancy. (Truth as redundancy is the theory of truth that holds that the expression 'to be true' does not add meaning to a statement. According to this view, this expression is used merely to emphasise or endorse what is being asserted.) See Davidson (1984b, 40-46). As we shall see, Davidson has changed his mind in later years and seems to have discarded truth as correspondence, thus denying the possibility of presenting the predicate 'to be true' as non-trivial or non-redundant. See, for instance, Davidson (1996, 263-278).

assertability[95]. Hence, Davidson maintains two conflicting aims: he seeks to reject the empiricist dualism between conceptual scheme and reality without giving up the notion of truth as correspondence.

Rorty's arguments against Davidson develop along similar lines: he claims that Davidson confusingly tries to reduce the notion of truth as correspondence to its minimal expression. As a result, the property of being true is void of explanatory value in that affirming the truth of a statement no longer relates our judgements to something external to them[96]. But, Rorty observes, Davidson uses obsolete language and, as a consequence, continues to advocate the possibility of reconciling coherence and Tarskian correspondence, and is oblivious of the minimal or trivial sense of truth that his project should embrace[97]. Rorty suggests that Davidson's perspective be re-interpreted as a dismissal of any attempt at offering a non-trivial sense of truth. Thus, Davidson's theory can be rendered consistent with his own anti-empiricist view. Davidson took on board some of Rorty's criticism, as is reflected in his *Afterthoughts, 1987* to *A Coherence Theory of Truth and Knowledge*. In this later work Davidson admits that he should not have presented his project as an attempt to show that coherence leads to correspondence[98]. He further admits that claiming the impossibility of going beyond internal evidence prevents advocating a correspondence theory that somehow links words to objects[99]. In addition, he notes that he should never have called his theory a coherentist theory because the notion of internal coherence among beliefs can only be understood as a negative thesis, namely, that it is impossible to find justification beyond coherence. According to Davidson, transforming this thesis into a

---

[95] The distinction between epistemic and non-epistemic theories of truth is due to Putnam. Theories of truth as assertability are epistemic, whereas theories of truth as correspondence are non-epistemic. See Putnam (1981, 49-56).

[96] Rorty (1993, 333-336).

[97] In this sense, Rorty claims that his interpretation of Davidson's position has to deal with the fact that Davidson presents his theory as an attempt to show how coherence leads to correspondence. Rorty accuses Davidson of not realising that correspondence without confrontation does not reconcile coherence with correspondence. Rather, correspondence without confrontation obliterates the very idea of correspondence. Thus, in order to preserve the achievement of Davidson's programme, we are urged to ignore, for example, Davidson's claim that despite 'we cannot get outside our beliefs and our language so as to find some test other than coherence we nevertheless can have knowledge and talk about an objective public world which is not of our making' (Rorty, 1993, 342). Rorty urges Davidson to abandon his attempt to show that coherence leads to correspondence because this idea is mistaken. See Rorty (1993, 342-345). See also Davidson (1993b, 309).

[98] Davidson (1990, 134; 1996, 263-278).

[99] Davidson (1990, 134-135).

positive view leads to idealism, the theory that claims that truth and reality are constructs of the mind, and that, therefore, ideas and beliefs are all that exists[100]. Thus, Davidson comes to the conclusion that his perspective has little to do with a genuine coherence theory. For this reason, he would accept no form of theory of truth as assertability[101]. In short, Davidson ultimately advocates a minimal or trivial sense of truth. But he does not join sceptics because, in his opinion, arguing that beliefs are veridical by nature enables him not 'to abandon the attempt to provide a general justification for knowledge claims'[102].

It is not clear to me how Davidson could overcome the sceptic 'anything goes' by minimising the notion of truth. As argued by Putnam in response to theories of truth as redundancy, to deny that there is a property of truth or correctness, not in the realist sense but in any sense, is to deny that our judgements and assertions are judgements and assertions. Along Putnam's line of criticism, these judgements would be no more than mere noise[103]. I believe Putnam's criticism to be appropriate because the objectivity postulate requires that we be able to discriminate (at least partially) arguments that are correct with respect to a certain phenomenon from those which are not.

Davidson leaves unanswered the question what does eliminating truth as correspondence and maintaining that beliefs are veridical by definition accrue to the possibility of offering a general justification to our judgements[104]. He simply insists that he need not assume a theory of truth as assertability. It could be argued that precisely this is Davidson's mistake if his aim is to distance himself from Rorty's scepticism once he has taken on board Rorty's criticism. Consequently, it appears that Davidson's terms are not appropriate to discuss and account for the distinction between interpretation and invention without falling into realism. Does this then mean that there is no way of making sense of this dichotomy? Is every attempt doomed to fall into scepticism? I do not believe this to be the case. In order to offer a negative answer to these questions, we should adequately reconstruct a theory of truth as assertability that successfully demonstrates the following three points: a) that the acceptability of a coherence theory requires neither that coherence be compatible with correspondence nor a trivial sense of truth; b) that truth as assertability does not necessarily lead to idealism; c) that a theory of truth as assertability can offer (non-arbitrary) criteria to guarantee that some

100 Davidson (1990, 135).
101 Davidson (1990, 136).
102 Davidson (1990, 137).
103 Putnam (1983, xiv-xv; 1990, 113-114).
104 Davidson (1990, 136-137).

judgements are more correct than others. Such a reconstruction of a theory of truth as assertability will be the aim of the coming chapter.

4.6 FINAL REMARKS

We have pointed out that the viability of the dichotomy between interpretation and invention requires that it be established in terms of objectivity. External objectivity is meaningless because it requires assuming semantic realism. We have analysed Ronald Dworkin's proposal on internal objectivity. Moreover, we have considered Stanley Fish's objections to this proposal, and drawn attention to the fact that in order to succeed in refuting Fish's objections, the philosophical grounds of Dworkin's theory on internal objectivity should be sound. To this end, we have explored two alternatives that seek to provide arguments for a general justification of judgements within a conceptual scheme, both of which seem to fail: Quine's holism and Davidson's epistemic coherentism. Quine's holism is still too close to empiricism and leads to scepticism. Davidson's coherence theory is of anti-empiricist descent but equally unsuccessful because 'correspondence without confrontation' does not work if we do not abandon the idea of correspondence itself. Moreover, Davidson's later turn towards a notion of truth as redundancy appears to place him back into scepticism or pragmatism.

In order to make sense of the claim that after an evaluation process we have reached the correct answer (not only because we believe it so, but because this is indeed the best answer), a thesis that seeks to incorporate internal objectivity must assign a significant role to the notion of truth. Without an explanatory idea of correctness or truth we are eventually bound to accept that we cannot evaluate judgements, and therefore, that no interpretation is better than any other. Putnam and Dworkin seem to endorse an explanatory sense of 'truth', and replace correspondence with coherence. Dworkin appeals to narrative consistency as the criterion of truth for legal statements, whereas Putnam devises a notion of truth as coherence under ideal epistemic conditions. As we shall see, neither of these proposals leads to idealism because an idealist or solipsist position requires a genuinely correspondentist (non-epistemic) sense of truth[105]. Doubts may leap to mind as to what is the concept of truth supported by Dworkin given that on some occasions he asserts that adding 'truly' or 'objectively' to a statement such as that

---

105 To our purposes, it suffices to note that in order to make such an assertion we need to adopt externalism. In other words, we ought to concede that we can go outside our own beliefs to confirm (regardless of our beliefs) that mental states are the only entities that exist. This amounts to replacing an ontology of uninterpreted objects with an ontology of uninterpreted beliefs.

slavery is unjust does not alter the meaning of the original statement[106]. I would like to stress that this view should not be mistaken for a minimal notion of truth. Dworkin argues that truth or correctness are notions internal to a particular language game and clearly in opposition to an externalist view[107]. The language of truth serves the clarification of the meaning of judgements as judgements about what the practice demands, and not as judgements about our emotions or tastes. As will be shown in Chapter 5, Dworkin seems to consider that internal objectivity is successful as a justification to why some judgements appear to be more correct than others[108]. Thus, Dworkin does not advocate that a particular argument about the practice is either correct or true only because it is an argument, or else, it is not even an argument, as we ought to conclude if we assume truth as redundancy. Dworkin's theory leads to the claim that the truth-value of a proposition depends on how it coheres with the best theory about the object of interpretation. This results from substituting truth as correspondence with truth as assertability or truth as coherence.

In the next chapter we will turn to an investigation of the parallelism between Putnam's and Dworkin's theories. We will analyse the advantages of these positions to account for a genuine distinction between interpretation and invention. For this reason, we will postpone answering the question about how an interpretive theory such as Dworkin's may refute Fish's sceptical criticism and yet avoid semantic realism.

---

[106] See, for instance, Dworkin (1986, 81-83; 1985, 172).

[107] Consider the statements 'slavery is unjust' and 'slavery is really unjust'. Dworkin claims that the second statement is not linking language to something independent of conceptual schemes. The term 'really' only adds that what is being claimed is the result of the best argument about what is being interpreted. It is in this sense that Dworkin claims there to be no difference between the two judgements. Therefore, in identifying these two statements, Dworkin is not sacrificing the possibility of objective justification of statements. He only makes this possibility internal to a certain theory. See Dworkin (1996, 103-108). For a discussion on the statement 'abortion is incorrect', see (1996, 96-99).

[108] Dworkin (1983, 299).

CHAPTER 5

COHERENCE IN LEGAL INTERPRETATION

5.1 INTRODUCTION

In the previous chapter we presented Dworkin's theory as an attempt to render the existence of objective restrictions to judgements about the legal practice compatible with the denial of semantic realism. Dworkin's strategy is based on two ideas: on the one hand, that every legal judgement is theory-dependent and internal to a particular social practice; on the other, that the correctness of legal judgements can and ought to be sought within the theory or interpretive scheme that gives rise to them. But hitherto we have only outlined the negative aspect of Dworkin's position, and the conclusion intended by the thesis of internal objectivity, namely, that there are genuine restrictions to interpretation. We shall now turn to investigate how Dworkin justifies this conclusion. It was pointed out that the justification of this conclusion requires addressing some issues regarding the problem of knowledge and the truth of legal propositions. We contended that neither empiricist holism nor Davidson's coherentism warrant objectivity, and therefore none of them overcome scepticism.

The main problem of these two theories is that they maintain a non-epistemic concept of truth, a non-trivial sense of correspondence. As we shall see in this chapter, the sceptical challenge can be successfully refuted. We noted that Rorty's pragmatism as well as Davidson's turn provide good arguments to abandon a strictly correspondentist theory of truth. However, this does not necessarily imply that we resort to a minimal or non-explanatory sense of 'truth'. Doing so would inevitably yield a discouraging picture in which arguments about what is demanded by the law do not interpret the legal practice, and in which there is no room for discussion, disagreement, and debate, in which arguments are then mere inventions resulting from interpreters' will and preferences[1]. Our legal language game would then become pointless because a language game is a game with rules and criteria, of right and wrong and successful and unsuccessful moves[2]. Sceptics thereby deny the possibility of asserting the existence of a social practice in which actions are perceived and understood in a converging way by participants.

At this point, we are urged to abandon such a crude vision, not because of its crudeness, but because of its unfeasibility. Scepticism uses externalism (that is, that its own judgements are theory-independent) to prove that this panorama is inescapable[3]. However, we also assumed that there is no external discourse independent of reasons and convictions to evaluate the correctness of our judgements. For this reason, neither the sceptical nor any other panorama is inescapable. Sceptics should provide convincing arguments for the inevitability of their picture and show that their point of view is the most correct one. I will argue that there are reasons to hold a more optimistic view that rejects both correspondence and truth as redundancy. This is the view that ascribes explanatory meaning to the term 'truth' and connects it to assertability and coherence instead of correspondence. In the previous chapter Dworkin and Putnam were shown to be circumscribed within this philosophical line of thought. If their claims obtain, their position will enable them to warrant that certain judgements are objectively correct. Before we undertake a detailed analysis of this position, it is worth noting a fundamental difference between Dworkin and Putnam: while Dworkin seems overwhelmingly optimistic about the possibility of always finding the right answer in interpretation, Putnam never intends to host such optimism[4]. This difference will prompt us to examine carefully the existing arguments to claim or deny not only global scepticism, but also partial scepticism as the best reconstructions of the legal practice.

5.2 TRUTH, ASSERTABILITY AND COHERENCE

Davidson's principle of charity shows that understanding a social practice requires optimising agreement in judgements. Thus, we need to be able to assume that other participants take to be true many of the propositions we consider true[5]. However, the

---

1 On this point see Putnam's (1995c, 74-75; 1996, 9-12) and Dworkin's (1991b, 360-364, 366-369) criticism to Rorty as a disillusioned metaphysical realist. For Rorty's sceptical position, see (1991b, 89-95).

2 See, for instance, Putnam (1992, 177-179).

3 See Putnam (1990, 32) and Dworkin (1996, 88; 1983, 302).

4 See Putnam (1995a, 6-7) and Dworkin (1985, 137-145; 1991a, 88-90).

5 Note that the first formulation of the principle of charity is due to Wilson (1959, 531).

principle of charity is of an epistemic character. It does not provide any information about the truth conditions of propositions. What makes participants' judgements true or false, correct or incorrect once correspondence is rated unintelligible?

Truth or correctness is our means of assessing each one of our assertions and those of other participants (for otherwise, our assertions would not have the character we attribute to them). If someone claimed that the death penalty is permitted in the Spanish Legal Order, one would point to her that she is wrong because her assertion is false. But just claiming that it is false does little for its truth or falsity. The original speaker may affirm the truth of her proposition and simply claim that her interlocutor is wrong. If this were all we could say about the truth or falsity of propositions, legal discussion would be extremely poor and limited. Views on matters may differ from one individual to the next. Sceptics contend that uttering these opinions is all that can be done regarding the truth of our judgements. This is unfortunate an interpretation of our language game in connection with a social phenomenon. Claiming that the death penalty is prohibited does not constitute an argument about its legal qualification. It is pointless even as a statement unless it can be backed up with argument. We often use the language of truth and falsity when debating. We tend not to assess the truthfulness of our judgements in private unless we are in doubt or reflecting about our beliefs after realising some misalignment between them[6]. The context of truth therefore appears not to be dissociated from that of the justification of judgements. For this reason, once we abandon the notion of correspondence, truth appears to be linked to the discursive force of arguments. When certain arguments cannot be defeated by any other argument, they momentarily act as a definitive test for the correctness of our assertions. We shall later see that this test is just a mechanism to distinguish between those conclusions, which result from a successful justificatory process from those which do not. Let us return to the discussion about the death penalty. If we claim that it is true that the death penalty is not permitted in the Spanish Legal Order, we are thereby claiming that we have sufficient arguments to prove so, and that the opposite view, namely that which contends that the death penalty is permitted, is wrong insofar that it is unable to refute our arguments. Thus, when using the term 'truth' we are not assuming to have accessed the reference of our judgements, but that we can offer the best theory or arguments about the issue in hand. What about the question whether the death penalty is really permitted in the Spanish legal system? In Putnam's own words, 'my view is that God

---

[6] This, however, does not mean that the term 'truth' can be meaningfully used only when there is controversy or doubt. I just wish to stress that it is most relevant in case of controversy.

himself, if he consented to answer the question [...], would say "I don't know"; not because His omniscience is limited, but because there is a limit to how far questions make sense'[7].

By no means should these preliminary remarks lead to the conclusion that the problem of the truth-value of legal propositions is a simple one. I just wish to emphasise that every intelligible position about the notion of truth should draw some kind of equivalence between truth and assertability: to claim that a statement is true is to assert that it can be justified[8].

This equivalence is a premise to the theory of truth as coherence. In line with antirealism this theory asserts that 'the contents of the statement is given, not by what renders it true or false independently of our knowledge, but by what we take as a legitimate ground for asserting it or for denying it'[9]. Hence, coherence theory can be seen as a philosophical enterprise that seeks to determine when is there legitimate

---

7 Putnam (1987, 19). In a similar sense, Dworkin (1985, 172) observes that 'we should account to ourselves for our own convictions as best as we can, standing ready to abandon those that do not survive reflective inspection. We should make such arguments to others, who do not share our opinions, as we can make with good faith and break off arguing when no further argument is appropriate. I do not mean that this is all we can do because we are creatures with limited access to true reality or with necessarily parochial viewpoints. I mean that we can give no sense to the idea that there is anything else we could do in deciding whether our judgements are "really" true'.

8 Putnam (1981, 55-56; 1990, 41-42, 114-115). Note that Putnam assumes the equivalence of truth and assertability by relating truth to rational acceptability in ideal epistemic conditions. The notion of truth as idealised assertability faces some difficulties to reject metaphysical realism and scepticism. The reason for this lies in that an idealisation of what is rationally acceptable dissociates truth from the agents' epistemic abilities and yet truth remains something internal to agents. This position breaches the thesis of internal realism for it renders truth theory-dependent but inaccessible. This, in turn, means giving in to sceptical criticism. However, Putnam view appears ambiguous on this point. We will take advantage of this ambiguity to present his internal realism as a position that postulates a theory-dependent and accessible notion of truth insofar as it is meaningful for the agents to think and act *as if* they were in ideal epistemic conditions. Such a position permits an intelligible notion of truth internal to a particular language game in which *as if* is the criterion to assess the correctness of judgements. This criterion is meaningful as long as *as if* cannot be replaced with something external to the language game that indicates whether or not we really are in ideal epistemic conditions, or know that we are in such conditions, or they obtain at all. Hence, we will pursue Putnam's remark (1981, 55) that 'we speak as if there were such things as epistemologically ideal conditions, and we call a statement "true" if it would be justified under such conditions'. In addition, we will assume his thesis that the specification of ideal or sufficient epistemic conditions is a question that can only be answered in the very process of inquiry. Putnam (1981, 55-56).

9 Dummet (1978, xxvii).

ground for asserting what we assert, and then, when is it the case that our judgements are true[10].

5.2.1 Coherentism as an epistemic theory, and as a theory of truth

To show the applicability of this philosophical perspective in legal interpretation we are urged to separate a theory of truth as coherence from epistemic coherentism. These are two versions of coherentism with different scope. But before we embark on an analysis of this point, it is worth noting and distancing ourselves from Raz's distinction between constitutive and epistemic coherence. In my opinion, this distinction does little to clarify the point at stake.

Constitutive coherence and epistemic coherence

In his well known article *The Relevance of Coherence*, Joseph Raz advocates differentiating two kinds of coherence: constitutive and epistemic coherence. This distinction purports to discriminate between a theory of truth as coherence and epistemic coherentism. However, I will show that his proposal does in fact not succeed in doing so.

Raz asserts that epistemic coherence is a mechanism to justify beliefs. Thus, a belief will be justified if it is the case that it coheres better than any other with the agent's body of beliefs[11]. Constitutive coherence, by contrast, is a criterion to assert or deny the truth of a proposition. According to Raz, the coherence attributed to the reference of propositions is what renders them true or false[12]. Thus, while epistemic coherence refers only to beliefs and their subjective justification within a body of convictions, constitutive coherence refers to the very nature of the phenomenon we seek to explain. Raz claims for this reason that in the legal context 'it is not always clearly understood that the jurisprudential theories of coherence are not epistemic, but constitutive'[13].

---

[10] It is important to note that coherence among beliefs can be adopted as a theory of truth only if truth and assertability are regarded as equivalent. Otherwise, coherence can only be thought of as an epistemic theory that often occurs in conjunction with what we will call 'optimistic semantic realism'. This position assumes that a coherent structure of beliefs yields the correspondence between judgements and the world. We have previously noted that Davidson's first approach to coherence theory as well as Quine's empiricist holism fit into this line of thought. In the legal context, Michael Moore is the most representative thinker. On this issue, see Moore (1985, 309-313). See also Peczenik (1989, 184-186) and his idea that if a theory is perfectly coherent, then it corresponds to truth-makers, that is, to the world.

[11] Raz (1992, 275-276).

[12] Raz (1992, 275, 282-283).

[13] Raz (1992, 283).

Moreover, he asserts, that legal theories based on constitutive coherence are more plausible than epistemic theories because 'we are now concerned not with coherence of beliefs but with the coherence of legal norms, rules, standards, doctrines, and principles'[14].

Raz's distinction presumes two different types of coherence being the basis for two diverging and separate versions of coherentism that, at times, seem irreconcilable. In addition, their explanatory purposes do not coincide[15]. This clear separation between both positions is bizarre. Its peculiarity seems to be due primarily to the obscurity of his characterisation of constitutive coherence. Constitutive coherence seems to be unrelated to the justification of someone's beliefs about law, but not so to the truth of these beliefs or of their propositional contents[16]. However, this truth can no longer be thought of as an adjustment between propositions within a propositional scheme because a propositional scheme is simply the contents of a scheme of beliefs. According to Raz, coherence between beliefs is a matter of epistemic coherence. However, epistemic coherence yields no information about the truth-value of legal propositions. The question then is what does constitutive coherence turn out to be, and what does it match? If the answer to this question is that constitutive coherence does not refer to the idea of adjustment, why should we call it 'coherence'?

Raz's proposal becomes more intelligible under the light that constitutive coherence does not refer to the contents of a particular conceptual scheme, that is, to a relationship between propositions, but to the very reference our judgements correspond with. Law as an object of interpretation is regarded by constitutive coherence as a coherent, orderly, and systematic structure by virtue of the nature of the legal phenomenon and

---

[14] Raz (1992, 284).

[15] Raz (1992, 275, 283). Raz discusses the consequences of a possible reconciliation between these two positions. In this sense, Raz (1992, 283) points out that 'the claim would be that if justified beliefs form a coherent whole then so does the reality they represent. The subjective and the objective, the beliefs and the reality they are about must, when the beliefs are true, mirror each other'. If rendering epistemic coherence compatible with constitutive coherence leads to this conclusion, this notion of constitutive coherence is not the one advocated by a coherence theory of truth. No advocate of a coherence theory of truth would admit that coherence permits access to the reference of judgements. In his definition of constitutive coherence, Raz seems to attribute to it a notion of truth as correspondence according to which everything that is external to judgements is coherent - Raz is not proposing a notion of truth that replaces correspondence. This ascription is most evident when he observes that the success of this theory relies heavily on whether law is in fact coherent or sufficiently coherent, Raz (1992, 284, 290-297).

[16] Raz (1992, 284).

not merely because we believe or need to believe it so[17]. Whether or not this view is right depends on whether or not law is in fact a coherent whole or, at least, a sufficiently coherent whole[18]. Raz's criticism to this position is that the legal phenomenon is constituted by authoritative acts that remain such acts even if they do not cohere with other acts and standards. Thus, for Raz, coherence cannot act as a criterion for truth of legal propositions. Raz claims that a coherence theory of law is not admissible as a version of law if it does not regard the existence of normative authorities as a fundamental element of the nature of law.[19]. However, this claim needs further justification. Why would a theory that does not do so not be a genuine theory of law? Given the choice of answers: a) because it does not reflect the reality of law; b) because it is not the best reconstruction of the legal phenomenon, Raz would presumably choose the first option. Notwithstanding, this answer would have no consequences for a constitutive coherence theory if such a theory were a theory of truth as coherence.

Raz presents constitutive coherentism as a form of correspondence theory of truth according to which the correctness of our judgements depends on something external to them that is itself coherent[20]. However, on some occasions, Raz seems to regard this position as an epistemic approach to the understanding of law that, nevertheless, deviates from epistemic coherence in that it develops along the lines of Davidson's

---

17 Raz seems to hold this position throughout his article (1992, 282-287, 290-297). It may be claimed that Raz's reconstruction of constitutive coherence is obscure because he simultaneously describes and criticises it: in addition to describing constitutive coherence, he reformulates its problematic elements such as, for instance, the assumption that the relation of fit within a body of beliefs can be taken as a criterion of truth for their propositional contents. Raz seeks to extend coherence to law as an uninterpreted phenomenon, and not to the theories or reconstructions of law as interpretations of this phenomenon. He thus establishes the distinction scheme-world that coherentists have long tried to deny. This enables Raz to distinguish propositions *of* law, i.e. those that report on what is prescribed by law, from propositions *about* law, those which reflect the contents of our legal beliefs or legal theories.

18 Raz claims that constitutive coherence is one way of accounting for the nature of law. This, according to this author, is equivalent to accounting for the nature of things independently of what agents think of them. For this reason, this position aims at showing that the legal phenomenon is, by nature, coherent. See Raz (1992, 283).

19 Raz (1992, 290-297).

20 His distinction between epistemic coherence as a subjective justification of beliefs on the one hand, and constitutive coherence as something that is predicated independently of conceptual schemes on the other, can only be grasped in these terms. Note that this version af a theory of truth as correspondence seems to be defended in the legal context by Peczenik. Peczenik (1989, 186) assumes the presence of an essential connection between correspondence and coherence: if a theory corresponds to the world, then it is highly coherent. He asserts that 'this thesis would be false had the world been chaotic. But if one assumes that the world is relatively ordered and stable, then it is plausible'.

principle of charity. Thus, constitutive coherence would argue that in order to grasp a social phenomenon coherence should be assumed. Raz contends that this assumption does not lead to the conclusion that law, as a product of human actions, beliefs, and will, be coherent[21]. I agree with Raz's claim, but not with the argument leading to it: his claim is correct, though not because this position falls into the fallacy of assuming that the coherence required to grasp something makes the reference a coherent whole, but because, as an epistemic theory, this version of constitutive coherentism merely seeks to evince when is it the case that a judgement about law is justified. It is not clear to me why Raz links this issue to constitutive coherence rather than to epistemic coherence. Clearly, Davidson's principle of charity is a strategy to justify beliefs, and this is precisely the role of epistemic coherence. Charity indicates which assumptions we should make to grasp something from the standpoint of our own conceptual scheme, that is, what is it we need for our beliefs to be justified. But charity remains silent as to the truth-value of our judgements[22]. The relationship between a body of justified beliefs and the truth of its contents depends on the theory of truth one adopts.

To conclude, Raz's reconstruction of constitutive coherence in my view does not represent a theory of truth as coherence. We will establish a distinction between a theory of truth as coherence and a coherentist epistemic theory. Raz seems little interested in this matter. For this reason, he constructs two versions of coherentism that bear little in common - they can each be separately analysed and assessed[23]. In contrast with Raz's idea of constitutive coherentism, identifying truth with assertability is the starting point of a theory of truth as coherence. The notion of truth as correspondence is thus replaced with a further explanatory notion of truth. Finally, this theory claims that coherence is a relation of fit among the propositional contents of beliefs.

Back to the point

A theory of truth as coherence takes adjustment between beliefs as the criterion to justify them[24]. But since it understands truth and assertability to be equivalent, it

---

21 Raz (1992, 289-290).

22 It was pointed out in Chapter 4 that Davidson maintained a notion of truth based on correspondence in much of his work even though he advocated epistemic coherentism.

23 If constitutive coherence were a theory of truth as coherence it would not be possible to assume that it is more plausible than an epistemic coherence theory, as constitutive coherence would then grant a broader scope to the adjustment among beliefs than epistemic coherence theory actually does.

24 In line with Alston, the following aspects characterise epistemic justification: a) it applies to beliefs; b) it is an evaluative concept, that is, it implies that there is something satisfactory or correct about the fact that an agent holds certain beliefs; c) its evaluative dimension is from an epistemic point of view only.

concludes that the truth-value of propositions does not transcend the justification offered by the relation of fit among beliefs. For this reason, an inquiry into whether the propositional contents of a belief is true or not is in fact an inquiry into how it coheres with the rest of beliefs in a conceptual scheme. It is clear that this position requires accepting some form of epistemic coherentism as a way to justify beliefs. Coherence can act as a criterion of truth only if it is possible to assume that a coherent scheme of convictions is internally justified. A relationship between epistemic theory and coherence theory of truth can be thus readily established. Epistemic coherentism need not specify what makes a proposition true. As an epistemic position, its main goal is to show that coherence is the best criterion to justify beliefs in a cognitive scheme. This epistemic approach has sometimes been reconciled, with different degrees of success, with a number of theories of truth. One of them, namely the coherence theory of truth, adopts coherence as the criterion for the justification of beliefs but, given that it identifies justification with truth, it uses coherence as a test for the truth of the propositional contents of beliefs.

Henceforth we will focus our attention on coherentism as a theory of truth. It is worth noting that coherence may become a test for truth only insofar as it is a plausible test for the justification of beliefs. Thus, a mechanism should be devised to go from coherence as justification to coherence as truth. To do this, we will be compelled to resort to the conceptual tools of epistemic coherentism[25].

Epistemic justification is a tool to assess beliefs that merely takes into account their adequacy to their 'aim at mazimizing truth and minimizing falsity in a large body of beliefs'; d) it is a matter of degree. For instance, if we relate justification to an agent's evidence for the truth of what she asserts, the extent to which her beliefs are justified depends on the strength and amount of evidence she possesses. See Alston (1989, 83-84).

25 Henceforth, whenever we consider coherence within an epistemic structure we will essentially focus on the relationships among beliefs. True, other mental states such as desires, intentions, and preferences are also part of human psychology. But it is of utmost importance to distinguish beliefs from these other states of mind when undertaking an analysis of theoretical reasoning. Theoretical reasoning involves a particular epistemic attitude and hence relates to our views of how things are. Here, beliefs and their interrelationships play a crucial role. Practical reasoning, by contrast, refers to actions and is therefore connected to what is the thing to do. For this reason, practical reasoning is directly linked to intentions, desires and preferences. Notwithstanding, the relationship between beliefs and intentions and desires is not to be overlooked or neglected. This connection will become clear when we inquire into the role of coherence in a practice such as the legal practice, in which participants conceive the existence of law as a reason for action, that is, as a criterion to evaluate their own behaviour as well as that of their peers. The epistemic standpoint, however, has some conceptual priority over the normative one insofar that, along Harman's line of argument, the formation of intentions presumes holding some beliefs. On this point and on the distinction between these two kinds of reasoning, see Harman (1986, 68, 113, 116).

5.3 THE THEORY OF TRUTH AS COHERENCE

We noted earlier that once we assume equivalence between truth and assertability, we are prompted to assume that truth does not transcend what we are entitled to assert. At the same time, denying every form of externalism leads to the conclusion that we cannot stand outside ourselves to access both other conceptual schemes and reality. Thus, although the truth-assertability of a judgement lies in its justification, it cannot embody its external justification, that justification independent of conceptual schemes. Neither can the truth-assertability of judgements become their subjective justification, if we associate subjective justification with individual voluntarism[26]. It is at this point important to recall that a belief can only be justified by other beliefs. Hence, truth-assertability is always internal to an epistemic structure. This, however, does not mean that it reflects individual preferences. Assertability tests the correctness of our judgements. In coherentist terms, however, this is a test concerning the relationship among beliefs in a body of convictions. This test indicates what this relationship should be like in order for the structure to be sufficiently sound to enable us to discriminate between what we are and are not entitled to assert.

As can easily be perceived from the above argument, the notion of justification endorsing assertability does not depend on each individual belief, but on the soundness of our epistemic structure as a whole. Any belief can be false, not on the grounds that it misrepresents reality, but because it may be unjustified[27]. The justification to each belief, in turn, should be measured in terms of a tightly interconnected body of mental states. This is the reason why, every philosophical position attempting to answer the question about how to refute semantic realism without falling into scepticism should provide a criterion to establish when a conceptual scheme is sufficiently sound. Complexity and coherence may become such criteria. For truth-assertability to make sense we need a sufficiently complex structure displaying coherence among its elements. If it is possible to combine complexity and coherence, we will have a sound epistemic scheme. But, how does soundness contribute towards assertability? It is certainly not an intermediary between our beliefs and the world; neither does it free our epistemic structure from being subject to review. Soundness enables us to claim that at

[26] As pointed out before, in social practice, these schemes tend to converge. Therefore, 'dependence of a scheme' here refers to a collection of individuals who share or presume they share some of the more basic aspects of their conceptual schemes.

[27] This means that we have no sufficient reasons or evidence within our conceptual structure to incorporate or maintain such a belief as part of our general scheme of beliefs. Moreover, as will be shown, in a holistic line, no specific belief can justify itself nor free itself from the need for justification.

a particular moment in time, our justifications and explanations are complete and satisfactory; that is, at this point there is no room for further argument because we have already provided the right interpretation[28]. In my opinion, this suffices to account for truth-assertability. To claim otherwise is not to reject that soundness be sufficient to truth as assertability. Rather, it implies rejecting this notion of truth in favour of the more implausible notion of truth as correspondence. Notwithstanding, it remains to be shown how coherence and complexity lead to the soundness of a scheme and how soundness, in turn, leads to truth-assertability.

5.3.1 Coherence and complexity

Coherence in the justification of beliefs

Coherence can be understood either as a property or as a relationship[29]. As a property, it is usually one said of a system of beliefs (i.e. of the propositional contents of a collection of mental states) that constitutes a unitary and harmonic whole[30]. Following BonJour, coherence as a property is measured not only in terms of consistency (i.e. non-contradiction) but in terms of inductive, justificatory, probabilistic, and explanatory links as well[31]. Consistency, as Peczenik stresses, is thus a necessary but not sufficient condition of coherence[32]. The latter tends to be evaluated in holistic

---

28 On this point, see Putnam's parallelism (1987, 79, 85-86) between ethical and scientific statements. See also Dworkin (1996, 117-118).

29 We will pay little attention to this distinction because to say of a system of beliefs that it is coherent requires that there be coherence relationships among the different beliefs. On this point, see Bender (1989, 2-3).

30 See Bender (1989, 2-5). About coherence as a property of a system of rules, see MacCormick (1984, 235-236), Peczenik (1989, 159-161), Gianformaggio (1990, 403-405), and Villa (1990, 432-433).

31 Note that from an internalist point of view, probability is to be interpreted in terms of confidence or of mutual support among beliefs. On the properties mentioned in the main text, see Goldman's account of BonJour's theory, Goldman (1989, 125). Similarly, Harman observes (1986, 32) that coherence 'includes not only consistency but also a network of relations among one's beliefs, especially relations of implication and explanation'. On this point see also the correlation Kress establishes between the higher or lower degree of coherence of a theory or system of beliefs on the one hand, and, on the other, the extent to which this theory or system displays consistency, comprehensiveness, completeness, monism, unity - internal relationships of justification, implication or mutual support, articulateness, and justifiability. Kress addresses each one of these properties separately and analyses the extent to which they can be considered conceptually linked to the idea of coherence. See Kress (1996, 533-534, 539-543).

32 Peczenik (1989, 158-159; 1992, 183). See also Alexy and Peczenik (1989, 130-131), Aarnio (1987, 199), and Villa (1990, 433) .

terms, that is, the epistemic scheme is conceived as a complex network of beliefs connected to each other in a variety of ways. Every element in this network is dependent on every other element, and liable to be revised to attain a balanced scheme[33]. Coherence as a property can be reduced to this global equilibrium. Perhaps for this reason, coherence can be presented as a rival to the classical notion of deductive system to account for our cognitive structures. It would then replace a reconstruction of the cognitive structure on the basis of axioms or ultimate foundations plus deductivility relations. Henceforth, however, we shall focus our attention on coherence as a relationship.

Coherence as a relationship refers to the connections of fit among beliefs, or between beliefs on the one hand, and the total body of belief on the other. We can evaluate this match in terms of either a horizontal or a vertical relationship. The horizontal dimension of coherence can be defined on the grounds of the notion of mutual support between beliefs. As pointed out by Raz, mutual support is a relationship among a number of beliefs in which possessing certain beliefs renders it more reasonable to possess certain other beliefs, and vice-versa[34]. Mutual support establishes a circular justification - none of the beliefs completely justifies other beliefs, and none is completely justified by others - and a symmetrical justification - every belief performs the same function relative to all other beliefs. Raz provides the following example to illustrate this idea:

> Suppose I believe (1) that John was seen going into Emily's house. Suppose further that I believe (2) that John has long wanted to visit Emily. My belief about John's desire to visit Emily tends to reinforce my belief that the reported sighting of John is correct. At the same time, if someone questions John's desire to visit Emily, I am likely to rely on the reported sighting as confirmation.[35]

It should be noted that two beliefs could be said to support each other mutually. But mutual support is relevant to justification only when it involves a wider range of beliefs. This horizontal aspect attributed to coherence is the basis for strict holism understood as antithetical to epistemic foundationalism[36]. Strict holism contends that

---

[33] Rawls' reflective equilibrium fits into this line of thought. We shall later explore this claim further. Coherence as a property of a system of beliefs can be taken to be the global equilibrium we are after when we readjust our initial and provisional justificatory basis in the process of incorporating new beliefs into our cognitive scheme. See Rawls (1971, 14-21, 43-53, 578-582).

[34] Raz (1992, 277-278). See also Sosa (1993, 395).

[35] Raz (1992, 277-278).

[36] Foundationalism, in Harman's words (1986, 29), 'holds that some of one's beliefs depend on others for their current justification; these other beliefs may depend on still others, until one gets to foundational

the justification for our beliefs lies, precisely, in the global relationship of mutual support among all the convictions in our body of belief.

Coherence in its vertical dimension establishes an asymmetrical and linear relationship of fit between different beliefs. It is assumed that there is a hierarchical structure or different levels of beliefs and coherence links the justification of each belief to its adjustment to higher-ranking beliefs. Vertical coherence must be distinguished from consistency and from logical deductivity. Whereas consistency merely demands non-contradiction, coherence requires some sort of dependence linkage. But this linkage is not necessarily one of logical deduction. According to MacCormick, coherence can be explained in terms of weak derivability. He uses the notion of weak derivability to clarify the relationship between principles and rules. However, this concept could also be useful to deal with the idea of vertical coherence between beliefs. In his opinion, weak deductivility requires that every rule be rooted in some principle or general value; that is, every rule has to have some principle as the reason for its existence. Thus, for instance, the rule that obliges drivers to use the safety belt is founded on the principle of road safety. This rule, nevertheless, rather than consisting in a logical derivation of this principle, is an acceptable or reasonable way of implementing the value of road safety[37].

Let us consider the case in which beliefs are differentiated according to their degree of firmness[38]. The inclusion and preservation of the least firm beliefs (those of which we are not sure that their propositional contents is true) in the epistemic structure

---

beliefs that do not depend on any further beliefs for their justification'. Broadly speaking, foundationalism is usually viewed as an epistemic position that seeks to justify our common beliefs in terms of something firmer and more stable than the beliefs themselves, be it beliefs that act as axioms, sensations, sensory stimuli, or brute facts. Thus, every form of foundationalism seeks to identify some sort of support for our epistemic structure that can stand by itself. See, for instance, Davidson (1993b, 312-313), Alston (1989, 19-32) and Kress (1996, 535).

[37] See MacCormick (1984, 235; 1978, 106-107). See also Villa (1990, 433).

[38] Here, we take firmness only as an example to illustrate the notion of vertical coherence. Surely other criteria are conceivable as a means of defining different hierarchical levels. For example, one could establish hierarchies according to the degree of abstraction, or the fundamentality of the contents of beliefs. However, throughout this chapter, firmness of beliefs and of a structure of beliefs will be portrayed as a main element in a coherentist perspective.

We pointed out in the previous chapter that the concept of belief as a disposition to assert that *p* does not necessarily require that beliefs be, exclusively, those mental states of absolute certainty about the truth of what we assert. This allows us to consider that some beliefs may act as a justification to other mental states that are beliefs too. In this sense, Harman (1986, 22) points out that beliefs are a matter of degree because one can feel more strongly about certain beliefs than about certain others. On the concept of belief as a disposition to assert *p*, see Alston (1989, 290).

requires that they fit or accord with firmer beliefs, i.e., with mental states that involve a higher or even total degree of certainty or confidence[39]. The firmest beliefs act as a justification of less firm ones. That is to say, firm beliefs act as a reason to preserve less firm beliefs in the epistemic structure because the former increase the reliability of the latter by offering evidence that transcends the mere possession of less firm beliefs. Coherence in its vertical sense accounts for the relation of fit between different hierarchical levels of beliefs. This idea has been taken to its most extreme form by foundationalism, which views vertical coherence as a sufficient criterion to justify our beliefs. According to this view, a belief is justified on the grounds of higher-ranking beliefs. These, in turn, are justified by beliefs of an even superior level, and so on till we reach foundational beliefs, which require no further justification.

Although there is a variety of ways to understand coherence and its role in the justification of beliefs, for our purposes it will suffice to think of coherence as a property and a relationship that can be either horizontal or vertical[40]. But once we characterise it in this way, we are hastened to examine whether coherence is an adequate criterion to justify beliefs at all. In my view, horizontal coherence is not sufficient to justify beliefs, for then we are adopting too strict a version of holism that views everything as always depending on everything else. Regardless of what it is that makes a belief more or less firm, this view neglects the fact that some beliefs are firmer

---

[39] According to Mosterín, 'to be certain about something' is not something than can be said of an object or idea, but only of an agent in accordance with his or her degree of confidence in the truth of a proposition or idea. Mosterín points to the importance of distinguishing between 'certainty' and 'what is certain'. Certainty is a property of the agent that results from certain subjective feelings and perceptions, whereas 'what is certain' refers to some objective truth, independent of the agent's opinion. See Mosterín (1987, 132-133). Regardless of whether Mosterín's distinction can be articulated similarly from an antirealist point of view, I would like to stress that certainty is: a) a property of the agent that b) refers to the truth of his assertions and c) is precisely the maximum degree of confidence about the truth of what is being asserted. Note that from the standpoint of truth-assertability, claiming that coherence ensures confidence in the truth of what is being stated does not mean introducing a notion of truth as correspondence of Davidson's kind. Confidence about the truth of a proposition can be understood in terms of confidence that we are legitimated to assert that proposition.

[40] We have devoted no attention to coherence as intelligibility, for instance. The reason for this is that I understand intelligibility not to be an alternative way of understanding coherence, but one of its consequences or advantages. Intelligibility indicates merely that something is within the reach of our understanding, that is, we can access it. Recall that this is the minimal condition required by the principle of charity to undertake any epistemic task. However, intelligibility should not be mistaken for justification - it is merely a pre-condition for justification. This can be easily grasped if we consider that to justify is to assess something as correct from a specific point of view. We can only do so if we understand what we are talking about. On coherence as intelligibility, see Raz (1992, 276-277) and Harman (1986, 65).

than others. Thus, although our reliance in our belief is dependent on the interconnections within our epistemic structure, it is nevertheless a matter of degree. Therefore, the relationship between beliefs is not always symmetrical nor of mutual support. Every structure of convictions should comprise a core part that we are more reluctant to review. As we shall see, this is an important point for the viability of a theory of truth as coherence.

Similarly, limiting coherence to its vertical sense seems insufficient too. Firstly, it would require accepting that some beliefs hold a privileged status - they justify themselves or do not need to be justified at all. Secondly, it would imply being oblivious of how some beliefs become firmer than others. This, in turn, leads to denying that a collection of beliefs forms a network of interconnections. In addition, coherence as a relationship needs to be linked to the idea of coherence as a general property of the global system. Including or maintaining one or several beliefs within this structure does not merely depend on their adjustment to other permanently well settled beliefs - the goal of this epistemic enterprise is to maximise the coherence of the whole as some sort of equilibrium.

Thus: for coherence to be a convincing criterion for the justification of beliefs, both vertical and horizontal coherence should be envisaged, and a close link between them should be acknowledged. This is precisely the aim of reflective equilibrium. Such a view succeeds in bringing together both dimensions of coherence on the grounds of the following two claims: a) since some beliefs are firmer or better settled than others, they act as a justification of less firm beliefs; and b) even the firmest beliefs can be revised and discarded as a result of the inclusion of further beliefs into the structure. This revision works in favour of the global coherence of the epistemic structure in which mutual support among all interrelated beliefs results in a compact network[41].

Dworkin's view comes close to reflective equilibrium in what regards the justification of beliefs about law. He writes:

> What we think, about anything important, is a structured and complex mix of different kinds of beliefs and convictions, some of which, in virtue of their content, act as check on others. No single one of these is absolutely foundational, in the sense of absolutely privileged, so that is can never be withdrawn in the face

41 This position reflects the thesis that we need to be confident in some of our beliefs whenever we undertake an epistemic enterprise. Otherwise, we could never advance as our convictions would be revisable at any point in time - it also reflects the idea that in the process of inquiry, given that beliefs as such are fallible, we may require readjustments in our epistemic network. This makes it possible for us to reach interpretive conclusions that take us beyond our starting point. In line with coherentist thought, it could be argued that precisely this is the basis for the evolution of knowledge.

of others. But as a system these convictions nevertheless check and constrain one another in a variety of ways[42].

Dworkin's holism also develops along the lines of the so-called "hermeneutic circle". According to Peczenik, the hermeneutic circle implies that 'the whole juristic content of a given cluster of legal norms can only be understood if one understands their mutual connections, the relevant legal concepts, legal theories, etc., while these connections, concepts and theories in their turn can be understood only by understanding the content of the legal norms. All this hangs together' [43]. Aarnio accounts for the same holistic perspective when he refers to the hermeneutic notion of "the circle of understanding". Following Gadamer, he contends:

> preunderstanding determines the way in which the details of the object are thematized. This way is reflected in the interpreter's conception of the totality that is constituted by the parts. The totality influences the interpretation of details, and so on. In hermeneutics, the essential thing is that the interpreter cannot break out this circle; the understanding is expressly produced by the progressive circular movement. The object has been understood when its details have been brought into harmony with each other, like the pieces of a puzzle. It is this harmony that is the criterion of whether or not the text has been interpreted correctly[44].

With this idea in mind, elucidating whether or not coherentism as presented above is successful in offering a justification to beliefs and in leading to a theory of truth as coherence will be of assistance to evaluate Dworkin's internal objectivity thesis.

From justification to truth-assertability

One of the main objections to coherence theory, both as a theory of truth as well as a justification to beliefs, turns on its circularity[45]. This is a particularly important criticism for if not refutable, it undermines coherentism as a philosophical alternative. Circularity arises when it is assumed that the justification of beliefs depends on other beliefs, and none of them is thought to occupy a privileged position. Thus, every belief requires a justification[46]. However, this circularity is in itself not a relevant problem if,

---

[42] Dworkin (1991b, 377; 1996, 119-120; 1983, 293-294; 1985, 169-170).

[43] Peczenik (1990, 300).

[44] Aarnio (1997, 103).

[45] See, for instance, Kirkham's criticism of Blanshard, Kirkham (1992, 104-112). See also Moser's remarks (1993, 63-75) on Dummet's theory, and Marmor's comments (1992, 78-84) to Dworkin's interpretive point of view.

[46] We already pointed out that this assumption can be found in Davidson's epistemic theory (1993b, 307-319).

as Dworkin suggests, semantic realism is abandoned[47]. Circularity is forceful an objection if it is seen to embody a vicious circle, and if it is viewed a sufficient reason to diminish the reliance on our epistemic structure.

Circularity could become problematic if justification is pursued within a reduced set of beliefs. However, an epistemic structure is usually complex. This complexity generates very wide circles in such a way that the interpreting agent cannot perceive them as circles. Thus, circularity need not prevent the success of coherentism.

It will be argued that the complexity of a coherent epistemic structure makes it possible to justify beliefs and to warrant the truth-assertability of judgements. Because of the structural reinforcement it entails, complexity increases our confidence in what we assert. Confidence, in turn, is related to the idea probability[48]. To be confident about something presupposes that the probability of error is rated to be low. We then have no reason to give up our judgement - our conclusions appear to be sufficiently justified and no further inquiry is necessary. It is useful here to appeal to a standard such as Harman's principle of conservatism: one is entitled to continue fully to believe something in the absence of a special reason not to do so[49]. This principle is the counter part of Harman's principle of positive undermining, according to which one should stop believing that *p* whenever one positively believes that one's reasons for believing that *p* are not good[50].

Accepting these two standards as a tool to assess beliefs from within a conceptual scheme leads to the conclusion that whenever an agent believes to have good reasons to believe that *p* and neither has, nor faces, good reasons to stop believing that *p*, in Dworkin's words, 'he'd better believe it'[51].

In short, confidence arising from coherence and complexity certainly does not permit an external nor definitive justification. The degree of confidence may vary. But at a given moment in time, this is the only way to reach a satisfactory justification or,

---

47 Dworkin (1985, 167-170).

48 See, for instance, Harman (1986, 45) and Mattey (1989, 42). Recall that introducing the notion of probability does not necessarily entail adopting a notion of truth as correspondence, since claiming that it is likely or unlikely that our beliefs are true directly reflects our willingness to keep them or to revise them.

49 Harman (1986, 46).

50 On these principles, see Harman (1986, 39-47).

51 See Dworkin (1996, 118).

for that matter, the only feasible conclusion from the internalist perspective that seeks to deny both externalism and voluntarism[52].

Is it possible to go from justification to truth-assertability? An affirmative answer to this question is conditional on the coming together of coherence and complexity. We are at this stage urged to investigate what is required for the above-mentioned step to be plausible. Justification relates to the connections among our judgements and it appears to be the case that any explanatory notion of truth should rely on something which is ultimately independent of at least some of these judgements, that is, something distinguishable from them and with which they couple. It is important to preserve the spirit of this idea for the notion of truth to remain meaningful. But in order to account for truth, we need not match judgements with states of affairs external to our conceptual schemes. Neither need we seek something different from our judgements with which they should correspond if they are to be true. It suffices to assume that we are able to distinguish and dissociate different types of judgements: some of them constitute our provisional ontology, whereas others enable us to develop theories about how to interpret and evaluate our provisional ontology. Ontological judgements, depending on their contents and strength, act as a test of correctness or as restrictions to interpretive judgements. The independence of these types of judgements is warranted only if the coherent structure is sufficiently complex, in other words, if the circular relationships that arise within it are sufficiently wide for the agent not to be aware of them.

This is Dworkin's and Putnam's strategy to advocate a coherence theory of truth. We observed previously that for Dworkin, an interpretive proposition is true if it coheres better than others with the whole of propositions that offer the best version of the object of interpretation[53]. This concept of truth is based upon the idea that facts

---

[52] In this respect it is interesting to draw attention to Gärdenfors' reflections (1988, 20) on the epistemic dynamics internal to a system of beliefs. He observes that 'from within a belief system there is no difference between knowledge and full belief. From the subject's point of view there is no way to tell whether she accepts something as knowledge, that is, has full belief in it, or whether her accepted knowledge is also true'. Although this author assumes a theory of truth as correspondence, it is nevertheless interesting to adopt his claim as the main idea of an internalist point of view about the relationship between the justification of beliefs and truth-assertability. See Gärdenfors (1988, 18-20). On the pre-eminence of confidence above empirical data and logical argument in general knowledge, see, for instance, Hardwig (1991, 693-708).

[53] Dworkin (1985, 138; 1986, 4-5; 1991a, 84-85). Hurley holds a similar position in this respect. She focuses her attention on the role played by coherence in the identification of what is, in moral terms, the thing to do. She understands her position to be also applicable to the domain of law. Hurley observes that the correctness or truth of a moral or legal proposition depends on whether or not the theory that displays

both restrict and are restricted by a particular interpretation. In Dworkin's view, this means that a theory displays different levels of interpretation in which certain judgements limit certain other judgements[54].

With a view to accounting for this point, and in response to scepticism in law and in art, Dworkin addresses the question about why is it commonplace to admit that facts restrict scientific theories. His answer to this question turns on the complexity of a coherence theory in the scientific domain that enables us to discriminate different levels of beliefs. In this respect, he claims:

> Facts check theories in science because the overall theoretical apparatus of science is complex enough to allow internal tensions, checks, and balances. This would be impossible if there were no functional distinctions within the system of scientific knowledge among various kinds and levels of belief. If we did not have special and discrete opinions about what counts as an observation, for example, we could not disprove established theories by fresh observations.[55]

For Dworkin, the distinction between levels of belief within a coherent structure warrants the notion of truth-assertability in Natural Sciences. He claims that therefore, any argument against the possibility of asserting the truth or falsity of our legal, aesthetic or ethical judgements can only be formulated in terms of a lack of complexity of our epistemic structures in these areas of knowledge. Dworkin does not agree with the latter claim, that is, he objects to the idea that our epistemic structures are not sufficiently complex in these areas. His theory of law as integrity tries to reflect this complexity as well as how some judgements can act as a test for others to yield interpretive conclusions[56].

Putnam's internal realism develops along similar lines[57]. On the one hand, Putnam insists that the truth of scientific theories is dependent on internal complexity and

---

the greatest coherence among the values to which it applies favours the truth of that proposition. See Hurley (1989, 193).

[54] Dworkin (1983, 310-313).

[55] Dworkin (1985, 170; 1983, 293-294; 1986, 236).

[56] See Dworkin (1983, 294-295, 310-313; 1991b, 376-377).

[57] It should be pointed out that, more recently, Putnam has changed his mind on this point. He has thus partially rejected the equivalence between truth and assertability that he had advocated in his early work *Reason, Truth and History*. Putnam has softened his internal realism and has admitted that occasionally truth may transcend what we are entitled to assert. He thus concludes that a proposition can be true and yet not verifiable or assertable. Notwithstanding, he persists in advocating the equivalence between truth and assertability for statements about social practices such as Ethics or Law. Here, in order to assert the truth or falsity of our judgements we need not appeal to a transcendent notion of truth. In this context, the mere possibility of distinguishing those statements that are acceptable form those that are not suffices to assert their truth or falsity. See, for instance, Putnam (1995a, 16-19; 1995b, 70-75). Thus, for the

coherence. On the other, he claims, this complexity can also be found in other areas of knowledge[58]. Furthermore, Putnam observes, the only test for our judgements about any phenomenon is that provided by two distinguishable but interrelated kinds of beliefs: theoretical beliefs, and experiential beliefs[59]. Both of these consist in mental states dependent on our mind and conceptual constructs. But they can be distinguished within an epistemic structure because, whether we consider the most experiential beliefs to be justified or not no longer depends on our will. In Putnam's opinion, this is precisely what enables experiential beliefs to act as an objective test to theoretical beliefs. However, according to the holistic line of thought adopted by Dworkin and Putnam, experiential beliefs restrict and are themselves restricted by each and every one of our conceptual options[60]. The confidence we gain in the correctness of these beliefs is directly dependent on their adjustment to our scheme of beliefs as a whole. Therefore, the degree of confidence may vary as we incorporate new beliefs into this highly interconnected network of beliefs. This, in turn, may compel us to review some judgement[61]. No belief is dissociated from other beliefs. It is precisely the

---

purposes of our discussion, we will adopt Putnam's original idea of internal realism for statements about social practices.

58 Putnam (1987, 20-21). From this perspective, and as Villa (1990, 445) points out, 'the conceptual dichotomy between "truth as the criterion of the empirical sciences and coherence as the criterion of the interpretive sciences", breaks down completely because coherence has a very much broader scope, in the sense that it applies even to empirical disciplines'.

59 Putnam (1981, 54-56).

60 Putnam (1981, 54-55, 102, 133-134). This puts Putnam in a position to legitimately claim that 'we cut up the world into objects when we introduce one or another scheme of description. Since the objects, and the signs are alike internal to the scheme of descriptions, it is possible to say what matches what'. Putnam (1981, 52). See also, Dworkin (1991b, 377).

61 As I have stressed, this kind of holism can be understood in terms of Rawls' reflective equilibrium. Every interpretation requires that we take as our starting point a quasi-axiomatic basis of convictions. This basis, however, is not strictly foundational. These convictions may be subject to later revisions once we put the whole of our epistemic structure at work to find a balance among our convictions as we incorporate new ones. For this reason, it is important to distinguish this point of view from a position such as Quine's, for whom statements with stimulus meaning eventually form a permanent foundational basis and hence, sensorial stimuli act as mediators between beliefs and reality. This basis ultimately seeks to set an external limit to the conceptual schemes that indicates the sufficiency of evidence for what we assert. Dworkin's and Putnam's holism implies a self-adjusting mechanism, both in the horizontal and the vertical dimensions of it; moreover, no belief holds a privileged position, and hence all of them are potentially subject to be revised. Concurrently, however, this kind of holism requires us to concede that some beliefs are better settled than others. These beliefs act as a test for truth only as long as they are not questioned or revised. See Rawls (1971, 14-21, 43-53, 578-582), Dworkin (1996, 119), Putnam (1987, 85-86), and Weinberger (1984, 231-232). See also Davidson's criticism of Quine's and Dummet's foundationalism, Davidson (1993b, 312-313).

interconnectedness of our epistemic structure what enables us to distinguish between different types of beliefs. If in some circumstances we consider that some of our beliefs cannot be reviewed, it is only because of their contents and because we consider the entire scheme of beliefs to be sound enough to objectively ensure that some judgements about a certain phenomenon are better than others.

From the interpretive point of view it makes sense to claim that the object of interpretation restricts its own interpretation: this assertion no longer presumes any form of metaphysical realism. This merely accounts for interpreters' perception of themselves as constrained as to the judgements they can make about the practice in which they participate. Sceptics pressed an objection to the circularity of the interpretive process, in particular to the fact that every interpreter is aware that she is free to make any reconstruction she likes and that his interpretive conclusions are the product of mere will. If the interpreter's epistemic structure is sufficiently sound and complex, the alleged vicious circle breaks down. The epistemic structure permits to differentiate between what one wishes to think and what one is entitled to think. Therefore, a thesis such as that of internal objectivity is, in my view, entirely justified and succeeds in its purpose: it permits a genuine distinction between interpretation and invention. Inevitably, some interpretations will be better than others, and there may even be some that are not at all acceptable as interpretations. If we deny that there be a criterion of truth that transcends what an individual or a group of individuals can think or justify, we are in a position to understand how coherence leads to truth-assertability.

The thesis of internal objectivity does not minimize the notion of truth. On the contrary, it seeks to make this notion meaningful and intelligible to the participants in the legal practice. The determination of the contents of such a practice is something internal to it. It is within the practice that we find more or less convincing arguments and more or less powerful reasons about what law is like and the conduct it demands. The discussion between participants focuses on which are the best arguments and reasons, i.e. what is the best way, to understand their interactions. These arguments are the only factor permitting the distinction between correct and incorrect judgements because no participant can, nor is required to, provide further evidence for her claims. However, these arguments are devised by the participants, and they reflect the participants' convictions, values, and reflections. No-thing falling outside their language game endows them with a sounder basis to assert their claims or to determine whose judgement is correct in the event of disagreement[62]. As Aarnio has stressed, 'the

---

[62] Dworkin (1985, 173-174).

interpreter is moving all the time *inside* the language without having a possibility to test the interpretation by reference to the empirical reality'[63]. Additionally, no mechanism is available to distinguish between the language game and the real world. Thus, Dworkin points out that, as participants, 'we should account to ourselves for our own convictions as best as we can, standing ready to abandon those that do not survive reflective inspection. We should make such arguments to others, who do not share our opinions, as we can make with good faith and break off arguing when no further argument is appropriate. I do not mean that this is all we can do because we are creatures with limited access to true reality or with necessarily parochial viewpoints. I mean that we can give no sense to the idea that there is anything else we could do in deciding whether our judgements are "really" true.'[64]. In short, as Wittgenstein would point out, after argument and controversy, all that remains is confidence in our judgements, some of which tend to converge among participants in the same practice. Moreover, confidence in our judgements depends on the soundness of our epistemic structure and ought to be explained on the basis of our form of life[65].

What we have presented hitherto does not seek to argue, in line with externalist idealism, that our world is made of beliefs exclusively[66]. Our language game includes facts that restrict our interpretations. These facts are what we are entitled to believe, but not our beliefs themselves. I wish to stress the distinction between the conviction that a certain judgement is correct only because it is believed so, and the conviction that a judgement is correct despite the fact that no absolute justification for it can readily be produced. We understand these interpretive facts as constituting the ontology that restricts what we can say about any phenomenon. There is no way we can step outside our own discursive context to elucidate what is the real nature of this ontology, that is, whether they are 'really' just beliefs, or 'really' facts independent of our judgements and our epistemic abilities.

---

63 Aarnio (1997, 109).

64 Dworkin (1985, 172). Dworkin insists (1996, 118) that 'I mean that any reason we think we have for abandoning a conviction is itself just another conviction, and that we can do no better for any claim, [...] that to see whether, after the best thought we find appropriate, we think it so'.

65 As a language game, a social practice is effectively only possible if we have confidence in something. On this point, see Putnam's references to Wittgenstein in Putnam (1992, 176-177).

66 We noted earlier that scepticism ultimately supports externalist idealism because it seeks to position itself at a pre-theoretical stage, and claims that beliefs are all that exists. Thus, sceptics advocate an uninterpreted world made of judgements and mental states exclusively. On this point see, for example, Putnam (1990, 32).

To sum up, we have analysed and supported the plausibility of internal objectivism as a thesis to refute the global sceptic challenge. We can therefore defend a weak form of discretion in adjudication and reject that judicial identification of law lack sufficient restrictions to distinguish between interpretation and invention. Consequently, we can deny that judges, as participants in the legal practice, in every case face the choice between alternatives typical of strong discretion. Internal objectivity has been used by Dworkin to reach a far more ambitious conclusion, namely that there always exists a single right legal answer. Can this conclusion be justified on the basis of the thesis of internal objectivity? Towards the end of this chapter we shall explore some arguments that yield a negative answer to this question. Let us first turn our attention to the appropriateness of applying coherentism to legal interpretation and adjudication.

5.4 COHERENCE IN LEGAL INTERPRETATION

5.4.1 Interpretive adjudication of norms

From an interpretive point of view of law the judge is no more than a participant in the legal practice. However, the judge's participation in the practice is twofold: interpretive and institutional. The interpretive dimension determines the judge's understanding of the practice he participates in; the institutional dimension, by contrast, determines his function within the practice. To be a judge is to fulfil the particular institutional role of normative adjudication; in other words, being a judge entails assuming the duty to settle conflicts by means of law[67]. If we presume that judges behave in accordance with their institutional role, we shall assume, too, that they take on the responsibility to use law as the means to settle legally relevant disputes[68]. From an interpretive standpoint, the judge should be able to distinguish between interpretation and invention if she is to carry out this responsibility. Judges interpret the material (typically acts and linguistic signs) they identify as participants in the practice. This material constitutes the pre-interpretive data to which they shall have to attribute meaning in the light of their particular understanding of law.

[67] On this point, see Hawkins' distinction (1992, 32-35) between the context of negotiation and that of adjudication. MacCormick, for example, argues that the role of a judge is different from that of a mediator because the judge assumes an institutional role, which takes law rather than equity or the particular circumstances of the case as the criterion to settle conflicts. See MacCormick (1978, 242) and Barak (1989, 229).

[68] See Dworkin (1991b, 380; 1986, 410-413).

If we agree that the arguments put forward in previous chapters refute externalism, adjudication cannot be viewed as an empirical nor as a semantic task that turns on the idea of social convention. Judges cannot be taken to represent the beliefs or propositional attitudes of a certain community if they, themselves, do not share or understand these beliefs and attitudes. Thus, their interpretive conclusions cannot embody the conventions about the legal nature of a particular normative source nor about the meaning of a linguistic act or inscription. Bodies of adjudication face the question about what is demanded by the law, and not about what participants believe is demanded by the law. A right legal answer to this question can only be obtained by judges if they possess a sufficiently complex and structured theory about the legal practice.

I agree with Dworkin that all we can request from judges is: a) commitment to the judicial role they assume[69]; b) willingness to engage in reflection about their beliefs, and readiness to admit to error; and c) the presumption that one legal argument is better than another legal argument if it fits better with the purpose or sense of our practice or legal language game[70]. Any demand beyond these three implies expecting bodies of adjudication to undertake an epistemically unfeasible task. I believe that, in this context, fewer demands yield better results. Thus, according to Kant's maxim that 'ought' implies 'can', any model of adjudication and of judges' institutional obligations should rest on a sound epistemic foundation[71].

An interpretive theory of law offers a plausible and epistemically accessible version of law and of the judicial function. From an interpretive point of view, judges are responsible for their decisions about what are citizens' rights and duties both in undisputed and in controversial cases[72]. To assert this responsibility accords with our idea that every judicial decision should be made on the basis of legal arguments and that the judge should aim at offering the best legal arguments[73].

---

69 This role is that of applying the law and standards of judicial action such as reasonableness, rationality and argumentative honesty. On these standards, see MacCormick (1978, 250-255), Raz (1972, 846-847), Hart (1980, 9) and Soper (1984, 3-9).

70 See Dworkin (1986, 86; 1985, 172; 1996, 118).

71 On Kant's maxim, see von Wright (1970, 124-131, 137-138).

72 In both cases the judge needs a theory of law that justifies her decisions and that is not arbitrary. As a participant fulfilling an institutional role, every judge needs to provide reasons based on general principles to prefer one legal perspective over any other. On this point, see Dworkin (1986, 265-266, 353-354, 410-413; 1991a, 88, 90).

73 This idea can be more easily grasped in terms of the distinction between the internal and the external justification of a legal argument. Internal justification is the demand that the conclusion of the argument be logically inferred or deduced from the premises invoked. External justification, in contrast, is related

However, an interpretive view of law is usually controversial because of its apparent incompatibility with the idea of 'law as authority'. We shall next devote some attention to clarifying the character of this alleged incompatibility.

5.4.2 Authority and coherence

One of the main objections to accepting a coherence theory of law is the widespread idea among positivists that law is the product of authoritative decisions[74]. According to this view, a legal system is the contents of normative acts performed by some authority that is accepted as such by the community[75]. Raz, for instance, understands a coherentist theory of law to be one contending that a legal system is a coherent set of norms. He presents the idea of law as authority as an alternative legal approach to coherentism and claims these two views to be incompatible with one another: either law is the product of authoritative normative acts, or it is a set of norms that form a unitary and coherent body. The incompatibility between the two lies in that coherence can only be ensured at the cost of excluding certain authoritative acts as part of law[76].

---

to the suitability of the chosen premises to carry out the judicial syllogism. Often, the 'legal justification' of a decision has been linked to its internal justification, and its moral justification has been related to the idea of external justification. From an interpretive point of view of law there is more to the legal justification of a judicial argument than just the formal correctness of the logical inference. Moreover, legal justification does not require that the normative premise be morally acceptable. The justification of the interpretive conclusion requires some legal criterion to select the normative premise. Therefore, some kind of external justification is needed. This specifically presumes the possibility of showing that it coheres vertically with a horizontally coherent collection of principles that offer the best justification of the legal practice as a whole. On the classical distinction between internal and external justification, see Wróblewski (1974, 33-34). On the idea that legal justification requires just internal justification when there is no right legal answer and that, otherwise, it demands external justification, see Aarnio (1990, 197-200), Atienza (1991, 45-46; 1993, 124-128).

74 Raz (1992, 293-297; 1979, 28-33) is one of the main avocates of this thesis.

75 This idea has been presented under different lights. Hart, for instance, considers that a legal system is made of a set of primary rules (i.e. rules that confer rights and impose duties upon the citizens) and a set of secondary rules (i.e. rules that confer power to introduce or eliminate primary rules, and to determine when primary rules have been broken) which has been granted the authority to guide conduct. However, as such, a system of rules is the product of an essentially judicial practice of acceptance and use of a set of criteria to determine what is law: a rule of recognition. According to Hart, in a complex society the rule of recognition embraces a constitution, legislative decisions, and judicial precedents, but there are other sources too. These criteria are sources of authority in the sense that they reflect who or what can generate binding patterns of conduct. See Hart (1994, 92-99, 100-104, 109-110, 116-117, 202-203).

76 Raz (1992, 284-285, 290-297). This conflict must not be mistaken for the classical debate about the authority of the legislator (as a representative of the citizenry) *vis-à-vis* the authority of the Constitution (as a collection of principles and values that restrict the freedom of public powers for the sake of the

Raz draws a comparison between these two options in terms of the structural nature of law given our linguistic conventions, and not as different interpretive theories of law. In line with Hart's position, Raz links the problem about what is law to the question about what the members of a community take as a criterion to evaluate their behaviour and that of their peers[77]. The underlying assumption here is that a community is immersed in a legal social practice when it is the case that participants accept as the criterion to assess conduct the prescriptions of those institutions that are regarded as authoritative[78].

We are urged to stress at this point that this approach relies on a particular conception of law, namely that which views it as a passive social practice. Participants need not hold a substantive position about the contents of law, that is, they are not required to hold a particular opinion about what is legally the thing to do, nor need they provide arguments to support their legal judgements. Participants should merely accept an authority that produces norms, and a different authority that applies them. Thus, although participants have a normative understanding of law and take legal rules as a criterion to assess the conduct of their peers as well as their own, they do not do so in virtue of the contents of the rules but in virtue of their origin. In the framework of this conception of the practice, the idea of normativity is reduced to the acceptance of

protection of individual rights). A Constitution may help to achieve coherence in the normative production because every legislative act and every judicial decision must conform to that set of principles. However, from a positivist point of view, the Constitution is a further authoritative legal source, which is pre-eminent over other sources. For this reason, the conflict between authority and coherence can also be found at the constitutional level. The problem that persists is, specifically, that either we concede the authority of the constitutional text, or we accept as the constitution only that part of the constitutional text that can be regarded as a coherent collection of standards of conduct.

77 These authors claim that law has normative force in the sense that the participants in the legal practice tend to take law as a reason to evaluate conduct. Hart asserts that this is the criterion that enables us to distinguish between a system of social rules and a set of habits of conduct. Hart draws the following distinction between social rules and habits: a) the existence of a habit simply requires that there be a certain regularity in conduct whereas social rules require, in addition, that deviations from the required conduct meet with criticism or reprobation; b) in contrast with habits, the criticism faced when behaviour deviates from the rule is considered to be justified; c) the existence of a social rule requires that some of those who comply with the rule (namely judges) accept the rule as a guide to conduct for everybody. These differences between habits and social rules emphasise what Hart called 'the internal aspect of rules'. The internal aspect of rules reflects the critical/reflective attitude of participants. It is necessary that judges display such an attitude for a practice governed by social rules to exist. Hart (1994, 55-57, 88-91, 116-117) and Raz (1990, 170-177).

78 'To have authority' is to be able to create binding patterns of conduct. On this point, see Raz (1979, 5-11, 18-21).

institutions that generate valid rules, i.e. rules whose binding force is due to their having been created by certain institutions[79].

However, when we attempt to answer the question about what is demanded by the law in each particular case, or what is its contents, this passive conception of the practice faces epistemic problems. Our aim is to elucidate, precisely, what was prescribed by the normative authority, that is, what is the propositional contents of the legislator's normative formulations or of judicial precedent or of the constitutional text[80]. Both Hart and Raz give an answer to this question by appealing again to the passivity of legal practice. Their argument turns on the settled use of language in a community as a criterion of truth of legal propositions[81]. These authors claim that we do not require a substantive judgement about what is demanded by the law in order to answer the question about what is prescribed by the authority. It suffices to accept a further authority, namely that of the majority of the members in the linguistic community and to reproduce the general use of language. Similarly, when there exists no settled use, we agree that judges choose between different alternatives for action on the basis of their own criteria and convictions[82].

The foregoing remarks reflect in broad terms the positivist view of law as authority. In the second chapter we pointed out the problems encountered by this perspective to

---

[79] It could be argued that Hart and Raz consider that for a legal system to exist, certain participants, namely judges, ought to display a particular attitude when facing rules. These two authors seem to agree that this attitude does not entail that judges believe in the moral correctness of the contents of the rule, but simply that they accept rules created by normative authorities as exclusionary reasons for action, i.e. reasons taken as a justification for actions that exclude prior to the deliberation process, other reasons that could have led to a different outcome. Thus, accepting a rule's binding force does not depend on its contents but on its origin. Hart repeatedly insisted that judges might accept this out of respect for tradition or their desire to identify with others, and not necessarily their moral beliefs. See Raz (1990, 73-76, 141-146; 1979, 153-157) and Hart (1982, 265-268; 1994, 243, 257). However, Raz has changed his mind on this point.

[80] Raz seems to acknowledge this problem when he claims that the idea of an authority and its intention when legislating is not relevant to determine the contents of law, but only to determine which statements should be endowed with propositional contents. This position admits the weakness of the idea of law as authority. If we adopt a semantic view of law as positivism typically does, to identify which rights and duties citizens have is to identify the propositional contents of normative texts. And if the propositional contents is no longer determined by the legislative will, the role of normative authorities in the definition of these rights and duties is minimal, or even irrelevant if we recall the sceptical challenge on rule-following. Accordingly, no statement or linguistic inscription can determine its own meaning. On this point, see Raz (1996, 256-268). See also Dworkin (1986, 317-338; 1991a, 87-88; 1985, 43-57, 154-158; 1991b, 374-377).

[81] See Hart (1994, 126-129) and Raz (1996, 262-268).

[82] See Hart (1994, 124-132).

account for the normativity of meaning. In addition, I would like to highlight that from this passive viewpoint of the practice, resorting to the widespread use of language does not yet answer the question about what it is the law demands. The contents of this language use remains to be determined. Here, given that conventions cannot identify themselves, we are left with two options only: either a) we accept a further authority, which, because the process repeats itself, requires us to accept yet one more, and so on; or, b) we change our conception of the practice and view it as an active social practice in which participants advocate a substantive position about which types of conduct are legally regulated on the grounds of arguments about why a particular theory of law is better than any other[83]. The former option in fact does not enable us to provide an answer to the question what is demanded by the law. However, if we assume the latter view, as common sense seems to suggest we do, we are actually adopting an interpretive view of law and every interpretation is constructive, i.e. every interpretation aims at portraying an object or event or sequence of events as the best example of its type. To provide a constructive interpretation is simply to apply a complex theory about the phenomenon in hand by adjusting the pre-interpretive material (the most formal convictions) to the epistemic and axiological apparatus that this theory is based on. Thus, one of the options leads to scepticism; the other, to coherence as a criterion of truth of legal propositions.

If we adopt the second option, as indeed coherentists would, we should return to the beginning of this section and refute the terms in which Raz discusses a coherence theory for law. Then, the plausibility of applying coherence in legal interpretation is no longer linked to the structural nature of law as determined by our linguistic conventions. From an epistemic point of view, coherence is necessary in every interpretation of law. Once we deny every form of externalism as a way to approach the contents of this social phenomenon, we are compelled to resort to the relationships among beliefs within an epistemic scheme. As has been hitherto argued, coherence emerges as the best candidate to justify our structure of beliefs and to claim the truth-assertability of our judgements.

---

[83] Although it can be argued that this turn is only necessary to answer the question about what the contents of this general use of language is, it takes us back to the initial question: what does law demand we do? As was already pointed out, adopting Davidson's principle of charity for interpretation does not enable us to dissociate the problem of what is it the members of a linguistic community think from that of what is it they do. In order to understand what they do, the interpreter need assume similarity between her conceptual scheme, her understanding of the world, and that of those whose linguistic conduct she seeks to interpret.

5.4.3 Coherence and the normative dimension of law

It is commonly assumed that law as an instrument to evaluate conduct has an important normative dimension that ought not to be neglected[84]. Legal practice as a normative practice embodies an idea of participation that does not permit to dissociate the position on what are our rights and duties from that on their axiological justification[85]. As

---

84 Throughout his work, Hart insists that any description of law should take into account the point of view of participants in the legal practice (the normativity of law). Hart argues (1994, 90) that a legal theory that does no account or explain the participants' normative attitude towards rules cannot properly reflect 'a whole dimension of the social life of those whom he is watching'. However, it is worth noting that in contrast with Dworkin, Hart claims that a theory of law may describe the beliefs and normative attitudes of the participants and yet not adopt an internal point of view. To clarify this point, Hart distinguishes between different types of statements about the legal practice on the basis of who produces them and the degree of internalisation they presume. The first such type of statements are those made by an external observer, who need not share the normative attitudes or the beliefs of participants. These are statements about law (descriptive statements), and should be clearly differentiated from internal statements. Internal statements are those statements produced by participants in the practice, that is, by individuals who accept its rules as a guide to assessing conducts and as justifying reasons for action. According to Hart, external statements fall into one of two further categories: those made by an external observer, which describe mere observable regularities in behaviour, and those by means of which the external observer describes the participants' attitudes and beliefs from an internal point of view. Hart claims that a theory of law does not require the observer to share the participants' normative attitudes, but its description of law should reflect the internal point of view. In *Essays on Bentham*, Hart includes a further type of statements: normative statements (which are not statements about participants' normative attitude). Statements made by lawyers and jurists (as opposed to judges, who are assumed to adopt the internal point of view) belong in this class of statements. Normative language is used in these statements and yet the rules are not taken to be justifying reasons for action. See Hart (1994, 89-91, 115-117; 1982, 153-157; 1983, 165-169) and Raz (1990, 171-177; 1979, 154-157). We pointed out in Chapter 2 that one of the main objections to positivism is that it regards legal theory to be something external to the practice, wherefore its statements are not committed to law as a justification for state coercion. The arguments explored after Chapter 2 aim at showing the unfeasibility of externalism as an approach to law. In my opinion, Dworkin would consequently be right in claiming that every description and understanding of the legal practice is interpretive because it involves a descriptive-justificatory viewpoint about the object of interpretation. See Dworkin (1985, 146-149; 1994b, 2-3). For evidence for this argument, see Putnam's views on the interrelationship between fact and value (1981, 127-135). See also Wittgenstein (1992, 9-91).

85 Although these two positions are dependent on one another within a normative practice, we could nevertheless distinguish between epistemic and axiological justifications. Epistemic justification evaluates beliefs to maximise the truthfulness of their propositional contents. Axiological justifications, in contrast, evaluate beliefs in terms of their conformity with certain values or standards of conduct. From an internalist point of view, whether or not a belief is epistemically justified depends on its degree of conformity with a structure of beliefs as a whole, whereas for it to be axiologically justified it needs to accord with an axiological structure or a scheme of values. Every epistemic structure is nevertheless often considered to be interrelated with an axiological structure, particularly as far as phenomena with a

proposed by Hart, to be a participant is to adopt the internal point of view. Hart asserts that holding this point of view is accepting certain guides of conduct. 'To accept' here means to use these rules as reasons to appraise or criticise behaviour, be it one's own or that of other participants. Hart associates the existence of the legal practice to the occurrence of this critical/reflective attitude on the part of at least some participants[86]. From the standpoint of interpretive theory as a theory clearly internal to the language game of law, the criterion of truth-coherence for legal statements ought to embrace within the notion of assertability what participants are both axiologically and epistemically entitled to assert[87]. If these two aspects are unified in our understanding of law, coherence should play a twofold role: it should act as a procedural criterion and as a justifying value.

The main purpose of Dworkin's idea of law as integrity is to account for this twofold role of coherence. Law as integrity aims at offering a constructive interpretation of the legal practice in terms of the judgements that, in his opinion, every judge-participant should possess to be able to produce an interpretive conclusion about its contents[88]. As pointed out above, this epistemic structure includes both formal and

---

normative dimension are concerned, that is, when participants understand their interactions to be binding or due acts. In this context, any belief about which conducts are legally regulated is in fact a belief about what is legally the thing to do. It can thus be claimed that the participants in the legal practice hold a normative point of view about their interactions. A great deal of literature concerned with the normativity of law has emerged and yielded fruitful debate about which kinds of reasons for action some participants need assume if a system of legal rules is to exist. This debate has re-opened the controversy on the connection between law and morality. See Hart (1982, 243-268) and Raz (1990, 162-177; 1979, 153-157). For discussion on these two authors concerning this point, see Nino (1985, 118-137; 1994, 79-81, 192-196), Bayón (1991), Garzón Valdés (1990, 119-124) and Redondo (1996). We shall not devote further attention to this issue. However, I would like to point to an interesting question: to what extent does the assumption that participating in the legal practice requires reasons dependent on the contents imply that these reasons are of a moral character? To answer this question we should elucidate the extent to which we can claim the autonomy of justificatory legal discourse. This would break down the idea of unity of practical discourse. See Putnam (1995a, 7) and Fried (1981, 35-58). This is precisely Coleman's interpretation (1995, 53-54) of the relationship between description and justification in Dworkin's interpretive theory.

86 Similarly to Raz, Hart considers that for a system of legal rules to exist, a critical/reflective attitude is not required from all of its participants, but just from some of them: judges. See Hart (1994, 114-117) and Raz (1990, 171).

87 In a broader sense, we could even say, following Villa (1990, 446, 447), that at the background of any holistic structure 'value judgements cohabit with theoretical statements mixed up with them (...). It is impossible to insulate the evaluative component from the whole theoretical framework'.

88 Dworkin notes that his interpretation of Hercules' reasoning is no more than what he considers to be his own opinions about which arguments are best. Thus, his claim that law as integrity should combine

substantive judgements[89]. Formal judgements shape what participants take to be the object of interpretation, whereas substantive judgements shape what participants assume as values that justify state coercion. In other words, substantive judgements reflect participants' normative understanding of the practice and the value or global purpose they attribute to it[90].

We pointed out in Chapter 3 that integrity, as narrative coherence, does not provide by itself an answer to the question about what is the best interpretation of law. It is only a means to presenting how we can obtain this answer. If our legal judgements undergo careful reflective examination to achieve global equilibrium in our scheme of legal beliefs, we may reach the correct answer. However, coherence is of no assistance to determine the right answer. The right answer depends on the contents of the convictions that fit horizontally and vertically into a scheme, that is, on what we take as our pre-interpretive ontology, and on what legal values we assume to globally justify state coercion. At the most abstract level, the contents of the convictions of different participants tends to converge. Notwithstanding, convergence is not the reason to accept certain judgements as right answers about the contents of law. The correctness of these judgements can only be evaluated in terms of the rest of legal judgements in our epistemic structure.

The substantive program of law as integrity is not merely the idea of coherence. Dworkin proposes that we take past decisions to be the pre-interpretive data and that we interpret them in the light of three standards: justice, equity, and due process. In Dworkin's opinion, these standards reflect our normative understanding of law. Coherence as a property and as a relationship is merely the means to reach interpretive conclusions by establishing an equilibrium within this structure.

Adopting coherence as a legal/political virtue should lead to the same conclusion. The commitment a fraternal community makes to speak with a single voice is not a

---

justice, equity and due process results from his interpretive convictions. Like any other judgement, this one is subject to debate and can be refuted by better arguments. See Dworkin (1986, 239-240).

89 For this reason, Dworkin points out that judgements about the contents of law are interpretive. They are the result of applying a complex theory that includes two dimensions: one tends to be more epistemic; the other, more substantive. It is important to define the character of these judgements on the basis of the idea of tendency because this reflects the thesis of interconnectedness of our judgements. This tendency is the result of interconnectedness and of the location of each judgement within the epistemic structure. On this point, see Dworkin (1985, 147-148).

90 Dworkin (1986, 67-68, 98-101).

value that contradicts the commitment to speak in terms of equity or justice[91]. To speak with a single voice is to be committed to reaching a unique solution that reflects the legal practice as a whole. But no-thing helps to determine what this solution must be.

The conclusion to be drawn from a theory of truth-coherence is that no interpretive solution is right or wrong or true or false only because it coheres or does not cohere with the epistemic structure in which it is embedded. Otherwise, we are assuming scepticism[92]. A judge or a legal theoretician such as Dworkin simply put forward their arguments and consider that they are most correct. Does this imply that the truth of propositions is ultimately independent of coherence? I think that a proper understanding of internalism leads to giving a negative answer to this question. An assessment of the adequacy of Dworkin's legal view, for example, requires that we address this issue in our own conceptual scheme and that we enquire whether or not law is the way Dworkin presents it. Our answer will be true if the relationships among our legal beliefs together with the soundness and complexity of our interpretive schemes enable us to reach a satisfactory justification to our judgements (the best reconstruction of the legal practice). Coherence then is the criterion of truth for a proposition about law. Dworkin's project will appeal to us if we share his epistemic structure or if we find his arguments convincing. This entails, specifically, that we agree with his understanding of what a political community is like. In addition, we should accept on the one hand, that law is related to the meaning of past institutional decisions, and, on the other, that the justifying context of law are the principles of equity, justice, and legality. Otherwise, we should provide arguments to show that Dworkin is mistaken, that is, that his reconstruction of the legal practice is wrong. But to do this we ought to develop an alternative reconstruction with the same interpretive goal, in other words, we ought to offer a picture of the legal practice as the best example of its kind[93].

---

91 On this notion of fraternal community, see Dworkin (1986, 206-216). It is not my intention to elucidate to what extent coherence should be adopted as a legal/political virtue. In connection with this point, we will assume Dworkin's position about what is required from a political community that has made a commitment to certain principles. Hurley's views on this issue are interesting too. She appeals to coherence as a means to warrant personal autonomy and to determine what is the thing to do in a democratic society. Hurley (1989, Ch. 15).

92 This position would have an externalist character and would imply scepticism because it would assume that there are just as many right or true positions as there are coherent schemes. However, such a claim is external to the conceptual schemes - and the plausibility of this kind of assertions is what we have been attempting to refute throughout this work.

93 Notwithstanding that this issue falls beyond the scope of this work, I pointed out in Chapter 2 that I find Dworkin's substantive project appealing. In my view, his argument against the claim that institutional

This approach to the truth conditions of legal propositions permits to dissociate the existence of a right answer from linguistic conventions and from the intentions of normative authorities. We will devote thorough consideration to the questions about how and to what extent is disagreement linked to the absence of right answer. Nevertheless, before we undertake these inquiries, we shall investigate if interpretive theory can plausibly maintain an optimistic thesis about the existence of right answers, as Dworkin indeed seeks to do.

5.5 RIGHT LEGAL ANSWERS AND STRONG DISCRETION

Once we reject the plausibility of global scepticism for law, the issue about the right answer or legal determinacy raises two further important questions to be treated separately. The first of them is whether we can find reasons to be always optimistic about the existence of a unique right legal answer. The second, what arguments can be put forward to establish a necessary link between hard cases as controversial cases and no right answer. We will devote thorough attention to these matters in Chapter 6. Notwithstanding, it is interesting at this point to highlight some aspects related to the first aforementioned question.

When we adopt a notion of truth-assertability on the grounds of coherence among legal beliefs or among their propositional contents, the existence of a unique right answer depends on the possibility of obtaining a single satisfactory interpretive conclusion within a particular conceptual scheme. In Dworkin's terms, we face a legal gap or a situation of no right answer when 'there are two interpretations, two ways to read a statute (for example), one way would give you the decision for the plaintiff in the case, the second reading would give the other decision, and there is no way to choose the better interpretation between the two'[94].

Dworkin claims that within the reduced epistemic context of a legal interpretation, we will never or hardly ever cease to be able to produce an answer or have an opinion

authorities may be mistaken about law is convincing: a decision is not legal just because it has been made by an institution that we regard as authoritative. Accepting authoritative decisions as exclusionary reasons entails precisely what needs to be proven: specifically, that such a reconstruction is epistemically plausible, and that it is better to view the legal practice as a passive practice than as a practice in which participants have their own convictions about which behaviours are legally regulated and assume that some arguments are better than others. I agree with Dworkin's denial of global scepticism as an acceptable interpretation. We cannot adopt scepticism because we presuppose that we are participants in a collective practice and, therefore, whenever we produce judgements about the law, we have an object to interpret.

[94] Dworkin (1991a, 88).

about which one of the competing interpretations is best[95]. For this reason, Dworkin maintains that it will always be possible to appeal to a single right legal answer. Objections to this thesis have repeatedly been pressed. I believe this point to be one of the weakest in his theory[96]. Its weakness becomes clear not in the framework of an alternative methodology of legal analysis, but from within the very interpretive parameters of his theory.

If we wish to assume an optimistic thesis about the existence of a single right legal answer, we shall have to disprove two arguments that lead to partial scepticism: firstly, we need to refute the incommensurability of interpretations; secondly, we shall have to show that two interpretations can never be equally good in their merits[97].

5.5.1 Incommensurability

From an interpretive point of view of law, the problem of incommensurability between interpretations may arise when it is not possible to structure our interpretive scheme so as to compare two alternatives. In this case, vertical and horizontal coherence do not suffice to select a single solution as the optimal solution. This situation occurs when one conceptual scheme can portray an object from different standpoints. Each one of these perspectives is the best interpretation of the object from that particular point of view[98]. Incommensurability then is a problem relating to the existence of more than one criterion against which to measure the different alternative interpretations. But our aim in this chapter is to analyse the problem of the existence of a variety of criteria in a single evaluative context. Clearly, if, say, we attempt to compare the technical quality

---

95 Dworkin (1985, 144-145; 1991a, 90).

96 See Finnis (1987, 371-374), Putnam (1995a, 6-7), Mackie (1984, 165, 168-169), Marmor (1992, 54 57) and Bix (1993, 96-106).

97 Dworkin denies the possibility of a tie between rival interpretations because in his view this claim makes no sense. Furthermore, he rejects incommensurability because he contends that it is always possible to embrace two interpretations according to the same parameters or criteria. See Dworkin (1991a, 89-90). Note that the purpose of this section is not whether or not it is possible to reject incommensurability between any two interpretations. This issue has been explored earlier when we considered global scepticism. Total incommensurability has advocates in every field of knowledge. Paradigmatic examples of this position are Feyerabend's critique of the scientific method, and the sceptical interpretation of the problem of rule-following in the context of the philosophy of language. These lines of argument have been adopted by deconstructionist approaches to legal theory such as that of *Critical Legal Studies*. See Putnam (1992, 124-128, 149-152; 1981, 113-119) for an argument on how global scepticism is self-defeating.

98 This is Finnis's internal criticism to Dworkin's thesis on the right answer. See Finnis (1987, 371-374) and Mackie (1984, 165).

of a soccer player such as Ronaldo with that of a painter such as Dalí, we encounter serious difficulties due to incommensurability because the domains in which we evaluate the technical achievements of these individuals are clearly different[99]. In my view, incommensurability should be treated separately from the problem Marmor brings to Dworkin's attention, namely that even if we accept that every legal interpretation depends on the value or purpose of the practice, it is not to be concluded that this value is of a moral or aesthetic character. Hence, Marmor stresses, different interpretations may attempt to adjust the practice to values or purposes of different characters. In consequence, they cannot be compared with one another[100]. However, Marmor's remarks are of little relevance to the problem of right answers from an interpretive viewpoint. Marmor assumes that our legal judgements can be radically or infinitely ambiguous in such a way that they may prevent a sensible formulation of the question what legal alternative is best. As we observed, for a social practice or language game to exist, a shared understanding of the general meaning of the interactions within it should occur. This entails not only that participants believe that there is a purpose to the practice, but that they share a single general understanding of this purpose. Marmor's argument leads to the conclusion that in such a situation participants cannot devise a view of law because they may have different practices in mind (different criteria of correctness), both when they act and when they interpret. This argument is in clear conflict with his support to the non-sceptical thesis of rule-following[101].

The problem of incommensurability is a real challenge to the optimistic thesis about the existence of a single right answer when we enquire about the comparability of different options within the same evaluative context. Accordingly, the problem turns on legal conceptions as ways to develop the interpretive concept rather than on the concept itself. It is worth noting, as Hurley does, that several alternatives can be commensurable in at least two senses: in a weak sense, there is commensurability when the agent can

---

[99] True, it is always logically possible to establish some comparative parameter between the two, but it would be hard to do so convincingly. In this case, I believe there to be better reasons to defend than to deny incommensurability. It should be conceded, however, that the question about whether we are within one or a number of evaluative contexts is a matter of degree and interpretation. See Dworkin (1996, 132-135; 1991a, 89).

[100] Marmor (1992, 54-57).

[101] A social practice of rule-following can only exist if there is no ambiguity in participants' understanding of their interactions at its most abstract level. This may embrace two situations: that in which different participants have different understandings of the practice, and that in which participants have an ambiguous understanding of their practice. In both of these cases, the idea of a social practice of rule-following is undermined.

choose one among different options regardless of whether or not she can compare them; to be commensurable in a strong sense requires a monist theory, a legal conception that reduces the purpose of the practice to a single value or standard[102]. According to strong commensurability, incommensurability will occur when the theory applied is pluralist, i.e. one that relates or adjusts different values that are not reducible to a single standard.

If we assume weak commensurability, we conclude that there is no room for incommensurability in adjudication. A judge can always reach a solution and decide between two options. However, when attempting to establish whether a right legal answer exists, weak commensurability is useless. The relevant question is no longer whether the judge can provide an answer to the conflict at stake, but whether she can provide an answer that accords with the law, that is, whether she can render a decision without exercising strong discretion. In order to assert the existence of a right legal answer and to deny the need for strong discretion we need to maintain strong commensurability.

Sometimes Dworkin seems to ground his optimistic thesis on weak commensurability[103]. He insists that a decision can be made even if two options at first appear difficult to compare. It is important to bear in mind that the problem of the right answer is not about making a decision, but about formulating a legal conclusion on the grounds of a particular theory or reconstruction of law[104]. For this reason, Dworkin ought to prove that strong incommensurability does not exist. However, there seem to be no good arguments to reject strong incommensurability if we assume, as indeed Dworkin does, a theory of law based on the equilibrium or coherence between three values: justice, equity, and due process. If these three substantive principles are irreducible to a single one and not measurable in terms of an axiologically superior value, we should acknowledge the impossibility of solving an irreducible conflict among these three principles[105].

---

[102] See Hurley (1989, 263-270), Bix (1993, 101-102) and Raz (1992, 286).

[103] Dworkin (1996, 137-138) replied to incommensurability by appealing to the need for decisions in the legal context. Moreover, he has often insisted that we will always have an opinion to readily choose between two alternatives. See Dworkin (1991a, 90).

[104] See, for example, Guastini's objections to Dworkin's model in Guastini (1983, 455).

[105] Some authors have devised perspectives to eliminate the incommensurability of values but they always assumed or added a structure that includes a meta-value or meta-criterion that allows for an intelligible comparison. The interesting question is whether it is possible to eliminate the problem of incommensurability when there are no such criteria readily available. On these proposals, see Raz (1991, 83-88) and Finnis (1990, 238-241).

In conclusion, an interpretive theory that takes coherence as a criterion of truth has no intrinsic reason to deny incommensurability as an interpretive possibility[106]. For this reason, the optimistic thesis about a right answer is not justifiable in case of incommensurability. Here, the judge will not be entitled to claim that there exists a single right legal answer. Under such circumstances, she has to exercise strong discretion to comply with her duty to render a decision.

We shall next investigate another of Dworkin's arguments in favour of his optimistic thesis, namely that a tie between interpretations is not plausible in the legal language game.

5.5.2 Tie between interpretations

Dworkin early on dismissed the idea that legal indeterminacy may arise from two interpretations being equally good. This situation is encountered when two comparable options display equal merits in terms of the criterion measuring their correctness or value[107]. Thus, two interpretations are equally correct when there are more epistemic reasons to justify their equality than to back up the conclusion that one is better than the other. It is important to elucidate whether there are epistemic reasons to conclude a tie between interpretations.

According to Currie, a tie presupposes the existence of different maximal interpretations so that none of them can be taken to be best[108]. Two different circumstances might lead to a tie: on the one hand, a tie may result from a lack of certainty or of sufficient evidence about which interpretation is best according to a particular criterion; on the other, it may result from the certainty or possession of sufficient evidence suggesting that two interpretations are, indeed, equally good.

In the first situation we lack epistemic reasons to legitimately ascertain which interpretive conclusion is best. But this does not mean that we possess sufficient evidence to assert that a tie, and therefore indeterminacy, be the most satisfactory solution. Here, no version of an object can be taken to be best. Not even the version claiming that there is no right answer can be said to be best. This problem has been tackled in legal thought taking as a starting point the notion of second or higher order vagueness, which reflects the following situation: when attempting to answer whether a

---

[106] Putnam, one of the exponents of the theory of truth as coherence, argues that a coherence theory should always assume incommensurability. He occasionally criticised Dworkin for being too naïve in this respect. See Putnam (1981, 72-73; 1995a, 6-7). See also Hurley (1989, 264-270).

[107] Dworkin (1991a, 89; 1985, 144).

[108] Currie (1993, 421).

given case falls within the scope of a particular concept, it may be the case that it is not possible to decide whether it belongs to its certainty zone, whether it is clearly excluded from it or whether it belongs to the penumbral zone of the concept. Second order vagueness reflects the problem that we may be unsure about the vagueness of a concept (or of a predicate) in a particular case, that is, its vagueness may be vague[109]. Second order vagueness implies indeterminacy in the judgement that there is a tie. This very judgement may itself be indeterminate, and so on and so forth.

However, regardless of whether it is possible to devise a way of overcoming this semantic difficulty, it is interesting to investigate how this problem may affect the thesis of partial indeterminacy and an optimistic view about the existence of right answers. Second order vagueness is an argument against the idea that it is always possible to determine when is it the case that a proposition has no truth-value. We should nevertheless differentiate between higher order potential and higher order actual vagueness. To assert that there is always room for uncertainty about the vagueness of a statement does not imply that we are never sure that it is vague. At times, we may possess sufficient evidence to conclude a tie between rival interpretations. On other occasions, however, we may not. For this reason, admitting potential higher order vagueness does not automatically undermine the thesis of partial indeterminacy of law. Neither is it an argument backing up this thesis.

By contrast, higher order vagueness creates some difficulties for an optimistic thesis that claims that any legal proposition is always either true or false. This claim should take into account the problem of second order vagueness. Dworkin admits that it may not be obvious whether or not a contract signed on a Sunday is sacrilegious. Then, it may be the case that we have no sufficient reasons to decide that the statement 'Tom's contract is sacrilegious' is true, false, or lacks truth-value[110]. In this case, we are not only not legitimated to claim indeterminacy: neither are we in a position to ascertain determinacy.

Dworkin has resorted to a further argument to reply to theses of partial indeterminacy and to support his optimism about the existence of right answers. He observes, I believe quite rightly, that an indeterministic conclusion cannot be obtained by default, that is, it cannot result from a lack of sufficient evidence to claim that a legal judgement is either true or false[111]. Every interpretive conclusion is the result of

---

[109] This problem may be reproduced ad infinitum. See Moreso (1998, 82-83), Raz (1979, 73-74) and Putnam (1975, 217; 1995b, 76-77). For a detailed analysis of this issue, see Sainsbury (1991, 167-182).

[110] See Endicott (1995) and Dworkin (1985, 405 footnote 3).

[111] Dworkin (1996, 129-139).

the best version of the legal practice. Therefore, an indeterministic conclusion should result from arguing that the version that yields this answer is the best version of law. Reaching a conclusion by excluding all alternative options is not acceptable from an interpretive point of view. Notwithstanding, as we shall stress in Chapter 6, taking Dworkin's observation into account does not imply agreeing with his optimistic thesis about right answers. The success of this epistemic thesis is conditional on there being no interpretive reasons to maintain partial indeterminacy in some cases. But what prevents the existence of such reasons? In this sense, Coleman writes:

> The decision that is supported by the balance of reasons is the correct one. There are no grounds for ruling out a priori the possibility that the balance of reasons in a given case might be in equipoise, not unambiguously favoring one decision over another. In that case, there is no right answer. There is nothing in the logic of reasons that entails that the balance of reasons must always favor one course of conduct over another, one judgement or decision over another. A fortiori, nothing in the nature of legal reasons entails the same thing[112]

Sometimes, internal scepticism, which Ronald Dworkin defines as the interpretive position that takes as the best reconstruction of law that which concludes that there is no right answer, may emerge as the best option on the grounds of epistemic and substantive reasons[113]. A system of beliefs was earlier defined as a dynamical structure that constantly incorporates new beliefs and rejects old ones. The aim of this activity is to reach global coherence or the equilibrium of the whole as a way of maximising the truth of its propositional contents. However, an epistemic structure has no mechanism to warrant that global equilibrium will eventually lead to a single option as the best interpretation. Let us recall Harman's principle of conservatism. According to this principle we are entitled to continue to hold our beliefs (in our case, the belief that there is a tie) as long as we have no special reason against doing so. Such a reason could

---

[112] Coleman (1995, 49). Coleman argues that Dworkin has by now abandoned the optimistic thesis about the existence of right answers. But Coleman's claim is not based on an explicit turn of Dworkin's view. Perhaps, Coleman intends to suggest that Dworkin should abandon his optimism because it is unjustified. Nothing in Dworkin's work suggests that he rejects one of his more controversial theses (and for that matter, one that he defends most fiercely). See, for example, his argument supporting the right answer in one of his most recent papers, Dworkin (1996, 129-139). Like Coleman, Kress (1996, 540-541) seeks to dissociate coherence from an optimistic thesis about the existence of right answers.

[113] See Dworkin's distinction between internal and external scepticism. External scepticism is an externalist position along the lines of what I have outlined in Chapters 4 and 5. According to external scepticism, it is pointless to claim the truth or falsity of a judgement. External scepticism concludes that discussions about what argument or interpretation is best simply reflect the expression of incommensurable opinions, or, even just noise. Dworkin (1986, 78-86; 1996, 89-94).

effectively only be the introspective realisation that there is insufficient evidence for our beliefs[114]. Furthermore, from an interpretive point of view, the existence of epistemic reasons to endorse a tie sets a limit on the possible substantive reasons to break the tie. A judge, for example, may rate two interpretations as equal in their merits and still believe that we would be much better off if the tie were broken. She can nevertheless not decide in favour of either of the two interpretations without being aware that she is inventing in the process of doing so. Here, she must exercise strong discretion if she wishes to reach a conclusion. At this point, the best version of law leads precisely to the conclusion of indeterminacy. Indeterminacy is all that the agent is entitled to assert.

We noted earlier that the plausibility of an optimistic thesis about the existence of a right answer should be carefully distinguished from the positivist link between hard cases and legal indeterminacy. Chapter 6 will address this last issue. On the basis of the exposition presented hitherto, it will be shown what are the reasons to dissociate hard cases from legal indeterminacy, even though it is plausible to reject optimism about the existence of right answers.

[114] On this principle see Harman (1986, 46).

CHAPTER 6

HARD CASES AND LEGAL DETERMINACY

6.1 INTRODUCTION

In foregoing chapters we examined mainly two views on the role of strong discretion in the application of law: Hartian positivism and Dworkin's interpretive theory. Both views posit similar conditions to assert that a case is a hard case. Notwithstanding, they disagree about the relationship between hard cases and legal indeterminacy, or absence of right answer, and hence, about the need for strong discretion. For Hartian positivism, hard cases, i.e. cases in which the truth-value of a proposition is considered to be controversial or uncertain, lead to legal indeterminacy. For this reason, settling hard cases requires the judge to exercise strong discretion[1].

The positivist approach to hard cases is grounded on a general semantic, ontological, and epistemic position. As a whole, this constitutes a view of law and reflects a specific understanding of the relationship between law and the language in which law is expressed. The following is an outline of the main positivist theses:

a) law is essentially a communicational phenomenon. Consequently, legal knowledge by and large consists in understanding the language in which law is expressed, or in identifying the truth conditions of legal propositions.

b) a proposition about law is true if there exist certain social facts (a rule of recognition and settled semantic conventions) that render it true.

c) these social facts depend on shared perceptions, social practices, linguistic conventions, or propositional attitudes in the legal community.

d) when there is no inter-subjective sufficient evidence to assert that a legal proposition is true or that it is false, it has no truth-value: we face a hard case.

e) the very possibility of normative communication requires that there exist non-controversial instances of the use of terms, the so-called easy cases.

---

[1] We pointed out previously that Hartian positivism regards judicial discretion as a restricted activity: it is interstitial legislation subject to constraints such as acceptability and reasonableness. Its strong character lies, specifically, in that it entails a choice between alternatives. On this point, see the characterisation of strong discretion presented in Chapter 1.

f) in easy cases, rule-following is possible because the contents of rules is determinate. To know the meaning of legal texts requires the ability to specify their instances of use. Thus, legal knowledge does not require interpretation as the substitution of one formulation of the rule for another.

g) legal language is inevitably of an open texture. This generates hard cases in the identification of law[2]. In these instances, rule-following is not possible because the contents of rules is indeterminate: literal or simple meaning does not embrace the case in hand. All we can do is stipulate a new meaning discretionarily.

Dworkin's position clearly differs from Hartian positivism in its views about the implications of the existence of hard cases upon the possibility for strong discretion. Dworkin claims that even in hard cases there is a single right legal answer and judges are legally obliged to identify it. In hard cases, very much like in easy ones, judges only need to exercise weak discretion. This approach to judicial activity in hard cases is circumscribed within a more general theory of law and legal knowledge: the interpretive theory of law. Dworkin's interpretive view of law is based on the following theses:

a) law is essentially an interpretive phenomenon. To know the law is to be able to offer the best version of the pre-interpretive data of the legal practice.

b) statements about law are theory-dependent - no legal reality permits the confrontation of our judgements. Moreover, the truth-value of legal propositions does not depend on the existence of a social convention.

c) a proposition about law is true if it coheres or fits into the larger group of propositions that offers the best version of the legal practice.

d) the best version of the legal practice is that explanation/justification of the pre-interpretive data that achieves the best balance between justice, equity, and legality; that is, the interpretation that displays the greatest degree of integrity in its formal and justifying dimensions.

e) in easy cases, the interpreter's conclusion about the contents of law is not controversial. Easy cases are not controversial because the participants perceive them as clear examples of the contents of their practice.

---

[2] We previously distinguished between vagueness and ambiguity as sources of semantic indeterminacy. Whereas vagueness entails widespread doubt or uncertainty about the truth-value of a proposition, ambiguity involves disagreement in the qualification of a proposition as true or false.

f) in contrast, hard cases are those in which interpretive conclusions are controversial. Several conceptions of what is required by the practice compete with one another.

g) hard cases do not generate a lack of right answer insofar that the interpreter is able to structure her interpretive scheme to reach a conclusion about what is demanded by the law.

These two theories appear to share some postulates and yet, they reach clearly diverging conclusions. Let us first note that both Hartian positivism and Dworkin's approach to law aim at rejecting semantic realism. Both approaches advocate a semantic theory based on the truth conditions of legal propositions. However, these truth conditions are not dependent on facts that transcend human epistemic abilities. In my view, the difference between the two approaches at this point is that positivism understands the collective epistemic abilities to provide the truth-value of legal propositions, whereas for Dworkin, the truth-value of propositions is to be established on the basis of coherence among the propositions in a particular interpretive scheme. Recall that participants tend to share this scheme at its most abstract level. From an interpretive point of view, differing interpretive conceptions and conclusions may occur within a single legal community. This, however, does not imply that legal propositions be indeterminate. For Hartian positivism, by contrast, from the existence of differing interpretations and conclusions it follows that the propositions in hand have no truth-value. This is so because the truth-value of a legal proposition is determined on the grounds of a unitary perception of the legal phenomenon. If this perception is not shared, there is no sufficient evidence to assert that the proposition is true or false.

What has been pointed out so far indicates that both theories advocate a theory of truth as assertability according to which only those propositions for which there is sufficient supportive evidence can be claimed either true or false. However, they differ as to what they consider to be evidence to assert or to deny the truth of a proposition. Hartian positivism supports a quantitative notion of evidence: the greater the number of particular schemes of interpretation that converge, the more evidence we have for our assertion. Thus, there will be sufficient evidence when the majority of competent members of the community agree on the truth-value of a certain proposition. If the community is divided in opinion, there is no sufficient evidence to warrant the truth or the falsity of the proposition and, consequently, it is indeterminate.

In contrast, Dworkin advocates a qualitative idea of evidence. Truth depends on the firmness of the beliefs on which a particular scheme of interpretation is grounded.

Firmness derives from coherence and from the possession of certain mental states that are independent of our will. Thus, there is sufficient evidence to assert the truth-value of a proposition when, having undergone an evaluative process, the interpreter can but conclude that hers is the right answer to the issue under consideration. Disagreement between interpreters is important to the extent that the arguments leading to the differing conclusions may convince an agent that her view is not sufficiently sound. Accordingly, this may induce her to change her views. However, if these are not convincing reasons to prove her mistake, she will continue to believe that there is a single right answer to the question in hand, and that her own embodies it best.

6.2 THE SCEPTICAL CHALLENGE

Before we turn our attention to the consequences of the differences between Hartian positivism and Dworkin's view of law in what regards judicial adjudication, let us stress one more aspect these two theories have in common: the claim that the sceptical thesis of 'anything goes' can be overcome. Hartian positivism puts forward two arguments for this claim. The first one is pragmatic in character: the existence of easy cases, in which legal propositions are either true or false, is indispensable for communication to be possible (recall that law is regarded as a communicational phenomenon)[3]. Its second argument is one that rests on a non-sceptical interpretation of the problem of rule-following: the fact that every rule is liable to multiple interpretations does not imply that it is not possible to grasp its meaning without interpretation (as substitution). There is a way to grasp the meaning of a rule that depends on the ability to identify its instances of use. This ability is linked to the existence of a shared linguistic practice, and ultimately, of a shared form of life[4].

By contrast, Dworkin replies to scepticism by observing that although the restrictions applying to the possible interpretations of the legal practice are scheme-dependent, they can nevertheless be perceived as genuine, that is, as objective restrictions. These internal restrictions thus become sufficient evidence for the truth of a proposition[5]. In fact, Dworkin dismisses any other kind of evidence. Moreover, he claims that scepticism cannot conclude by default that no right answer exists: the fact

3 See Hart (1994, 126).

4 Bix (1993, Ch.2) and Marmor (1992, 146-147) are the main advocates of this idea.

5 See, for instance, Dworkin (1986, 235-236). Recall that Dworkin defends a non-Wittgensteinian concept of interpretation. Thus, to interpret according to this author is not replacing one linguistic formulation for another, but a way of knowing or grasping a phenomenon from a particular perspective about its global sense.

that there is insufficient evidence to claim either the truth or the falsity of a proposition cannot acceptably lead to the conclusion that the proposition has no truth-value. Just like determinacy, indeterminacy should follow from the best interpretation of the practice - one should provide interpretive reasons to conclude indeterminacy[6]. Finally, Dworkin advocates an optimistic thesis about the possibility of each agent structuring his scheme of interpretive convictions in such a way that she is in general able to recognise one of the possible answers as the correct one.

In previous chapters we emphasised the most important problems encountered by both theories to warrant the plausibility of their main theses. It was pointed out that Hartian positivism meets with difficulties to overcome the sceptical challenge because its interpretation of rule-following is closely dependent on a shared linguistic use as the basis for meaning of legal terms and expressions. Moreover, we observed that it faces hardship to explain what is the mistake or epistemic defect of an interpretive agent who dissents from the majority view. The problem here is that a theory of truth-assertability should reject that the truth-value of propositions be linked to facts independent of our epistemic abilities to verify them. Therefore, to know if these truth conditions are met cannot consist in an accurate description of facts such as consensus or shared psychological states. Hartian positivism asserts that the truth-value of legal propositions transcends the epistemic abilities of each individual agent, but not those of the aggregate of speakers in a community. This thesis may lead to counter-intuitive conclusions. If the legal phenomenon is a product of collective invention as an aggregate of individual inventions, and if we admit that individual perceptions are fallible, the aggregate of individual perceptions must be fallible too. If, on the other hand, it is possible to distinguish between collective invention and the collection of individual inventions we are compelled to accept one of the following premises: either a) there is a subgroup of individuals which have epistemic authority over the rest of individuals in the group, in which case, the referent of legal propositions is constituted by the perceptions of the authoritative subgroup and their judgements are infallible; or b) the community as a whole constitutes an epistemic entity different from the sum of its individual members. None of these premises appears compatible with positivism, particularly if we take into account Hart's thesis of judicial fallibility[7], and the widespread rejection of collective entities as something non-metaphorical. It is nevertheless interesting to analyse the consequences of adopting either of these

---

[6] See Dworkin (1996, 129-139).
[7] Hart (1994, 141-147).

premises. Following the first one, knowing the meaning of legal terms and expressions is no more than accounting for the intentions and mental states of those individuals who have epistemic authority. This poses two problems: in addition to the difficulty in identifying which individuals possess such authority, we thus return to realist semantics about the truth conditions of legal propositions. The truth-value of propositions about law would then be determined by the mental states of these individuals regardless of interpreters' epistemic abilities to identify them correctly.

If, on the other hand, we adopt the second premise, namely that the community constitutes a separate entity, its members may all be mistaken as to the phenomenon the very community constructed. The members in a community may all be mistaken as to the collective facts constructed by the community to which they belong. This thesis seems to lead to realist semantics too because the truth-value of propositions in effect transcends the epistemic abilities of the aggregate of individuals who constitute the community. In my opinion, Hartian positivism does not escape either of these conclusions because, as was pointed out before, it does not offer a convincing answer to the problem of rule-following. Neither does it show how the idea of internal relationship between the rule and its instances of use avoids semantic realism and the sceptical challenge. In conclusion, positivism does not explain how the truth conditions of legal propositions can transcend individual epistemic abilities and yet not fall into some form of semantic realism.

The weakest point of Dworkin's theory is, by contrast, how to justify an optimistic thesis on the existence of a single right answer. We observed that a coherentist position about truth and legal knowledge does not warrant a unique right legal answer. This position defines the character of the right answer and it explains how it is possible to speak of objectivity disregarding semantic and metaphysical realism. It also seeks to prove that disagreement does not imply legal indeterminacy. But it does not guarantee the existence of a right answer in all cases. One may well continue to enquire what arguments justify the thesis that an agent can always structure her scheme of interpretive convictions in such a way that she will be able to reach a unique conclusion. As pointed out previously, a coherentist position is compatible with the assumption that a single conceptual scheme may provide sufficient evidence to claim that there are several equally correct answers to a particular question, or that there is none[8]. For this reason, although Dworkin's position provides good reasons not to take

[8] In this sense, see Putnam (1995a, 6; 1981, 49-54).

the global sceptical challenge seriously, it does not offer convincing arguments as to why the thesis of partial indeterminacy should be rejected.

The question relevant to legal adjudication is when is it possible to assume legal indeterminacy and, consequently, when do strongly discretionary decisions become necessary to comply with the duty to render a decision? Neither of these two theories provides an entirely satisfactory answer to this question. Hartian positivism does not overcome global scepticism. Dworkin's theory does not succeed in justifying an optimistic conclusion on the right answer, which would be plausible only if we accepted as implausible a theory as optimistic semantic realism.

It remains to be determined which one of these theories most effectively accounts for judicial activity in controversial cases. This is crucial to decide for any of these perspectives on the legal phenomenon. In my opinion, a theory of law ought to provide some explanation to controversial cases as a relevant aspect of every day legal life. It appears counter-intuitive to claim that something as commonplace as disagreements about the meaning of legal terms and expressions leads to legal indeterminacy[9].

When a case is controversial, each one of the views in conflict purport to provide *the* right legal answer. The underlying assumption is that a right legal answer exists. But such an assumption may simply be one of the rules of the legal language game. Each conception tries to offer legal arguments, and their conclusions reflect a particular understanding of law. The degree to which these arguments are convincing may vary, but it is important to distinguish between a bad legal argument and an extra-legal argument. It is rather odd to defend some legal claim on the grounds of aesthetic arguments, for instance. Likewise, it is unusual to advocate a particular legal claim by appealing to the lack of right answer. These remarks seem intuitively right. True, disagreement may render legal indeterminacy a mere illusion, but I venture this is a settled and firm illusion. It is the kind of illusion that a theory of truth-assertability may take as sufficient evidence to claim legal determinacy even in the event of disagreement. It does nevertheless not follow that there be sufficient evidence to assert that indeterminacy plays no part in the legal discourse. This conclusion appears counter-intuitive too. The point here is whether indeterminacy is a necessary consequence of disagreement and, therefore, whether cases that raise controversy about the contents of law ought to be considered instances of no right answer. Obviously, given the antirealist character of the theoretical proposals we are analysing, the answer

---

[9] On this point, see Brink (1988, 112-117; 1989, 188-191), Dworkin (1986, 45-46, Ch. IV; 1996, 136-139) and Stavropoulos (1996, Ch. V).

to this question greatly depends on the explanatory force of a positive or a negative thesis, that is, on what position better adapts to our legal convictions, as well as on the strength of the reasons provided to support it.

Hartian positivism opts for partial indeterminacy because of the limits language imposes upon what we can assert or deny. According to antirealist semantics, these limits are ultimately those imposed by our fictional legal ontology. However, positivism does not present reasons to justify a fictional ontology based on inter-subjective agreement. Its only argument is that communication is otherwise impossible. But this answer presumes the very claim it needs to prove: that law is a communicational and not an interpretive phenomenon, and, as such, controversial.

Clearly, a theory of legal determinacy should explain not only what permits communication and agreement, but also how disagreement prevents communication. Dworkin shows that disagreement does not prevent communication. He does so by resorting to the distinction between concept and conception. Legal disagreement arises between different conceptions about how to render meaningful a common shared idea. These general conceptions are different answers to the same question, namely what are the features that render law a justification to state coercion. Disagreement among conceptions is meaningful because each position may identify alternative proposals to reflect the contents of the legal practice. The question then is which among the possible versions of the legal phenomenon is the best interpretation of law as a justification for state coercion.

In my opinion, Dworkin's view displays some interesting features. Common sense suggests that disagreements about law are meaningful and legal in character. The fact that other interpretive agents hold positions that diverge from our own does not imply that our judgements about law be wrong, or that they do not even qualify as legal judgements. The arguments offered by other conceptions may convince us that we are mistaken. But only the realisation that our initial opinion was not sufficiently sound can urge us to change our views - our change of mind does not result from the fact that other agents have a different perception of the legal phenomenon[10].

This advantage of Dworkin's theory is marginal because the foregoing reflection is not necessarily correct. With a view to evaluating its correctness, one need assume a substantive position about what constitutes an acceptable understanding of law, and provide reasons for the relationship between disagreement and legal indeterminacy.

---

10 Dworkin points out that what counts as evidence for the truth of our opinions is not how popular they are. Neither is the degree of controversy they raise evidence for their falsity. See Dworkin (1996, 112-117).

6.3 JUSTIFIYING SEMANTIC INDETERMINACY

Recall that a theory of truth as assertability for legal statements connects the truth of a proposition to the sufficiency of evidence to justify its assertion. In this sense, this theory holds an epistemic view of the concept of truth. However, antirealist semantics imply a specific ontological position about the existence of the reference of legal propositions[11]. Thus, the facts we designate by means of legal language result from our social practice: *esse est percipi* or *esse est concipi*[12]. From this viewpoint, legal facts are theoretical-conceptual constructs - they are artefacts or fictional objects internal to the language game of law. These objects could therefore be considered a product of imagination. As pointed out by Dummet,

> To say that fictional characters are the creations of the imagination is to say that a statement about a fictional character can be true only if it is imagined as being true, that a fictional character can have only those properties which it is part of the story that he has; to say that something in as object of sense – that for it *esse est percipi* – is to say that it has only those properties it is perceived as having: in both cases, the ontological thesis is a ground for rejecting the law of excluded middle as applied to statements about those objects. Thus, we cannot separate the question of the ontological status of a class of objects from the question of the correct notion of truth for statements about those objects, i.e. of the kind of thing in virtue of which such statements are true, when they are true.[13]

Taking the relationship between semantics and ontology into consideration, semantic indeterminacy generates ontological indeterminacy. Legal facts are the product of the language in which we express judgements. Therefore, the limits to legal ontology are imposed by our perceptions of objects and events, and the available

---

[11] As noted by Dummet (1978, 229) with regard to mathematical objects, it is not possible to regard mathematical reality as something external to or independent of the agent if we assess the truth-value of mathematical statements in terms of antirealist semantics. On the relationship between semantics and ontology see also Hierro Pescador (1986, 400-401) and Marmor (1995, 194-195). From the viewpoint of antirealist semantics it is not necessary to assume a robust ontology for descriptive judgements to make sense.

[12] These two Latin phrases mean that objects are what we *perceive* or *conceive* them to be. Thus, propositions designating objects do not refer to a reality independent of our language, judgements and perceptions. See Dummet (1978, 228-230). To illustrate this idea, Marmor observes that Michaelangelo's David (the statue) is a cultural construct. As such, it is dependent on our knowledge. If we consider this statue as a physical object whose properties are independent of our epistemic abilities, we will be speaking of a piece of marble. But a piece of marble is of no interest to interpreters: it is the statue they are concerned with. See Marmor (1995, 194-195).

[13] Dummet (1978, 230).

evidence[14]. For this reason, ontological determinacy is conditional on how our judgements endorse a deterministic or an indeterministic position.

Recall that antirealism need not assume that legal determinacy depends on shared perceptions or individual stipulations. It can overcome the difficulties in maintaining either or both of the foregoing criteria by assuming that legal determinacy depends on the best theory of law. Here, the best theory of law establishes the truth conditions of legal propositions and constitutes the ontology of law[15]. This idea is reflected in Dworkin's claim that legal facts are not 'hard facts' but facts of narrative consistency[16]. Legal ontology is a conceptual construct, a fictional fact, and its existence depends on the possibility of devising the best version of the novel or of the legal history that coheres best with the pre-interpretive data[17]. Dworkin insists that, precisely for this reason, a defence of ontological indeterminacy, (even of partial ontological indeterminacy), should be based on some substantive position. The version of the legal history that concludes that legal ontology is indeterminate on a particular point should emerge as the best version of the legal history[18]. Indeterminacy cannot be the result of

---

[14] Demonstrability does not depend on facts, but on argument. It is therefore important to distinguish between a verificationist theory of meaning and antirealist semantics. The latter does not claim that a correct method of verification enables us to bridge the gap between our beliefs and the real world, facilitating access to reality or to a significant part thereof, as this would entail presuming optimistic realism. As some authors have pointed out in their objections to verificationism in general, and logical positivism in particular, this would entail presuming optimistic realism. In contrast, truth as assertability claims on the one hand, that the truth-value of our judgements depends on what we can assert, and, on the other, that evidence is what constitutes our ontology. Thus, truth as assertability does not contend that we may access reality through our judgements. See Wright (1993, 280-288).

[15] If we take this point into consideration, this position becomes compatible with Putnam's semantics and his internal realism given that we are not denying that meaning can be established by the reference of terms. Putnam argues that meaning does not depend on our mental states and conventions, but rather on their reference. Moreover, he insists that the reference is determined by the best theory. This position can be redirected towards the idea that a theory of meaning is an ontological theory. Hence, endowing a term with meaning entails presenting the designated object in its best light. In this sense, meaning is not connected to the mere existence of an individual or collective mental state, but to the object construed from those beliefs that cohere with the best theory. Precisely for this reason, meaning does not change when a belief changes, but only when the theory as a whole ceases to be the best theory, and is therefore replaced with a different theory. In this case, the ontology, too, changes. On this point, see Putnam (1975, 245-247, 268-271; 1981, 22-25, 49-54) and Brink (1988, 116-119).

[16] On this point, see Dworkin (1985, 137-145; 1986, 228-238; 1991b, 377-382).

[17] We noted in Chapter 5 that pre-interpretive data are conceptual constructs too. The truth of statements about pre-interpretive data depends on assertability.

[18] I would like to stress that from this point of view, semantic indeterminacy leads to ontological indeterminacy: the semantic and ontological levels collapse into one and the same thing.

excluding all other options. Legal reasons to support it as a better version than determinacy ought to be provided[19].

In my view, overlooking these remarks leads to semantic realism. If our evidence is not what leads us to assume ontological indeterminacy, and, ultimately, what generates this indeterminacy, we should have some criterion independent of our epistemic abilities.

Hartian positivism asserts partial indeterminacy on the basis of the thesis of the social sources of law. This thesis leads to the conclusion that the absence of a shared perception of what counts as law is sufficient a reason to assert its indeterminacy. The thesis of the social sources of law does not emerge as an interpretive view of the legal phenomenon[20]. Notwithstanding, current positivists insist on the antirealist nature of interpretive theory. But, are these two claims compatible with one another at all?

Positivism assumes a more restrictive view of the legal phenomenon than Dworkin does. The social sources of law limit the possible judgements about law. But what kind of limitation is this? Two possible answers leap to mind: either it is an interpretive limitation, i.e. dependent on which version of law is thought to be best, or else it is one set by the legal ontology itself upon the judgements we can make about it. The first alternative requires positivists to show why the version that advocates indeterminacy in the event of disagreement is sounder than that endorsing determinacy. Positivism fails to provide convincing reasons to argue so; and the second alternative takes us away from an antirealist position about law.

Dworkin proposes the following example to clarify this point. He observes that in the scientific context, an explanation has been offered to the question why disagreement about objects should be regarded as suspicious. Many a scientist assume that the properties of objects cause uniform judgements about them. If, say, a group of individuals claim to have seen a unicorn but they all clearly disagree as to its description, disagreement is a good reason or evidence to discard the existence of such

---

19 Note that in order to assume legal ontology as a form of fictional ontology we should accept that both its determinacy and indeterminacy depend on the available evidence. Thus, the legal ontology will be indeterminate only as long as we can provide sufficient evidence to claim this to be the case. See Dworkin (1996, 129-131).

20 In this sense, Hart present his legal theory as a semantic theory, in contrast with an interpretive one. Indeterminacy then arises when we lack shared semantic criteria to determine the contents of law. An interpretive reading of Hart would yield the conclusion that indeterminacy is posited as a result of the demands of the legal practice. Such an interpretation would argue that the very practice dictates that disagreement about the contents of law should count as legal indeterminacy. On this point, see Hart (1994, 124-132) and Stavropoulos (1996, 162).

a being. This conclusion follows from the realist assumption in the scientific domain that if unicorns existed, their properties would provoke the same reactions and judgements in all individuals exposed to them[21].

By contrast, if we assume an antirealist position to deal with statements about law, we need not presume that there is an object whose properties generate agreement in our legal judgements. Therefore, we lack reasons based on this presumption to conclude that the existence of divided opinion is evidence for indeterminacy in legal ontology. If at all, this conclusion ought to result from interpretive arguments[22].

These considerations raise the question about whether the positivist thesis of partial legal indeterminacy ultimately relies on a realist view of law. (Note the difference between this and legal realism as a sceptical theory.) If this were to be the case, then the restrictions imposed by the social sources thesis upon what can be claimed about law are similar in kind to causal restrictions set by the existence of unicorns upon scientific judgements[23]. This conclusion would render the positivism inconsistent for maintaining both the thesis of the social sources of law and antirealist semantics[24].

Alternatively, one could conceive positivism as an interpretive theory of law. Such a reading of positivism raises the following two issues: on the one hand, the ultimate role of the thesis of the social sources of law within positivism. This thesis seems to

---

[21] See Dworkin (1996, 113-114).

[22] See Dworkin (1996, 136-139).

[23] Dworkin has repeatedly pressed objections to positivism on account of its thesis of demonstrability as the criterion of truth for legal propositions. According to this criterion, only 'hard facts' are demonstrable. Thus, demonstrability does not depend on our judgements and perceptions about law, but on judgements and perceptions that manage to reflect the true nature of legal ontology. On Hartian positivism, Dworkin (1985, 138) writes that 'if we believe that no proposition can be true except in virtue of some fact that makes it true, and that there are no facts in the world but hard facts, then the demonstrability thesis follows from that metaphysics. The proposition could rationally be believed to be true, even though its truth is not demonstrated when all the hard facts are known or stipulated, only if there were something else in the world in virtue of which it could possibly be true. But if there is nothing else, then the proposition cannot rationally be believed to be true; the failure of hard facts to make it true would have exhausted all hope of making it true'. Note that this perspective coincides with the realist view on unicorns. It is a realist perspective because it assumes that what makes propositions true or false are the facts they describe (these are the facts that generate and justify judgements). Thus, only if the very ontology is indeterminate, is there room for indeterminacy in the truth conditions of propositions. See Dworkin (1985, 137-139; 1986, 228-238).

[24] As pointed out previously, antirealist semantics should reject metaphysical realism. Consequently, antirealist semantics may not assume that consensus or the occurrence of shared psychological states determine the truth value of a proposition, for then, consensus or mental states would be independent of our epistemic abilities to verify them.

lose all its strength if positivism is considered to be an interpretive theory. Therefore, it could no longer be taken to characterise positivism[25]. Current positivism could appear not to offer a positivist theory of law anymore. On the other hand, positivism has not provided reasons other than the thesis of sources to advocate the partial indeterminacy of law as a better option than determinacy when there is disagreement[26].

These difficulties prevent the success of positivism over Dworkin's interpretive theory. Thus, its partial indeterminacy thesis does not justify why an interpreter capable of structuring her legal convictions into a coherent scheme should concede that, in case of disagreement, there is no right answer to the question in hand.

Interpretive theory has a further advantage in its explanatory output. It was pointed out in previous chapters that even to defend partial legal determinacy, the sceptical challenge of 'anything goes' for the problem of rule-following ought to be overcome. According to scepticism, any act can be viewed to conform and to conflict with the rule. The contents of the rule is determined only to the extent that its use *a posteriori* generates general consensus. Consequently, rules cannot be followed on the basis of restrictions established prior to application.

Overcoming the sceptical challenge entails proving that: a) there exists an internal relationship between the rule and its instances of use, which determines which acts can be seen as following the rule. Every mediator should be discarded; b) what is the nature of this internal relationship.

Hartian positivism does not offer an answer to these questions and therefore, its theory of meaning as use does not escape the following dilemma: either consensus is thought to determine the contents of the rule only *a posteriori* (that is, it adopts the sceptical position), or else we understand that consensus as a fact is what predetermines the contents of the rule. In the latter case we meet with the sceptical challenge, for every past event can be described in a multiplicity of ways.

---

25 At least, it could be argued that a reformulation of this thesis is needed for it to conform to an interpretive view of law. This is an important challenge which positivism seems so far not to have overcome. Current versions of positivism appear to adhere to the thesis of the social sources posited by Joseph Raz (see Marmor 1992, 8, 90). Recall Raz's insistence on the idea that the contents of law depends on facts about human conduct which can be described in neutral terms. For Raz, only this kind of facts can be the basis for the truth of a statement about what is legally the thing to do. See Raz (1979, 37-52).

26 Stavropoulos (1996, 200-201) points out that interpretive positivism fails to provide a coherent justification as to why there is no law in case of controversy. It is at this point relevant to recall that in his Postscript to *The Concept of Law*, Hart denies the possibility of viewing his legal theory as an interpretive approach to law. He claims his theory does not purport to develop a particular conception of law based on the purpose or goal of the legal practice. See Hart (1994, 248-250).

Dworkin's interpretive model appears as a more suitable candidate to provide an answer to the problem of rule-following that avoids the foregoing dilemma. It will succeed only if it can provide reasons to show how the internal relationship between the rule and its instances of use comes into existence. It should therefore render plausible the claim that in order to know if a certain act conforms with the rule we ought to turn to the criteria used in the act of application. If Dworkin's approach to law answers these questions, it shall similarly be able to explain why in controversial cases, rule-following can still be invoked. This, in turn, will provide arguments to deny that the resolution of such cases always requires the judge to exercise strong discretion.

6.4 RULE-FOLLOWING AND THE INTERNAL RELATIONSHIP

As pointed out in Chapter 2, a non-sceptical interpretation of rule-following resorts to the notion of internal relationship between the rule and its instances of use. This interpretation attempts to avoid the sceptical challenge by denying the need for mediators between rules and acts. Consequently, neither agreement nor interpretation as substitution may constitute the criterion for semantic determinacy. It is pointless to invoke rules if they themselves do not embody standards of correctness[27]. What renders the series 1000, 1002, 1004, 1006 a correct application of the rule n+2 cannot be the fact that most of us would follow this sequence in this way, nor the fact that there exists a particular interpretation of this rule that views this sequence as an instance of use of the rule. The non-sceptical view insists that in order to assert that a rule is being followed we should resort to the criteria used in the act of use.

Accordingly, rule-following is confined to the particular circumstances surrounding each instance of use, and hence, to the criterion guiding each action as it relates to the rule. This may lead to conclude that rule-following is essentially an individual or subjective matter: the belief that a rule is being followed suffices to actually follow it, regardless of the reaction that an identical formulation of the rule would provoke in other agents. This view of rule-following is questionable, for it appears to prevent objectivity in rule-following. As a conclusion, this is a rather unsatisfactory one as the ultimate goal of rule-following is to show that the contents of the rule is partially predetermined and that, consequently, the rule somehow guides its own instances of use. For this reason, a suitable answer to this problem should address the following question: how can the idea of internal relationship without mediators preserve objectivity?

---

[27] See Baker and Hacker (1994, 248).

With a view to answering this question, one should carefully analyse the relevant aspects of the thesis of internal relationship. Firstly, the very notion that a rule is being followed suggests that action is not arbitrary, but grounded on a rule. Undeniably, no act can conform to the rule if no rule exists. Neither can an act conform to the rule if the agent that performs the act is not aware of the existence of the rule. This is a particularly important point. It shows that, although rule-following requires uniform behaviour within a group of agents, there is more to it than mere regularity in conduct. The occurrence of a sequence of actions is not indicative of rule-following since convergence does not permit to distinguish between actual rule-following and the mere appearance that a rule is being followed.

An example by Putnam helps to illustrate this point. Imagine that an ant is crawling on a patch of sand, and it is leaving a visible spoor behind. If its spoor happens to outline something that looks like a caricature of Winston Churchill we will hardly be tempted to think that the ant drew a portrait of this politician. The fact that the spoor resembles Churchill is not sufficient to attribute to the ant the purpose to draw a caricature[28]. We understand that in order that someone may produce a piece of art, he or she ought to display the intention to produce such a work and possess the knowledge about how to do so. Clearly, an ant lacks all of these abilities. Similarly, rule-following cannot be claimed on the basis of homogeneous behaviour only. As was pointed out in Chapter 2, the mastery of a certain technique is necessary, as is the capability to put it into practice. The mere existence of instances of use does not show that a rule is being followed. Consequently, the internal relationship cannot be that the instances of use determine the contents of the rule. This relationship should arise from the existence of a practice of use, which can only emerge if a particular technique is mastered. This is the second relevant aspect of the thesis of the internal relationship.

In Hacker and Baker's terms, to master a technique is to possess a particular ability, namely that of recognising which acts reflect a correct application of the rule, and which ones do not. Hence, it is impossible to master a rule-following technique (that is, to have the skill to use the rule in the practice) without having grasped the rule, the criterion of correctness[29]. We should nevertheless consider the question about what is required to grasp this criterion, and about what allows us to distinguish between the belief that a rule is being followed and an actual instance of rule-following.

---

[28] Putnam (1981, 1-2). See also Baker and Hacker (1994, 162-164).

[29] Baker and Hacker (1994, 161-164).

This issue takes us to a further relevant aspect of the thesis of internal relationship: objectivity[30]. The thesis of the internal relationship makes sense only if it is possible to show that the rule and its instances of use can be objectively related to one another. In other words, we are urged to show that there is a way to predetermine without resort to facts, metaphysical entities, or collective conventions, which acts embody a correct application of the rule. These latter criteria can only preserve objectivity at the cost of undermining the very notion of internal relationship. Objectivity should therefore be warranted by some element internal to the process of knowing and applying a rule.

Pettit writes that although a non-sceptical answer to the problem of rule-following ought to give consideration to the fact that any act of use may be seen as an instance of a multiplicity of rules, it should nevertheless not assume that the actual interpreters see this to be the case. An agent may consider that one or a number of instances exemplify a particular rule. Under the right circumstances, this suffices to assert that a rule is being followed[31]. For Pettit, the concept of exemplification is constituted by three elements: one or more examples, a rule, and an agent who views those examples as instances of application of the rule[32].

From this point of view, no agent means no rule-following. Moreover, there is no rule-following unless the agent has the conviction that his acts embody the rule or accord with it. For this reason, a direct relationship between rules and acts makes sense only within a certain type of scheme of interpretation. Any attempt to explain this relationship requires us to assume some sort of mediator. Precisely a mediator is what a non-sceptical interpretation of rule-following seeks to avoid. Notwithstanding, this approach to the internal relationship should provide a criterion to warrant objectivity. The lack of objectivity prevents the distinction between actual rule-following, and the mere belief that a rule is being followed. Pettit, for instance, resorts to the idea of inclination. Rule-following presupposes a specific inclination or disposition (which need not even be conscious) to associate a sequence of examples to a particular rule[33].

---

[30] Hacker and Baker consider that rule-following requires three factors: regularity in conduct, a criterion of correctness, and objectivity. See Baker and Hacker (1994, 162-164).

[31] See Pettit (1990, 9, 13).

[32] Pettit observes that a clear distinction is to be drawn between exemplification and instantiation. The latter connects two elements only: the rule and its instances of use, whereas the former links the three elements mentioned in the main text. Hence, a particular act of application of the rule can be an instance of several rules, but an act does not exemplify a number of rules if the agent does not perceive it so, Pettit (1990, 9). Note that Pettit's view does not entail an intermediary between the rule and the acts. It focuses on the assumptions required to claim that an act of use exemplifies the rule.

[33] Pettit (1990, 10-16).

However, there is more to the possibility of rule-following than just a mere inclination. According to Pettit, this disposition should manifest itself under certain particular circumstances. Firstly, the agent should be aware of the possibility of having grasped the rule incorrectly in her act of use because the rule (not her beliefs) is the criterion to assess conduct; secondly, she should be able to explain intertemporal and interpersonal discrepancies in the application of the rule on the basis of some element that affects the correct understanding of the rule[34].

Pettit's conditions seem to suggest that rule-following requires that the agent does not identify the rule with her inclination (of which she need not be aware), but that she realises the presence of the rule on the basis of her inclination. The rule, not the mere inclination to behave in a certain manner, is the criterion of correctness for the acts of application[35].

However, Pettit adds a further condition to rule-following which, in my view, could lead precisely to the position he seeks to refute. Pettit indicates that in the case of public rules, (rules embedded in social practices) rule-following can only exist in a context of general agreement on the contents of the rule[36]. Therefore, he claims, a conditioned individual inclination does not suffice to distinguish between the belief that a public rule is being followed and actual rule-following: the individual inclination should coincide with the collective disposition to perceive certain acts as instances of use of the rule. In line with Davidson's principle of charity, Pettit concludes that if a rule is to be public, rule-following can only be asserted if all the agents acknowledge that the rule is being followed. To do so, they shall share the same perception of the rule[37].

This position is ambiguous in that it may lead to the conclusion that following public rules does not require that individuals grasp the criterion of correctness, but that they adjust their behaviour to that of the group. This would introduce an external mediator between rules and acts. As was pointed out, it may yield the thesis that the

---

34 Pettit (1990, 13-15).

35 Note that the rule is the justifying reason to act, whereas the inclination may only embody an explanation as to why one acts in a particular way. Thus, we are not purporting to claim that inclination acts as an intermediary between the rule and its acts of use.

36 Pettit (1990, 19-21). Following McGinn (1984, 192) we will speak of public rules when it is the case that which rules a person follows is ascertainable by others on the basis of public criteria such as behaviour and context.

37 Pettit (1990, 20-21). Pettit concedes that rule-following is possible as long as there is an intertemporal interaction, that is, a standardised inclination to act consistently throughout time. Intersubjective interaction is not always necessary. However, if rules are public, intertemporal interaction is insufficient to speak of rule-following.

meaning of a rule is determined by agreement and hence, that the objectivity inherent in regulated actions lies precisely in the social dimension of the use of rules. For this reason, Pettit's attempt to refute scepticism seems to fail.

When speaking of public rules, the first person singular becomes the first person plural. However, the acts of use continue to relate to the rule, not to what speakers think or believe. The rule is a public rule because it is the object of discussion about how a group of individuals should act if they are to conform to the standard of correctness that identifies the practice they share.

Certainly, some elements in Pettit's proposal elucidate the necessary assumptions to claim a mediator-free internal relationship between the rule and its instances of use. In order to establish such a relationship, it is important to consider the point of view of the acting agents and their inclination to regard a certain line of action as an exemplification of a the rule. Furthermore, agents should be able to explain interpersonal discrepancies and recognise the possibility of being mistaken. These remarks allow us to differentiate rule-following from shared practices. To follow a rule is to master a technique, that is, to possess a criterion of correctness internal to the practice of use. To appeal to a criterion such as shared perceptions to determine whether a rule has been complied with or broken entails advocating a criterion of correctness external to rule-following[38].

Pettit argues that this reconstruction of the internal relationship between the rule and the acts is not useful to account for public rule-following[39]. Here, a collective inclination to perceive a sequence of cases as exemplifications of the rule is required. It is precisely at this point, I think, that Pettit is too strict with regard to public rule-following. Is it imperative that all speakers have an inclination to react similarly to an instance of use for a rule to be public? If so, disagreements about law make no sense. If there is no shared inclination, there is no rule to follow because the very existence of a public rule requires that individual dispositions converge. Thus, it is conceptually impossible to claim disagreement on a single normative pattern.

It may be relevant at this point to investigate whether this conclusion is absolutely necessary for public rule-following, or whether it can be shown that participants may hold different beliefs about something and still speak of the same object. The latter situation would render the following two theses plausible: a) rule-following is possible

[38] On this point, see Baker and Hacker (1994, 164).
[39] Pettit (1990, 19).

even in the event of disagreement; b) disagreement about the contents of public rules does not imply their indeterminacy.

Interpretive theory can deal with this issue and yet avoid falling into scepticism or realist semantics. It is important to bear in mind that the right answer is internal to a particular theory. This postulate is similar in character to the one positing that the criterion of correctness is internal to a rule-following technique. Thus, an inquiry into the determinacy of rules is, in fact, an inquiry into the theory embraced or the whole of propositions that an agent is entitled to assert. A theory is not separable form the agents that endorse it and their perceptions and beliefs. To speak of a version of law is to speak of interpreters who defend a view of law.

This idea is essential to elucidate the scope of the right answer. A criterion of correctness internal to a theory, that is, internal to a scheme of perception, can be qualified as really correct only if we assume an intermediary between the rule and its instances of use[40]. I have repeatedly insisted that I do not seek to advocate that our judgements constitute reality. All we can do is trust our strongest or better-settled beliefs - only the entire body of beliefs can act as a criterion to assume or to discard new beliefs into our interpretive scheme. Once we confront judgements with the whole body of beliefs, we reach 'the truth for us', the only intelligible truth from an antirealist point of view.

Dworkin has supported this idea throughout. Recall his thesis about the impossibility of adopting an external approach to a phenomenon: every descriptive statement presupposes a certain position about the object being described and, consequently, the correctness of the statement is internal to some theory. Dworkin claims that when we speak of mountains in ordinary language, they exist in the language game. In this game, there is apparently no obstacle to claim that the existence of mountains does not depend on what we think, or that they are part of reality. These appreciations are the mere product of our convictions about mountains. To assert the existence of mountains is merely to speak of these objects and to attribute certain properties to them[41]. But it is illusory to believe that there is a level of discourse external to ordinary language that may indicate whether or not mountains really exist in 'the world out there' regardless of the language game. For Dworkin, a statement such as

---

40 On this point, see Pears (1991, 280-281).

41 Dworkin claims that in ordinary language, the claims 'slavery is unjust' and 'slavery is really unjust' are actually equivalent. On this point, see Dworkin (1986, 73-76; 1996, 91-94).

'mountains exist' has the same meaning in ordinary language as it does in philosophical archimedean discourse. Both statements are internal in character[42].

The thesis of internalism does not rely on an antirealist perspective based upon inter-subjective agreement or on socially shared perceptions as a criterion to determine the truth conditions of legal propositions. Meaning or rule-following does not depend on a social perception about which are the rules of the language game in a particular context, but on the very participation in this language game. Therefore, the contents of rules does not rest on agreement. Participants address the question about the right answer from some particular viewpoint about the language game and the actions required by it. For this reason, this question leads to the comparison between a proposition and the whole of propositions that conform the scheme of interpretation from within which the question is asked.

Concerning this point, Dworkin writes:

> That is not a question of where a burden of proof lies, but of what, considering each possibility as fully as we can, and noting its implications for the rest of what we think, we find that we believe. Of course I do not mean that our convictions are right just because we find them irresistible, or that our inability to think anything else is a reason or ground or argument supporting our judgement. On the contrary, these suggestions are forms of the skepticism I am opposing. I mean that any reason we think we have for abandoning a conviction is itself just another conviction, and that we can do no better for any claim, [...] than to see whether, after the best thought we find appropriate, we think it so. If you can't help believing something, steadily and wholeheartedly, you'd better believe it. Not, as I just said, because the fact of your belief argues for its own truth, but because you cannot think any argument a decisive refutation of a belief it does not even dent. In the beginning, and in the end, is the conviction.[43]

This is a very fruitful approach to legal determinacy because the correctness of a judgement about law is not dependent on an intermediary between the rule and the acting agents but on the soundness of the interpretive scheme within which the judgement is produced. Our beliefs can be undermined by disagreement among agents, but deviation from the majority view does not imply that the judgement be incorrect. If an agent who is aware of the possibility of being mistaken and who gives consideration to the arguments supporting alternative conclusions can but think that her judgement is correct, there is no reason why she should abandon it. McGinn observes that the reasons backing up descriptive judgements come to an end and no further rational foundation can be found for them, not even the test of community conformity. According to this author, Wittgenstein successfully showed why the normativity of meaning requires no

---

[42] See Dworkin (1991b, 361-363; 1996, 94-99).

[43] Dworkin (1996, 118).

more reasons than those the agent is able to provide[44]. This is all that can be said about right answers and determinacy of rules. Beyond this internal criterion only external mediators can be ascertained. This, however, does not imply that interpretive theory lead to radical subjectivism. Firstly, we are referring to social practices and to participants in a collective enterprise. This means that their judgements do not produce in isolation. Participants' beliefs and thoughts cannot be detached from their social environment, nor can they be explained disregarding what participants share. Secondly, an internal view blurs the distinction between subjective and objective[45]. To ascribe meaning is to present an object in its best light[46]. The best theory constitutes the truth-conditions of legal propositions. However, criteria to determine what is the best theory are agent-dependent. The correctness of judgements depends on the subject. But as noted in Chapters 4 and 5, this dependence is not dependence on the agent's will: she does not choose her perception of the legal phenomenon because she does not choose to believe that a certain version of law is the soundest. At some point, the interpreter cannot help thinking the way she does - for her, this becomes an objective or genuine restriction to the possibility of interpreting the practice differently. If no reason evinces that she is mistaken, her version of law is, objectively, the best theory. Hence, it fixes the meaning of statements about law. This objectivity, however, is not external objectivity derived from certain facts, but internal objectivity of the scheme of interpretation. These restrictions are not subjective if we understand subjective to refer to anything that an agent constructs on the basis of her individual choice or stipulation. Internal objectivity should be differentiated from subjectivity as individual will[47].

My exposition so far may lead to think that interpretive theory does not distinguish between following private and following public rules. One possible objection to internalism is that it does not warrant communication nor the possibility for a community to follow the same rules. Recall, however, that rejecting agreement as the semantic criterion does not mean that agreement plays no role in the ascription of

---

44 McGinn (1984, 84).

45 Scepticism, by contrast, defends the dichotomy between subjective and objective on the grounds of a realist notion of objectivity that derives from the occurrence of certain facts that are independent of our epistemic abilities. This leads to 'anything goes'. If only objective criteria (objective in a realist sense) can determine the correctness of judgements about law, and it is the case that such criteria do not exist, then their correctness will be entirely dependent on individual will. In this sense, see Dworkin (1986, 78-85).

46 Dworkin (1986, 49-53).

47 Scepticism defends the notion of subjectivity as individual will. See, for instance, Fish (1982, 553-555) and Rorty (1991a, xxiii).

meaning. Neither does it imply that the perception of the convictions of the rest of the participants has no influence on the agent's judgements.

6.5 AGREEMENT, DISAGREEMENT, AND RIGHT ANSWERS

What is the role of agreement in the determination of the contents of law? There are several answers to this question, none of which regards agreement as the criterion of meaning.

Firstly, Hacker and Baker claim that agreement is a pre-requisite for our language game to exist. But this pre-requisite need not be one of our rules of action nor need it be the criterion determining when is it the case that a rule of the language game is being followed correctly[48]. Thus, although agreement may be conceived as a condition endowing the idea of rules with meaning in certain language games[49], it need not be the criterion fixing its contents. The criterion of correctness is internal to the practice of rule-following. Hence, the debate about meaning is circumscribed within the internal domain.

Secondly, we should elucidate how much disagreement can a social practice endure before it breaks down as such a practice. This question can be rephrased in terms of Wittgenstein's idea of forms of life: what is the extent to which views within a form of life may diverge if we want to speak of a single form of life[50]?

According to McGinn, a strong community thesis of meaning holds that following a rule is adjusting one's behaviour to a particular standard of conduct determined by social agreement. Rejecting this thesis does not necessarily imply denying every possible kind of relationship between rule-following and the idea that meaning ought to be interpersonally accessible[51]. It is important to distinguish between 'what is shared' on the one hand, and what is 'shareable' on the other. Following public rules, and indeed their very existence, could be subject to two different restrictions: a) that the contents of the rule be in fact shared, and b) that its contents be shareable.

---

[48] Baker and Hacker (1994, 234, 248).

[49] We are here referring to certain kinds of language games only because, as pointed out in Chapter 2, there seems to be no conceptual obstacle to claim that an isolated individual can follow rules provided she is able to compare her present behaviour with her past decisions and the intentions that endorsed them. See McGinn (1984, 192-200) and Baker and Hacker (1994, 171-179).

[50] As observed by Hacker and Baker, this question cannot be answered in full because doing so would require a very precise notion of form of life and of what counts as language. For the purposes of the present work, the relevant point is to demonstrate that the mere existence of disagreement does not necessarily imply diverging forms of life. On this point, see Baker and Hacker (1994, 243).

[51] On the strong community thesis see McGinn (1984, 192-195).

The first restriction is based on the already rejected thesis that the meaning of terms and expressions is determined by agreement in the community. The second constraint, by contrast, assumes that following a public rule requires the logical possibility that its contents be shareable with, and, communicable to, other agents. For rule-following is not only linked to the mastery of a technique, but also to the possibility of showing and teaching this technique to others[52].

An agent follows a rule only if she is able to provide reasons for her behaviour or for the correctness of her judgements about the rule[53]. She ought to be able to justify her position as the best way to specify the contents of the rule, and to apply it to actual cases. The need for justification emerges from the idea that meaning depends on the best theory, and, in general, from the very notion of knowledge. As Aarnio points out, 'if I aver that I know something, I must be prepared to present justification for my position (...). Knowledge presupposes the possibility of doubt as well as justification'[54]. For this reason, any judgement should be subject to confrontation and criticism. Thus, according to Pettit, an agent who follows a rule ought to be ready to admit that she might have grasped it incorrectly[55]. However, this demand for justification does not imply that all participants in a practice must react to the formulation of the rule in the same way, but merely that they assume that the judgements about the practice are communicable and subject to discussion.

This is a particularly important assumption in the context of a collective enterprise, where participants act with a particular goal or purpose. If it were the case that the judgements of different participants could not be communicated, the very idea of collective practice would break down. We would then encounter a collection of individual practices. However, this discouraging hypothesis does not make sense unless

---

52 In this sense, Hacker and Baker claim that if one is not able to explain or show the technique one is using and just waits for inspiration or an internal voice to lead him or her to the correct result, one is not exhibiting a technique of use. See Baker and Hacker (1994, 164-165) and McDowell (1993, 273).

53 A justification is not a proof. Justifying a judgement does not demand intersubjective valid evidence for its truth. An agent provides a justification of her position when, having assessed all the possible alternatives, she cannot help concluding that her judgement is the correct one. It is pointless to search for reasons beyond this to justify the truth of his judgements. Therefore, an agent is entitled to assert something even though she might not be able to demonstrate to other agents that hers is the correct view. Consequently, the truth-value of propositions does not depend on its intersubjective demonstrability or general consensus, for this would entail, precisely, adopting agreement as a criterion of meaning. On this point, see Dworkin's attack (1985, 137-139) to the positivist thesis of demonstrability, and McGinn (1984, 72-73).

54 See Aarnio (1987, 214-215).

55 See Pettit (1990, 10-16).

it is an interpretive conclusion. A judgement about law reflects an interpretation of a social phenomenon. The following questions await answer: what reasons can be put forward to convince a particular agent that she is mistaken in her views, and that there is no social phenomenon to interpret but only her own particular and isolated construct? Why should an agent assume that she actually never communicates? Why should she accept that her actions and expressions are meaningless for the agents she interacts with?

This sceptical scenario is possible. However, if we do not presume realist semantics, the truth of such a scenario depends on the evidence we have for it. In my opinion, scepticism fails to provide such evidence[56]. The alternative panorama assumes *prima facie* about the communicability of our legal judgements. Here, we communicate and disagree about the contents of the legal phenomenon. These are substantive and not conceptual disagreements since we are able to explain our discrepancies in terms of either our own mistakes, or those of other participants, and we are able to recognise alternative positions as conceptions about what the legal practice requires us to do. In this context, it will be possible to discuss meaningfully which approach offers better arguments[57].

This scenario, however, need not be oblivious of the existence of conceptual disagreement when speakers use language to refer to different things. But there is no ground to conclude that hard cases always arise from conceptual and not from substantive disagreements. It could be argued that there are compelling reasons to assume that conceptual disagreements are marginal: if it were otherwise, each participant would assume either that she has identical opinions to the rest of the participants in the practice or that communication is impossible. Why should we not allow for some logical space between incommunication or absurd error, and shared perceptions? This space reproduces the platitude that debate and discussion are possible, as is convincing other individuals that they are mistaken (or, for that matter, convincing ourselves that our position is not sound).

This is a *prima facie* assumption because it is possible that at some point differences can no longer be explained in terms of a mistaken interpretation of the practice. This takes us back to the question how much disagreement can judgements about some aspect of the practice endure for it to prevail as a shared practice.

---

[56] On this point, see Dworkin (1986, 76-86).

[57] See Dworkin (1986, 85-86, 412-413).

In my view, Dworkin's distinction between concept and conception offers a useful answer to this question. Controversy about our conceptions as a sub-interpretation of a more abstract idea that we call 'the concept' does not generate incommunication because we are not required to reach identical conclusions to legal questions[58]. Incommunication emerges when we do not share the most fundamental ideas about some social institution, that is, when we do not share the concept. In these cases, certain interpretations may appear absurd or may be seen not even to qualify as interpretations. We then encounter different practices immersed in different interpretive paradigms. Thus, although the distinction between concept and conception allows for the logical space referred to above, the notion of concept does not prevent the possibility that there is no practice of common use. This does not imply that whenever we have sufficient evidence to claim that the concept is not shared, we automatically face an instance of no right answer for such a conclusion would prompt the idea that shared perceptions act as intermediaries between the rules and the acts of use (the thesis of law-communication). All we can conclude is that we can no longer claim the shared character of this answer - there are different practices of use with regard to that particular point, there exist several languages and forms of life. Here, agents follow a rule, but not the same one because they do not even share the interpretive concept accounting for the purpose of the practice.

This situation would entail the existence of irresolvable controversy as far as the contents of law is concerned, and this would lead to incommunication. But, although only individual practices can be appealed to, rules are not indeterminate. Thus, a right answer would continue to exist insofar as the agent is capable of structuring her scheme of convictions to reach a legal conclusion. However, we would be prompted to conclude that we no longer have public rules and that, therefore, our attempt to view a social practice as a collective purpose has failed for the very idea of participant breaks down at this point.

---

[58] Dworkin pointed out that the distinction between concept and conception is not of a semantic nature, but of an interpretive one. For Dworkin, the distinction between concept and conception is not one between the intension and the extension of the meaning of a term. Rather, they represent different levels of abstraction in the interpretation of social phenomena, that is, different degrees of concretion of our perceptions of these phenomena. However, the denial of the semantic nature of this distinction can be redirected towards a denial of conventionalist semantics. In this sense, Dworkin's position can be seen to posit constructivist semantics in which the concepts we use reflect our worldview. For this reason, to assign meaning is to offer an interpretation about how things are under the light of some substantive theory about them. See Dworkin (1986, 49-55, 70-76).

True, nothing guarantees that our practices remain stable throughout time. Existing interpretive paradigms may disappear and new ones that generate new practices of use emerge. All in all, our agreements of conviction are as stable as our opinions and justifications. But our beliefs are often firm, and so are our reasons to believe that we hold meaningful discussions with other participants. This is the context in which the question about what is it the legal practice demands should be placed.

The absence of right answers should be sought in those instances in which the agent cannot justify that the best theory of law leads to a univocal legal solution. In these cases, coherence between the propositions in a conceptual scheme is not a sufficient criterion to select one option as most suitable. Here, law is indeterminate. To make a decision, strong discretion must be exercised, and this involves a justified choice among different admissible alternatives for action.

Dworkin's typical optimism leads him to argue that indeterminacy cannot be a conclusion reached by default. Because there always exist different reasons to support a positive or a negative decision, noting that there is a tie between two legal interpretations is not sufficient to conclude a third option: indeterminacy. Moreover, he claims, there is a further argument in favour of determinacy: the peculiarity of legal discourse. Law requires making decisions. Precisely this requirement renders indeterminacy even less justifiable[59].

This optimistic view places very high expectations on an interpreter attempting to answer the question about which is the right answer. On some occasions, indeterminacy is the most suitable alternative because it is endorsed by interpretive reasons. Firstly, in accord with Dworkin's own theory, the very distinction between interpretation and invention requires the agent to be aware that she is interpreting, that is, that she is assigning meaning to some social institution in the light of the best version of this institution. Therefore, in case of tie or incommensurability between different alternatives, the agent cannot justify her decision on the grounds of the best theory because precisely the best theory leads to the conclusion that the two options are incommensurable or equal in their merits. Here, a solution other than indeterminacy would lead the interpreter to renounce the best theory and to realise that she is in fact inventing.

Secondly, if we turn our attention to adjudication, the fact that judges are by law obliged to make decisions about the rights and duties of citizens is not a good argument against the thesis of partial indeterminacy. The judicial obligation to render a decision

---

59 See Dworkin (1996, 137-138).

should not be mistaken with the judicial obligation to decide according to the law. In contrast with what Dworkin seems to argue, choosing indeterminacy as the best option does not prevent that a decision be made. The decision, however, will not be a legal decision because the answer will eventually rest on a genuine stipulation, either of the contents of the answer, or of the reasons that endorse a certain choice. Therefore, in Dworkin's own terms, when a judge can but honestly believe that law is indeterminate on some point, it is best she believes it so. Thus, the grounds for the truth of a judgement about legal indeterminacy are identical to those for the truth of the opposite judgement. Denying this point involves either embracing scepticism or accepting some sort of intermediary between the rule and its instances of use.

6.6 FINAL REMARKS

Legal positivism has been portrayed as a semantic position that advocates a conventionalist theory of meaning. For this reason, it views hard cases as the limits of law. Legal propositions lack truth-value in hard cases and the judge must therefore exercise strong discretion in order to provide an answer to these cases. Several deficiencies of this approach have been identified. Objectivity is warranted at the expense of undermining the internal relationship between the rule and its acts of use.

Ronald Dworkin's alternative is not merely the broadening of the legal phenomenology[60]. This would imply that interpretive theory does not succeed in offering an answer to the problem of rule-following either. The question at this point is not how far we can or want to stretch our legal ontology. We have seen that an alternative to conventionalist semantics ought to account for the mediator-free internal relationship between the rule and its acts of use. Dworkin's position, or at least the version of his theory that has been defended here, allows for this. This version evinces the relevance of weak discretion in the resolution of hard cases. Disagreement is not sufficient for interpreters to abandon their belief in the existence of a right answer. In line with antirealism, this is not a sufficient reason to deny the existence of such an answer. The semantic criterion is the best theory, and the best theory is independent of agreement in the legal community - it depends on the best legal argument, on the degree of soundness of the answer as rated from within the interpretive scheme. Weak discretion is the mechanism to reach this answer because it demands that the interpreter assess the coherence of her judgements and consider carefully the possible alternatives on the basis of a complex theory about the rights and duties of citizens, and about how

---

[60] Gavison (1987, 29-32) and Coleman (1984, 35-47) present views in contrast with this one.

to recognise them in each particular case. According to antirealist semantics, we cannot request from interpreters more than what they are able to identify and justify once they have taken law seriously.

Two consequences relevant to the role of judges in legal adjudication follow: on the one hand, adjudication as a cognitive activity that the judge is expected to carry out neutrally (i.e. regardless of her interpretive judgements, presuppositions and convictions about law) loses its plausibility; on the other, the judge becomes responsible for the decisions she makes both in controversial and in non-controversial cases.

However, the same arguments that yield the link between weak discretion and hard cases can be put forward to back up the technical necessity for strong discretion when an interpretive scheme cannot reach a single right legal answer. In these cases, the judge must inevitably choose between alternatives in exactly the same way a conscious legislator would, given that she can no longer back up her choice with legal argument. It is not disagreement but the limit to our ability to imagine how things are and to present them in their best light what leads to the need for strong discretion. Surely, limits remain, but to consider that they rule wherever disagreement and controversy rule would suggest disheartening scepticism about the potential of human imagination.

BIBLIOGRAPHY

AARNIO, A. (1987), *The Rational as Reasonable*, D. Reidel Publishing Company, Dordrecht.

AARNIO, A. (1990), "La tesis de la única respuesta correcta y el principio regulativo del razonamiento jurídico", *DOXA*, n. 8, 23-38.

AARNIO, A. (1991), *Lo racional como razonable*, Centro de Estudios Constitucionales, Madrid, (transl. E. Garzón Valdés).

AARNIO, A. (1997), *Reason and Authority. A Treatise on the Dynamic Paradigm of Legal Dogmatics*, Ashgate/Dartmouth, Aldershot.

AFRIAT, S. N. (1987), *Logic of Choice and Economic Theory*, Clarendon Press, Oxford.

ALCHOURRÓN, C., and BULYGIN, E. (1971), *Normative Systems*, Springer-Verlang, New York.

ALCHOURRÓN, C., and BULYGIN, E. (1979), *Sobre la existencia de las normas jurídicas*, Universidad de Carabobo, Valencia, Venezuela.

ALEXY, R. (1989), *A Theory of Legal Argumentation*, Clarendon Press, Oxford.

ALEXY, R. (1993), *Teoría de los derechos fundamentales*, Centro de Estudios Constitucionales, Madrid, (transl. E. Garzón Valdés).

ALEXY, R., and PECZENIK, A. (1990), "The Concept of Coherence and Its Significance for Discursive Rationality", *Ratio Juris*, 130-147.

ALSTON, W. (1989), *Epistemic Justification*, Cornell University Press, Ithaca.

ATIENZA, M. (1991), *Las razones del Derecho. Teorías de la argumentación jurídica*, Centro de Estudios Constitucionales, Madrid.

ATIENZA, M. (1993), *Tras la Justicia. Una introducción al Derecho y al razonamiento jurídico*, Ariel, Barcelona.

ATIENZA, M., and RUÍZ MANERO, J., (1991) "Sobre principios y reglas", *DOXA*, n. 10, 101-119.

AUSTIN, J. L. (1976), *How to Do Things with Words*, Oxford University Press, Oxford, second edition.

BAKER, G. (1977), "Defeasibility and Meaning", in Hacker, P., and Raz, J., (eds.) *Law, Morality, and Society. Essays in Honour of H.L.A. Hart,* Clarendon Press, Oxford, 26-57.

BAKER, G., and HACKER, P. (1992), *Wittgenstein. Meaning and Understanding*, Blackwell, Oxford.

BAKER, G., and HACKER, P. (1994), *Wittgenstein. Rules, Grammar and Necessity*, Blackwell, Oxford.

BARAK, A. (1989), *Judicial Discretion*, Yale University Press, New Haven.

BAYÓN, J. C. (1991), *La normatividad del Derecho: deber jurídico y razones para la acción*, Centro de Estudios Constitucionales, Madrid.

BAYÓN, J. C. (1996), "Proposiciones normativas e indeterminación del Derecho", paper prepared for the Congress on Philosophy and Legal Theory, Vaquerías, Córdoba, Argentina, October.

BELL, J. (1992), "Discretionary Decision-Making: A Jurisprudential View", in Hawkins, K., (ed.) *The Uses of Discretion*, Clarendon Press, Oxford, 89-111.

BENDER, J. (1989), "Coherence, Justification, and Knowledge: The Current Debate", in Bender, J., (ed.) *The Current State of Coherence Theory*, Kluwer, Dordrecht, 1-14.

BIX, B. (1991), "H. L. A. Hart and the 'Open Texture' of Language", *Law and Philosophy*, n. 10, 51-72.

BIX, B. (1993), *Law, Language, and Legal Determinacy*, Clarendon Press, Oxford.

BIX, B. (1995), "Questions in Legal Interpretation", in Marmor, A., (ed.) *Law and Interpretation*, Clarendon Press, Oxford, 137-154.

BLACKBURN, S. (1981), "Reply: Rule-Following and Moral Realism", in Holtzman, St., and Leich, Ch. (ed.) *Wittgenstein: To Follow a Rule*, Routledge & Kegan Paul, London, 163-190.

BOBBIO, N. (1991), *El problema del positivismo jurídico*, Fontamara, México (transl. E. Garzón Valdés).

BRINK, D. (1988), "Legal Theory, Legal Interpretation and Judicial Review", *Philosophy and Public Affairs*, v. 17, 105-148.

BRINK, D. (1989), "Semantics and Legal Interpretation (Further Thoughts)", *Canadian Journal of Law and Jurisprudence*, v. 2, n.2, 181-191.

BRINT, M., and WEAVER, W. (1991), (eds.) *Pragmatism in Law and Society*, Westview Press, Oxford.

BULYGIN, E. (1991a), "El concepto de vigencia en Ross", in Alchourrón, C., and Bulygin, E., *Análisis Lógico y Derecho*, Centro de Estudios Constitucionales, Madrid.

BULYGIN, E. (1991b), "Sentencia judicial y creación de derecho", in Alchourrón, C., and Bulygin, E., *Análisis Lógico y Derecho*, Centro de Estudios Constitucionales, Madrid, 355-369.

BURROWS, J. (1976), "Statutes and Judicial Discretion", *New Zealand Universities Law Review*, v. 7, 1-22.

CALSAMIGLIA, A. (1992), "El concepto de integridad en Dworkin", *DOXA*, n. 12, 155-176.

CARDOZO, B. (1921), *The Nature of the Judicial Process,* Yale University Press, New Haven.

CARNAP, R. (1947), *Meaning and Necessity*, The University of Chicago Press, Chicago.

CARNAP, R. (1971), *The Logical Syntax of Language*, Routledge & Kegan Paul, London.

CARRIÓ, G. (1965), *Notas sobre Derecho y lenguaje*, Abeledo-Perrot, Buenos Aires.

COHEN, J. (1992), *An Essay on Belief and Acceptance*, Clarendon Press, Oxford.

COHEN, M. (1984), (ed.) *Ronald Dworkin and Contemporary Jurisprudence*, Rowman and Allanheld, New Jersey.

COLEMAN, J. (1984), "Negative and Positive Positivism", in Cohen, M., (ed.) *Ronald Dworkin and Contemporary Jurisprudence*, Rowman and Allanheld, New Jersey, 28-48.

COLEMAN, J. (1995), "Truth and Objectivity in Law", *Legal Theory*, n. 1, 33-68.

COLEMAN, J., and LEITER, B. (1995), "Determinacy, Objectivity, and Authority", in Marmor, A., (ed.) *Law and Interpretation*, Clarendon Press, Oxford, 203-278.

CONKLIN, W. (1981), "Clear Cases", *University of Toronto Law Journal*, v. 31, 231-248.

CURRIE, G. (1991), "Work and Text", *MIND*, v. 100, 325-339.

CURRIE, G. (1993), "Interpretation and Objectivity", *MIND*, v. 102, n. 407, 413-428.

DAVIDSON, D. (1984a), "First Person Authority", *Dialetica*, v. 38, n.2, 101-111.

DAVIDSON, D. (1984b), *Inquiries into Truth and Interpretation*, Clarendon Press, Oxford.

DAVIDSON, D. (1990), "Afterthoughts, 1987", in the edition of "A Coherence Theory of Truth and Knowledge" in Malachowski, A., (ed.) *Reading Rorty*, Basil Blackwell, Oxford, 120-138.

DAVIDSON, D. (1993a), "Empirical Content", in LePore, E. (ed.), *Truth and Interpretation*, Blackwell, Oxford, 320-332.

DAVIDSON, D. (1993b), "A Coherence Theory of Truth and Knowledge", in LePore, E. (ed.), *Truth and Interpretation*, Blackwell, Oxford, 107-119.

DAVIDSON, D. (1996), "The Folly of Trying to Define Truth", *The Journal of Philosophy*, v. XCIII, n. 6, 263-278.

DAVIS, K. (1969), *Discretionary Justice: a Preliminary Enquiry*, University of Illinois Press, Urbana.

DICEY, A. (1945), *An Introduction to the Study of the Law of the Constitution,* Macmillan, London.

DUMMETT, M. (1978), *Truth and Other Enigmas*, Duckworth, London.

DUMMETT, M. (1993), "'A Nice Derangement of Epitaphs': Some Comments on Davidson and Hacking", in LePore, E., (ed.), *Truth and Interpretation*, Blackwell, Oxford, 459-476.

DWORKIN, R. (1963), "Judicial Discretion", *The Journal of Philosophy*, v. 50, n. 21, 624-638.

DWORKIN, R. (1977), *Taking Rights Seriously*, Duckworth, London.

DWORKIN, R. (1983), "My Reply to Stanley Fish (and Walter Benn Michaels): Please Don't Talk About Objectivity Any More", in *The Politics of Interpretation*, The University of Chicago Press, Chicago, 287-313.

DWORKIN, R. (1984), "A Reply by Ronald Dworkin", in Cohen, M., (ed.) *Ronald Dworkin and Contemporary Jurisprudence*, Rowman and Allanheld, New Jersey, 247-300.

DWORKIN, R. (1985), *A Matter of Principle*, Harvard University Press, Cambridge, Massachusetts.

DWORKIN, R. (1986), *Law's Empire*, The Belknap Press of Harvard University Press, Cambridge, Massachusetts.

DWORKIN, R. (1987), "Legal Theory and the Problem of Sense", in Gavison, R., (ed.), *Issues in Contemporary Legal Philosophy*, Clarendon Press, Oxford, 9-34.

DWORKIN, R. (1991a), "On Gaps in the Law", in Amselek, P., and MacCormick, N., (eds.), *Controversies about Law and Ontology*, Edinburgh University Press, Edinburgh, 84-90.

DWORKIN, R. (1991b), "Pragmatism, Right Answers, and True Banality", in Brint, M., and Weaver, W., (eds.), *Pragmatism in Law and Society*, Westview Press, Oxford, 359-388.

DWORKIN, R. (1993), *Life's Dominion*, Alfred Knopf, New York.

DWORKIN, R. (1994a), "Law, Philosophy and Interpretation", *ARSP*, v. 80, 463-475.

DWORKIN, R. (1994b), "Reply to Hart Draft", (unpublished manuscript).

DWORKIN, R. (1996), "Objectivity and Truth: You'd Better Believe It", *Philosophy and Public Affairs*, v. 25, n. 2, 87-139.

EBBS, G. (1997), *Rule-Following and Realism*, Harvard University Press, Cambridge, Massachusetts.

ENDICOTT, T. (1994), "Putting Interpretation in Its Place", *Law and Philosophy*, n. 13, 1-29.

ENDICOTT, T. (1997), "Ronald Dworkin y las consecuencias de la vaguedad", *DOXA*, n. 19, (transl. J.J. Moreso and P. Navarro), 375-383.

FARAGO, J. (1980), "Intractable Cases: The Role of Uncertainty in the Concept of Law", *New York University Law Review*, v. 55, 195-240.

FINNIS, J. (1987), "On Reason and Authority in *Law's Empire*", *Law and Philosophy*, n. 6, 357-380.

FINNIS, J. (1990), "Concluding Reflections", *Cleveland State Law Review*, n. 38.

FISH, S. (1982), "Working on the Chain Gang: Interpretation in Law and Literature", *Texas Law Review*, v. 60, 551-568.

FISH, S. (1983), "Wrong Again", *Texas Law Review*, v. 62, 299-316.

FISH, S. (1987), "Still Wrong After All These Years", *Law and Philosophy*, v. 6, n. 3, 401-418.

FISS, O. (1982), "Objectivity and Interpretation", *Stanford Law Review*, v. 34, 739-763.

FRANK, J. (1930), *Law and the Modern Mind*, Anchor Books, New York.

FRANK, J. (1949), *Courts on Trial. Myth and Reality in American Justice*, Princeton University Press, Princeton.

FREGE, G. (1993), "On Sense and Reference", in Moore, A. (ed.) *Meaning and Reference*, Oxford University Press, Oxford, 23-42.

FRIED, Ch. (1981), "The Artificial Reasons of the Law or: What Lawyers Know", *Texas Law Review*, v. 60, 35-58.

FULLER, L. (1958), "Positivism and the Fidelity to Law: A Reply to Professor Hart", *Harvard Law Review*, n. 71, 630-672.

FULLER, L. (1978), "The Forms and Limits of Adjudication", *Harvard Law Review*, v. 92.

GALLIE, W. (1956), "Essentially Contested Concepts", *Proceedings of the Aristotelian Society*, n. 56, 167-198.

GALLIGAN, D. (1986), *Discretionary Powers*, Clarendon Press, Oxford.

GÄRDENFORS, P. (1988), *Knowledge in Flux*, The MIT Press, Cambridge, Massachusetts.

GARZON VALDES, E. (1990), "Algo más acerca de la relación entre Derecho y Moral", *DOXA*, n. 8, 111-130.

GAVISON, R. (1987), "Comment" in Gavison, R., (ed.) *Issues in Contemporary Legal Philosophy*, Clarendon Press, Oxford, 21-34.

GIANFORMAGGIO, L. (1990), "Legal Certainty, Coherence and Consensus", in Nerhot, P., (ed.) *Law, Interpretation and Reality*, Kluwer Academic Publishers, Dordrecht, 402-430.

GOLDMAN, A. (1989), "BonJour's Coherentism", in Bender, J., (ed.) *The Current State of Coherence Theories*, Kluwer Academic Publishers, Dordrecht, 125-133.

GREENAWALT, K. (1975), "Discretion and Judicial Decision: The Elusive Quest for the Fetters that Bind the Judges", *Columbia Law Review*, v. 75, 359-398.

GREENAWALT, K. (1977), "Policy Rights and Judicial Decision", *Georgia Law Review*, v. 11, n. 5, 991-1053.

GREENAWALT, K. (1992), *Law and Objectivity*, Oxford University Press, Oxford.

GRICE, H. (1989), *Studies in the Way of Words*, Harvard University Press, Cambridge, Massachusetts.

GUASTINI, R. (1983), "Soluzioni dubbie. Lacune e interpretazione secondo Dworkin. Con un'appendice bibliográfica", in *Materiali per una storia della cultura giuridica*, XII, n. 2.

GUEST, S. (1992), *Ronald Dworkin,* Edinburgh University Press, Edinburgh.

HACKER, P. (1977), "Hart's Philosophy of Law" in Hacker, P. and Raz, J., (eds.), *Law, Morality and Society. Essays in Honour of H.L.A. Hart,* Clarendon Press, Oxford, 1-25.

HACKER, P. (1988), "Language, Rules, and Pseudo-Rules", *Language and Communication*, n. 8, 159-175.

HARDWIG, J. (1991), "The Role of Trust in Knowledge", *The Journal of Philosophy*, v. LXXXVIII, n. 12, 693-708.

HARMAN, G. (1986), *Change in View*, The MIT Press, Cambridge, Massachusetts.

HART, H., and Sacks, A. (1958), *The Legal Process: Basic Problems in the Making and Application of Law*, Tentative Edition.

HART, H. L. A. (1958), "Positivism and the Separation of Law and Morals", *Harvard Law Review*, v. 71, 593-630.

HART, H. L. A. (1980), "El Nuevo desafío al positivismo jurídico", *Sistema*, n. 36, 1980, 3-19.

HART, H. L. A. (1982), *Essays on Bentham. Studies in Jurisprudence and Political Theory*, Clarendon Press, Oxford.

HART, H. L. A. (1983), *Essays in Jurisprudence and Philosophy*, Clarendon Press, Oxford.

HART, H. L. A. (1994), *The Concept of Law*, Clarendon Press, Oxford, second edition with a Postscript.

HAWKINS, K. (1992), "The Use of Legal Discretion: Perspectives from Law and Social Science", in Hawkins, K., (ed.) *The Uses of Discretion*, Clarendon Press, Oxford, 11-46.

HAYEK, F. (1960), *The Constitution of Liberty*, Routledge, London.

HIERRO PESCADOR, J. (1986), *Principios de Filosofía del Lenguaje*, Alianza Editorial, Madrid.

HOFFSMASTER, B. (1982), "Understanding Judicial Discretion", *Law and Philosophy*, v. 1, 21-55.

HOLLIS, M. and SUDGEN, R. (1993), "Rationality in Action", in *MIND*, v. 102, n. 405.

HURLEY, S. (1989), *Natural Reasons*, Oxford University Press, Oxford.

HURLEY, S. (1990), "Coherence, Hypothetical Cases, and Precedent", *Oxford Journal of Legal Studies* v. 10, n. 2, 221-251.

ISAACS, N. (1933), "The Limits of Judicial Discretion", *The Yale Law Journal*, v. 32, 339-352.

KADISH, M., and KADISH, S. (1973), *Discretion to Disobey*, Stanford University Press, Stanford.

KELSEN, H., (1970), *Pure Theory of Law*, University of California Press, Berkeley.

KIRKHAM, R. (1992), *Theories of Truth*, The MIT Press, Cambridge, Massachusetts.

KNAPP, S. (1991), "Practice, Purpose, and Interpretive Controversy", in Brint, M. and Weaver, W. (eds.) *Pragmatism in Law and Society*, Westview Press, Oxford, 323-342.

KRESS, K. (1989), "Legal Indeterminacy", *California Law Review*, v. 77, 243-337.

KRESS, K. (1996), "Coherence", in Patterson, D., *A Companion to Philosophy of Law and Legal Theory*, Blackwell, Oxford, 533-552.

KRIPKE, S. (1980), *Naming and Necessity*, Blackwell, Oxford.

KRIPKE, S. (1982), *Wittgenstein on Rules and Private Language*, Basil Blackwell, Oxford.

LAPORTA, F. (1985), "El principio de igualdad: Introducción a su análisis", *Sistema*, n. 67.

LEMPER, R. (1992), "Discretion in a Behavioural Perspective: The Case of a Public Housing Eviction Board", in Hawkins, K., (ed.) *The Uses of Discretion*, Clarendon Press, Oxford, 185-230.

LLEWELYN, K. (1951), *The Bramble Bush*, Oceana Publications, New York.

LORD HODSON, *Judicial Discretion and Its Exercise*, The Holdsworth Club, Birmingham, 1961.

LUCAS, J. R., *Responsibility*, Clarendon Press, Oxford, 1993.

LUZZATI, C. (1990a), "Discretion and 'Indeterminacy' in Kelsen's Theory of Legal Interpretation", in Gianformaggio, L. (ed.) *Hans Kelsen's Legal Theory. A Diachronic Point of View, Analisi e Diritto*, Giappichelli Editore, Torino, 123-137.

LUZZATI, C. (1990b), *La vaghezza delle norme*, Dott. A. Giuffrè Editore, Milano.

LYONS, J. (1981), *Language, Meaning, and Context*, Fontana, London.

MACCORMICK, N. (1978), *Legal Reasoning and Legal Theory*, Clarendon Press, Oxford.

MACCORMICK, N. (1982), "Legal Reasoning and Practical Reason", *Midwest Studies in Philosophy*, v. VII, 271-286.

MACCORMICK, N. (1984), "Coherence in Legal Justification", in Peczencik, A., Lindahl, L., and Roermund, B., (eds.) *Theory of Legal Science*, Reidel, Dordrecht.

MACCORMICK, N. (1991), "On 'Open Texture' in Law", in Amselek, P., and MacCormick, N., (eds.), *Controversies about Law and Ontology*, Edinburgh University Press, Edinburgh, 72-83.

MACCORMICK, N., and WEINBERGER, O. (1986), *An Institutional Theory of Law. New Approaches to Legal Positivism,* Reidel, Dordrecht.

MACKIE, J. (1984), "The Third Theory of Law", in Cohen, M., (ed.) *Ronald Dworkin and Contemporary Jurisprudence*, Rowman & Allanheld, New Jersey, 161-170

MARMOR, A. (1992), *Interpretation and Legal Theory*, Clarendon Press, Oxford.

MARMOR, A. (1995), "Three Concepts of Objectivity", in Marmor, A. (ed.), *Law and Interpretation*, Clarendon Press, Oxford, 177-202.

MARMOR, A. (1996), "On Convention", *Synthese*, v. 107, 533-552.

MATTEY, G. (1989), "Personal Coherence, Objectivity, and Reliability", in Bender, J., (ed.) *The Current State of Coherence Theory*, Kluwer, Dordrecht, 38-51.

MCDOWELL, J. (1976), "Truth Conditions, Bivalence and Verificationism", in Evans G., and McDowell, J. (eds.), *Truth and Meaning. Essays in Semantics*, Oxford University Press, Oxford, 43-66.

MCDOWELL, J. (1981), "Non-Cognitivism and Rule-Following", in Holtzman, S. and Leich, Ch. (eds.) *Wittgenstein: To Follow a Rule*, Routledge, London, 141-162.

MCDOWELL, J. (1993), "Wittgenstein on Following a Rule", in Moore, A. (ed.), *Meaning and Reference*, Oxford University Press, Oxford, 257-293.

MCGINN, C. (1984), *Wittgenstein on Meaning*, Basil Blackwell, Oxford.

MENDONCA, D. (1997), *Interpretación y aplicación del derecho*, Universidad de Almeria, Almeria.

MOORE, M. (1985), "A Natural Law Theory of Interpretation", *Southern California Law Review*, v. 58, 277-398.

MOORE, M. (1992), "Law as a Functional Kind", in George, R., *Natural Law Theories*, Oxford University Press, Oxford, 188-244.

MOORE, M. (1995), "Interpreting Interpretation", in Marmor, A. (ed.), *Law and Interpretation*, Clarendon Press, Oxford, 1-29.

MORESO, J. J. (1996), "Leguaje jurídico", in Garzón Valdés, E., and Laporta, F., (eds.) *El derecho y la justicia*, Enciclopedia iberoamericana de filosofía, Trotta, Madrid, 105-116.

MORESO, J. J. (1998), *Legal Indeterminacy and Constitutional Interpretation*, Kluwer Academic Publishers, Dordrecht.

MOSER, P. (1993), *Philosophy After Objectivity*, Oxford University Press, Oxford.

MOSTERÍN, J. (1987), *Racionalidad y acción humana*, Alianza Universidad, Madrid, second edition.

MURPHY, C. (1990), *Descent Into Subjectivity*, Longwood Academic, Wakefield.

NAVARRO, P. (1993), "Sistema jurídico, casos difíciles y conocimiento del derecho", *DOXA*, n. 14, 243-268.

NINO, C. S. (1985), *La validez del Derecho*, Astrea, Buenos Aires.

NINO, C. S. (1994), *Derecho, moral y política*, Ariel, Barcelona.

PÁRAMO, J. R., de (1984), *H.L.A. Hart y la teoría analítica del Derecho*, Centro de Estudios Constitucionales, Madrid.

PARENT, W. (1980), "Interpretation and Justification in Hard Cases", *Georgia Law Review*, v. 15, 99-142.

PATTENDEN, R. (1990), *Judicial Discretion and Criminal Litigation,* Clarendon Press, Oxford.

PATTERSON, D. (1996), *Law and Truth*, Oxford University Press, Oxford.

PEARS, D. (1991), "Wittgenstein's Account of Rule-Following", *Synthese,* v. 87, n. 2, 273-283.

PECZENIK, A. (1989), *On Law and Reason*, Kluwer Academic Publishers, Dordrecht.

PECZENIK, A. (1990), "Coherence, Truth and Rightness in the Law", in NERHOT, P. (ed.), *Law, Interpretation and Reality. Essays in Epistemology, Hermeneutics and Jurisprudence*, Kluwer Academic Publishers, Dordrecht.

PECZENIK, A., LINDAHL, L., and VAN ROERMUND, B. (1984), (eds.), *Theory of Legal Science*, Reidel Publishing Company, Dordrecht.

PECZENIK, A. (1992), "Legal Collision Norms and Moral Considerations", in *Coherence and Conflict in Law*, Serie Rechtsfilosofie en Rechtstheorie 7, Kluwer Law and taxation Publishers, Deventer.

PETTIT, P. (1990), "The Reality of Rule-Following", *MIND*, v. 99, 1-21.

PRIETO, L. (1987), *Ideología e interpretación jurídica*, Tecnos, Madrid.

PRIETO, L. (1992), *Sobre principios y normas: Problemas del razonamiento jurídico*, Civitas, Madrid.

PUTNAM, H. (1975), "The Meaning of 'Meaning' ", in *Mind, Language and Reality. Philosophical Papers v. 2,* Cambridge University Press, Cambridge, 215-271.

PUTNAM, H. (1981), *Reason, Truth and History*, Cambridge University Press, Cambridge.

PUTNAM, H. (1983), *Realism and Reason*, Cambridge University Press, Cambridge.

PUTNAM, H. (1987), *The Many Faces of Realism*, Open Court, Illinois.

PUTNAM, H. (1990), *Realism with a Human Face*, Harvard University Press, Cambridge, Massachusetts.

PUTNAM, H. (1992), *Renewing Philosophy*, Harvard University Press, Cambridge, Massachusetts.

PUTNAM, H. (1995a), "Are Moral and Legal Values Made or Discovered?", *Legal Theory*, n. 1, 1-19.

PUTNAM, H. (1995b), "Replies", *Legal Theory*, n. 1, 69-80.

PUTNAM, H. (1995c), *Pragmatism*, Blackwell, Oxford.

QUINE, W. V. O. (1953), "Two Dogmas of Empiricism", in *From a Logical Point of View*, Harvard University Press, Cambridge, Massachusetts, 20-46.

QUINE, W. V. O. (1960), *Word and Object*, The MIT Press, Cambridge, Massachusetts.

QUINE, W. V. O. (1975), The Nature of Natural Knowledge", in Guttenplan, S., (ed.) *Mind and Language*, Clarendon Press, Oxford.

RAWLS, J. (1971), *A Theory of Justice*, Harvard University Press, Cambridge, Massachusetts.

RAZ, J. (1972), "Legal Principles and the Limits of Law", *The Yale Law Journal*, v. 81, n. 5, 823-854.

RAZ, J. (1979), *The Authority of Law. Essays on Law and Morality*, Clarendon Press, Oxford.

RAZ, J. (1986), "Dworkin: A New Link in the Chain", *California Law Review*, n. 74, 1103-1119.

RAZ, J. (1990), *Practical Reasons and Norms*, Princeton University Press, Princeton.

RAZ, J. (1991), "Mixing Values", *Proceedings of the Aristotelian Society*, v. 65.

RAZ, J. (1992), "The Relevance of Coherence", *Boston University Law Review*, v. 72, n. 2, 273-321.

RAZ, J. (1995), "Interpretation without Retrieval", in Marmor, A., (ed.) *Law and Interpretation*, Clarendon Press, Oxford, 155-176.

RAZ, J. (1996), "Intention in Interpretation", in George, R. (ed.), *The Autonomy of Law. Essays on Legal Positivism*, Clarendon Press, Oxford, 249-286.

REDONDO, C. (1996), *La noción de razón para la acción en el análisis jurídico*, Centro de Estudios Constitucionales, Madrid.

REDONDO, C. (1997), "Teorías del Derecho e indeterminación normativa" in *DOXA* v. 20, 177-196.

RORTY, R. (1980), *Philosophy and the Mirror of Nature*, Basil Blackwell, Oxford.

RORTY, R. (1991a), *The Consequences of Pragmatism*, Harvester Wheatsheaf, New York.

RORTY, R. (1991b), "The Banality of Pragmatism and the Poetry of Justice", in Brint, M. and Weaver, W. (eds.) *Pragmatism in Law and Society*, Westview Press, Oxford, 89-98.

RORTY, R. (1993), "Pragmatism, Davidson and Truth", in LePore, E. (ed.) *Truth and Interpretation*, Blackwell, Oxford, 333-355.

ROSENBERG, M. (1971), "Judicial Discretion of the Trial Court, Viewed From Abowe", *Syracuse Law Review*, v. 22, n. 3, 635-667.

ROSS, A. (1958), *On Law and Justice*, Stevens & Sons Limited, London.

RUÍZ MANERO, J. (1990), *Jurisdicción y normas. Dos estudios sobre función jurisdiccional y teoría del Derecho*, Centro de Estudios Constitucionales, Madrid.

SAINSBURY, R. (1991), "Is There Higher-Order Vagueness?", *The Philosophical Quarterly*, n. 41, 167-182.

SARTORIUS, R. (1968), "The Justification of the Judicial Decision", *Ethics*, v. 78, n. 3, 171-187.

SARTORIUS, R. (1971), "Social Policy and Judicial Legislation", *American Philosophical Quarterly*, v. 8, n. 2, 151-160.

SCHAUER, F. (1985), "Easy Cases", *Southern California Law Review*, v. 58, 399-440.

SCHAUER, F. (1988), "Formalism", *The Yale Law Journal*, v. 97, 509-548.

SCHAUER, F. (1991), *Playing by the Rules. A Philosophical Examination of Rule-Based Decision-Making in Law and Life*, Clarendon Press, Oxford.

SCHAUER, F. (1992), "Rule-Following Argument", in Patterson, D., *Wittgenstein and Legal Theory*, Westview Press, Oxford, 225-230.

SEARLE, J. (1969), *Speech Acts*, Cambridge University Press, Cambridge.

SEARLE, J. (1983), *Intentionality*, Cambridge University Press, Cambridge.

SEARLE, J. (1995), *The Construction of Social Reality*, The Free Press, New York.

SHAPIRO, D. L. (1985), "Jurisdiction and Discretion", *New York University Law Review*, v. 60, n. 4, 543-590.

SHINER, R. (1992a), *Norm and Nature,* Clarendon Press, Oxford.

SHINER, R. (1992b), "The Acceptance of a Legal System", in Patterson, D. (ed.), *Wittgenstein and Legal Theory*, Westview Press, Oxford, 59-84.

SKOLIMOWSKI, H. (1979), *Racionalidad Evolutiva*, Cuadernos Teorema, Valencia, (transl. C. García Trevijano and F. Soto).

SKUBIK, D. W. (1990), *At the Intersection of Legality and Morality. Hartian Law as Natural Law*, Peter Lang Publishing, New York.

SOPER, P. (1984), "Legal Theory and the Obligation of a Judge: The Hart/Dworkin Dispute", in Cohen, M., (ed.) *Ronald Dworkin and Contemporary Jurisprudence*, Rowman & Allanheld, New Jersey, 3-27.

SOSA, E. (1993), "'Circular' Coherence and 'Absurd' Foundations", in LePore, E. (ed.), *Truth and Interpretation*, Blackwell, Oxford, 387-397.

STAVROPOULOS, N. (1996), *Objectivity in Law*, Clarendon Press, Oxford.

TARSKI, A. (1960), "La concepción semántica de la verdad y los fundamentos de la semántica", in Bunge, M., (ed.) *Antología semántica*, Nueva visión, Buenos Aires, 11-157.

TRAYNOR, R. (1978), "The Limits of Judicial Creativity", *The Hastings Law Journal*, v. 29, 1025-1040.

VILLA, V. (1990), "Normative Coherence and Epistemological Presuppositions of Justification", in NERHOT, P. (ed.), *Law, Interpretation and Reality. Essays in Epistemology, Hermeneutics and Jurisprudence*, Kluwer Academic Publishers, Dordrecht.

WAISMANN, F. (1951), "Verifiability", in Flew, A. (ed.), *Logic and Language*, Blackwell, Oxford, 117-144.

WALUCHOW, W. (1983), "Strong Discretion", The Philosophical Quarterly, v. 33, n.133, 321-339.

WALUCHOW, W. (1994), *Inclusive Legal Positivism*, Clarendon Press, Oxford.

WASSERSTROM, R. (1961), *The Judicial Decision*, Stanford University Press, Stanford.

WEINBERGER, O. (1984), "Objectivity and Rationality in Lawyer's Reasoning", in PECZENIK, A., LINDAHL, L., and VAN ROERMUND, B. (eds.), *Theory of Legal Science*, Reidel Publishing Company, Dordrecht.

WELLMAN, C. (1988), "Judicial Discretion and Constitutional Law", *Rechtstheorie*, n. 19, 153-165.

WILSON, N. (1959), "Substances without Substrata", in *Review of Metaphysics*, XII.

WITTGENSTEIN, L. (1953), *Philosophical Investigations*, Basil Blackwell, Oxford, (transl. G. E. M. Anscombe).

WITTGENSTEIN, L. (1992), *Observaciones a La Rama Dorada de Frazer*, Tecnos, Madrid, (transl. J. Sádaba).

WRIGHT, C. (1993), *Realism, Meaning and Truth*, Blackwell, Oxford, second edition.

WRIGHT, G. H. von (1970), *Norma y acción*, Tecnos, Madrid, (transl. P. García).

WRÓBLEWSKI, J. (1974), "Legal Syllogism and Rationality of Judicial Decision", *Rechtstheorie*, n. 5, 33-46.

WRÓBLEWSKI, J. (1988), *Constitución y teoría general del Derecho*, Cuadernos Cívitas, Madrid.

WRÓBLEWSKI, J. (1989), *Sentido y hecho en el derecho*, Servicio Editorial del Pais Vasco, San Sebastián.

YABLON, Ch. (1987), "Law and Metaphysics", *The Yale Law Journal*, v. 96, 613-642.

Law and Philosophy Library

1. E. Bulygin, J.-L. Gardies and I. Niiniluoto (eds.): *Man, Law and Modern Forms of Life.* With an Introduction by M.D. Bayles. 1985 ISBN 90-277-1869-5
2. W. Sadurski: *Giving Desert Its Due.* Social Justice and Legal Theory. 1985 ISBN 90-277-1941-1
3. N. MacCormick and O. Weinberger: *An Institutional Theory of Law.* New Approaches to Legal Positivism. 1986 ISBN 90-277-2079-7
4. A. Aarnio: *The Rational as Reasonable.* A Treatise on Legal Justification. 1987 ISBN 90-277-2276-5
5. M.D. Bayles: *Principles of Law.* A Normative Analysis. 1987 ISBN 90-277-2412-1; Pb: 90-277-2413-X
6. A. Soeteman: *Logic in Law.* Remarks on Logic and Rationality in Normative Reasoning, Especially in Law. 1989 ISBN 0-7923-0042-4
7. C.T. Sistare: *Responsibility and Criminal Liability.* 1989 ISBN 0-7923-0396-2
8. A. Peczenik: *On Law and Reason.* 1989 ISBN 0-7923-0444-6
9. W. Sadurski: *Moral Pluralism and Legal Neutrality.* 1990 ISBN 0-7923-0565-5
10. M.D. Bayles: *Procedural Justice.* Allocating to Individuals. 1990 ISBN 0-7923-0567-1
11. P. Nerhot (ed.): *Law, Interpretation and Reality.* Essays in Epistemology, Hermeneutics and Jurisprudence. 1990 ISBN 0-7923-0593-0
12. A.W. Norrie: *Law, Ideology and Punishment.* Retrieval and Critique of the Liberal Ideal of Criminal Justice. 1991 ISBN 0-7923-1013-6
13. P. Nerhot (ed.): *Legal Knowledge and Analogy.* Fragments of Legal Epistemology, Hermeneutics and Linguistics. 1991 ISBN 0-7923-1065-9
14. O. Weinberger: *Law, Institution and Legal Politics.* Fundamental Problems of Legal Theory and Social Philosophy. 1991 ISBN 0-7923-1143-4
15. J. Wróblewski: *The Judicial Application of Law.* Edited by Z. Bańkowski and N. MacCormick. 1992 ISBN 0-7923-1569-3
16. T. Wilhelmsson: *Critical Studies in Private Law.* A Treatise on Need-Rational Principles in Modern Law. 1992 ISBN 0-7923-1659-2
17. M.D. Bayles: *Hart's Legal Philosophy.* An Examination. 1992 ISBN 0-7923-1981-8
18. D.W.P. Ruiter: *Institutional Legal Facts.* Legal Powers and their Effects. 1993 ISBN 0-7923-2441-2
19. J. Schonsheck: *On Criminalization.* An Essay in the Philosophy of the Criminal Law. 1994 ISBN 0-7923-2663-6
20. R.P. Malloy and J. Evensky (eds.): *Adam Smith and the Philosophy of Law and Economics.* 1994 ISBN 0-7923-2796-9
21. Z. Bańkowski, I. White and U. Hahn (eds.): *Informatics and the Foundations of Legal Reasoning.* 1995 ISBN 0-7923-3455-8

Law and Philosophy Library

22. E. Lagerspetz: *The Opposite Mirrors*. An Essay on the Conventionalist Theory of Institutions. 1995 ISBN 0-7923-3325-X
23. M. van Hees: *Rights and Decisions*. Formal Models of Law and Liberalism. 1995 ISBN 0-7923-3754-9
24. B. Anderson: *"Discovery" in Legal Decision-Making*. 1996 ISBN 0-7923-3981-9
25. S. Urbina: *Reason, Democracy, Society*. A Study on the Basis of Legal Thinking. 1996 ISBN 0-7923-4262-3
26. E. Attwooll: *The Tapestry of the Law*. Scotland, Legal Culture and Legal Theory. 1997 ISBN 0-7923-4310-7
27. J.C. Hage: *Reasoning with Rules*. An Essay on Legal Reasoning and Its Underlying Logic. 1997 ISBN 0-7923-4325-5
28. R.A. Hillman: *The Richness of Contract Law*. An Analysis and Critique of Contemporary Theories of Contract Law. 1997 ISBN 0-7923-4336-0; 0-7923-5063-4 (Pb)
29. C. Wellman: *An Approach to Rights*. Studies in the Philosophy of Law and Morals. 1997 ISBN 0-7923-4467-7
30. B. van Roermund: *Law, Narrative and Reality*. An Essay in Intercepting Politics. 1997 ISBN 0-7923-4621-1
31. I. Ward: *Kantianism, Postmodernism and Critical Legal Thought*. 1997 ISBN 0-7923-4745-5
32. H. Prakken: *Logical Tools for Modelling Legal Argument*. A Study of Defeasible Reasoning in Law. 1997 ISBN 0-7923-4776-5
33. T. May: *Autonomy, Authority and Moral Responsibility*. 1998 ISBN 0-7923-4851-6
34. M. Atienza and J.R. Manero: *A Theory of Legal Sentences*. 1998 ISBN 0-7923-4856-7
35. E.A. Christodoulidis: *Law and Reflexive Politics*. 1998 ISBN 0-7923-4954-7
36. L.M.M. Royakkers: *Extending Deontic Logic for the Formalisation of Legal Rules*. 1998 ISBN 0-7923-4982-2
37. J.J. Moreso: *Legal Indeterminacy and Constitutional Interpretation*. 1998 ISBN 0-7923-5156-8
38. W. Sadurski: *Freedom of Speech and Its Limits*. 1999 ISBN 0-7923-5523-7
39. J. Wolenski (ed.): *Kazimierz Opalek Selected Papers in Legal Philosophy*. 1999 ISBN 0-7923-5732-9
40. H.P. Visser 't Hooft: *Justice to Future Generations and the Environment*. 1999 ISBN 0-7923-5756-6
41. L.J. Wintgens (ed.): *The Law in Philosophical Perspectives*. My Philosophy of Law. 1999 ISBN 0-7923-5796-5
42. A.R. Lodder: *DiaLaw*. On Legal Justification and Dialogical Models of Argumentation. 1999 ISBN 0-7923-5830-9
43. C. Redondo: *Reasons for Action and the Law*. 1999 ISBN 0-7923-5912-7

Law and Philosophy Library

44. M. Friedman, L. May, K. Parsons and J. Stiff (eds.): *Rights and Reason.* Essays in Honor of Carl Wellman. 2000 ISBN 0-7923-6198-9
45. G.C. Christie: *The Notion of an Ideal Audience in Legal Argument.* 2000 ISBN 0-7923-6283-7
46. R.S. Summers: *Essays in Legal Theory.* 2000 ISBN 0-7923-6367-1
47. M. van Hees: *Legal Reductionism and Freedom.* 2000 ISBN 0-7923-6491-0
48. R. Gargarella: *The Scepter of Reason.* Public Discussion and Political Radicalism in the Origins of Constitutionalism. 2000 ISBN 0-7923-6508-9
49. M. Iglesias Vila: *Facing Judicial Discretion.* Legal Knowledge and Right Answers Revisited. 2001 ISBN 0-7923-6778-2

KLUWER ACADEMIC PUBLISHERS – DORDRECHT / BOSTON / LONDON